Charlemagne's Tablecloth

Also by Nichola Fletcher

Game For All
(Victor Gollancz / Peter Crawley)

Charlemagne's Tablecloth

A Piquant History of Feasting

NICHOLA FLETCHER

St. Martin's Press ✷ New York

www.stmartins.com

ISBN 0-312-34068-0
EAN 978-0-312-34068-1

First published in Great Britain by Weidenfeld & Nicolson
in association with Peter Crawley

First Edition: August 2005

10 9 8 7 6 5 4 3 2 1

For John
for Stella
and
for Martha

MENU

vii

Menu cards lend an air of theatricality to a meal and, of course, antici-pation. To quote one eighteenth-century French diner: '*C'est l'ensemble des mots et des mets qui nous font saliver; c'est un plaisir avant le plaisir, un préliminaire en soi, pratiquement un rite de passage.*' ('It is an assembly of words and dishes that make us salivate; it is a pleasure before the pleasures, a starter in itself, practically a rite of passage.') The quotation was jotted down on an old menu displayed at an exhibition of menus in Saulieu, Burgundy.

ACKNOWLEDGEMENTS

The writing of this book has been like a feast in reverse. I began by consuming innumerable courses of choice pieces of information, savouring and enjoying each one in turn. And afterwards I had to construct out of them a feast of words. Like most major feasts, the task required input from a great many people, and I am profoundly grateful for the help, enthusiasm and moral support I have received.

Firstly I should like to thank my publisher Peter Crawley for his tenacious faith in the concept of this book. As editors, publishing houses and style of book came, went and returned, he was the only constant, reassuring and always sensible factor – the sort of publisher authors dream of having. My thanks are also due to the team at Weidenfeld & Nicolson for transforming my ambitious ideas into a manageable book.

I am grateful beyond measure for the kind help that has been given, sometimes by strangers, often by friends both old and new, for many friendships have been made or strengthened as a result of my research. So many people have contributed ideas, references, information and practical help that it is impossible to thank everyone individually. Where their help can be linked to a particular chapter, I have acknowledged it in the sources of information at the end of the book; but the masses of suggestions, ideas and quirky snippets will be recognised by their contributors who will, I hope, approve of how I used their offerings. I should particularly like to mention the members of The Guild of Food Writers' discussion group who have clarified points and speedily supplied information when requested – my thanks to you all.

I am greatly indebted to those who so generously gave me board, lodging and hospitality. In no particular order, I thank Ian Murray and Annie Good, Susie Lendrum, Emi Kazuko, Nicholas Mellor, Marlena Spieler and Alan McLaughlin, Louise Cattrell and Alex McLennan, Sophie and Mark Dorber, Deh-ta Hsiung, and Isabel Rutherford. Whenever I was stuck with a classical issue I turned to my cousin Oliver Nicholson whose singular sense of humour always cheers me up. David Clarkson, as well as making sure my computer hums along contentedly, helped me with the pictures for this book – without him there would be many empty pages. Gillian Riley has been kindness beyond measure in providing moral support and in allowing me to use her extensive library forby. And it was Mike Longstaffe who rescued the swan pie in the middle of the night. The Belgian Tourist Board arranged a splendid trip to Saint-Hubert; and the Philadelphia Tourist Convention generously hosted a trip to that historic city. To the Kevoch Choir, to John and Kate MacSween and to Rob Kesseler, I add my thanks for including me in their special events. Mauri Nieminen of the Kahnen reindeer research station in Finland provided the reindeer milk indispensable for one of my feasts – I thank him for his kindness. Without libraries and museums this book would not have been possible. In particular I should like to acknowledge the Special Collections department at the Brotherton Library in Leeds; the British Library, particularly Beth McKillop; the National Library of Scotland – a haven for me; and Alison Sheridan of National Museums of Scotland. Alex Fraser initially told me I should write this book and I shall always remain grateful for his suggestion. Anthony Turner has diligently copy-edited my manuscript – I hope his retirement comes as a pleasant contrast.

Although it is a cliché to thank your family for its forbearance, it is essential to do so. All books require sacrifices, and this author's family has been the recipient of neglect and bad temper during difficult times. Stella, Martha and John, bless you for your help, your understanding and your enthusiasm.

Acknowledgements for permission to use copyright material

Strenuous efforts have been made to clear the necessary copyright for reproduction. However, in one or two cases it proved impossible to discover who held the copyright or whether indeed the works were still covered by copyright. Rather than leave out works which I feel sure the authors and artists would have been happy to see reproduced, I have included them but should be delighted to make any necessary alterations in future editions.

The quotation on p. 131 is reprinted by permission of the publisher from *The Paris of Henry Navarre as Seen by Pierre de L'Estoile: Selections from his* Mémoires-Journaux, translated and edited by Nancy Lyman Roelker (Cambridge, Mass.: Harvard University Press, Copyright © 1958 by the President and Fellows of Harvard College, Copyright renewed 1986 by Nancy Lyman Roelker).

The quotation from 'Burger Heaven' by Jason Epstein is reproduced by kind permission of the New York Times Syndicate.

The quotations from *The Cuisine of Hungary* by George Lang are reproduced by kind permission of Penguin Books Ltd.

The quotation from 'A Piece of Pie' by Damon Runyon comes from *Runyon on Broadway* and is reproduced by kind permission of Constable & Robinson Publishing.

The quotation from Champlain's 'The Order of Good Cheer' is reproduced by kind permission of the Champlain Society.

The translation from *Le Mercure galant* appears in *Savouring the Past* by Barbara Ketchum Wheaton and is reproduced with her kind permission.

The translation of the Giacomo Castelvestro quotation appears in *The Fruit, Herbs and Vegetables of Italy* by Gillian Riley and is reproduced with her kind permission.

My thanks to Sue Style for her quotation on Treberwurstfrasse; to Margaret Shaida for her quotation on Escudella; and to Marc Millon for his passage on Thanksgiving.

Picture Credits

Harley 4380 f. 1, *Masquerade at the French Court*, and Harley 4379 f. 3, *Queen Isabel Enters Paris*, are reproduced by permission of the British Library.

Photograph *Dr Wilson, Lt Bowers & Cherry-Garrard on return from Cape Crozier* by Herbert Ponting on the British Antarctic Expedition, 1910–13 (Leader Capt. R. F. Scott) reproduced by permission of the Scott Polar Research Institute, University of Cambridge.

Photograph *Killing a pig in Portugal* by Nichola Fletcher.

Photograph *Bawdy Tudor drinking cup* reproduced by permission of the Museum of London.

Chazen itchi and *Ichigo ichie* Japanese calligraphies were made by Emi Kazuko.

Painting *A Feast in the Bath* from an anonymous fifteenth-century Burgundian miniature, Dep. Breslau 2, Band 2, Bl. 244r., reproduced with kind permission from the Staatsbibliothek zu Berlin. Bildarchiv Preussischer Kulturbesitz.

Photograph *Gathered*, Lawson Park, 2000, by Jenny Brownrigg reproduced by permission of Rob Kesseler.

Photograph of the painting *The inauguration of Robert Burns as Poet Laureate of the Lodge Canongate Kilwinning* by Antonia Reeve and reproduced by kind permission of the Grand Lodge of Scotland.

Photograph *C. K. G. Billings' horseback dinner at Sherry's, 1903* reproduced with permission from the Museum of the City of New York, the Byron Collection.

Days of the Dead skeletons photographs from the exhibition *Heaven and Hell* reproduced by kind permission of National Museums of Scotland.

Photograph *Days of the Dead stall* copyright Ron O'Donnell, and reproduced with his permission.

Photograph *After the feast* copyright Tatyana Jakovskaya of Sharmanka Kinetic Theatre and reproduced with her permission.

Engraving *Die Hirsch Pastet* reproduced by permission of the Special Collections, Brotherton Library, University of Leeds.

Painting *The Banquet at Casa Nani*, Pietro Longhi, Ca' Rezzonico, Museo del Settecento, Venice; Painting *Banquet in Thames Tunnel*, attr. George Jones, 1827, Ironbridge Gorge Museum, Telford; Mosaic *Preparations for a Banquet*, Louvre, Paris; Painting *Persian Garden*, Bibliothèque Nationale, Paris; Illustration *How the Noble King Alexander was Poisoned*, Musée de la Ville de Paris; Illustration *Banqueting Scene*, Bibliothèque Nationale, Paris; Painting *The Meal Stall*, Pieter Aertsen, 1551; Mosaic *The Costume Banquet*, Musée National du Bardo, Tunisia; Illustration *The Gathering before the Stag Hunt*, Bibliothèque Nationale, Paris; Painting *Three Prize Pigs outside a Sty*; Painting *Plan of a tea garden*, private collection; Painting *A Fete at Bermondsey*; Joris Hoefnagel, 1570, Hatfield House; Painting *Peasant Wedding*, Pieter Brueghel, 1568, Kunsthistorisches Museum, Vienna; *Scene of cannibalism*, from 'American Tertia Pars ...', 1592 (colour engraving), Theodore de Bry (1528–98), Service historique de Vincennes, France, Lauros/Giraudon. All reproduced by permission of the Bridgeman Art Library, London.

Illustration *Les Voeux du banquet du paon*; Engraving, *Dog-meat, cat-meat, rat ...* Vierge, 1871; Engraving *Harvest Home*, 1843; Engraving *Meleagris gallopavo*, John Johnston, 1650; Engraving *Kilted Scotsmen drink the health of the duke of Rothsay*, 1872; Engraving *An excess of food and drink at Christmas*, George Cruikshank. All reproduced by permission of Mary Evans Picture Library.

Painting *Cockaigne*, Pieter Brueghel, Alte Pinakothek, Munich; Painting *Large Food Display*, Georg Flegel, Alte Pinakothek, Munich; Painting *Sumptuous Still Life*, Jans Davidsz de Heem, 1648, Museum Boymans-van Beuningen, Rotterdam; Wood cut *Cannibalism amongst Indians*, 1558. All reproduced by permission of akg-images.

Charlemagne's
Tablecloth

I

What is a feast?

However far back you may go in time, the gastronomical value of food always outweighs its alimentary value, and it is in joy, not in pain, that man has found his spirit.

GASTON BACHELARD

The Emperor Charlemagne had an asbestos tablecloth. He would impress his dinner guests by throwing it in the fire after the feast so all the crumbs would burn away and he could put it back on the table clean and white. The full story of Charlemagne's bizarre tablecloth is told at the end of the book; it was just one of dozens of colourful anecdotes that mention of a subject like this inevitably elicits. Everyone I spoke to had something to contribute, and as well as pouring forth excited memories, fantasies, aspirations, myths and tantalising snippets, they had questions about what prompts a feast and how some of the great historic events were organised. There were also discussions about what constitutes a feast; whether all feasts have common elements; and, inevitably, whether there is still a place for feasts or whether the notion of such spectacular magnificence is outdated – a barbaric squandering of resources when we are overfed anyway.

What do we learn from reading about culinary entertainments? Mostly we learn about ourselves: how inventive we can be, how sometimes we are individualists and sometimes conformists. We are social creatures, we love to eat, we love to show off and we love to laugh; you don't have to be Aristotle or Rabelais to recognise this,[1] and with few exceptions feasts are to provide pleasure, to have fun. Nevertheless, simply to make a collection of every notable feast there had ever been would make tedious reading. Instead, by grouping examples together (for certain occasions prompt a feast in every society), or by using an event to illustrate a particular element of the feast, be it an 'ingredient' or the reason for staging the event, I have covered the main categories of feasting. Even if a particular feast appears unique it usually conforms to at least one type. In and amongst are some oddities I enjoyed and one or two examples of the magiric art that I staged myself. However, attempting to arrange subjects as diverse as these into any logical sequence presents problems. Whether arranged by calendar or life events, by geography, chronology, culture or social distinctions, there are in all cases too many that either simply don't fit or else fit into several categories. So I present them as a series of essays, each in itself a complete unit though there are obviously connections between some events. There is, purposely, no particular order about the chapters except that each seems to follow on from the other either as a complement or a stimulating contrast. Therefore this book may be read as a many-coursed feast from start to finish, or dipped into as a series of appetisers.

But what is a feast – exquisite refinement or gargantuan excess? Opinions differ. Once when I was foolish enough to refuse a second helping by quoting John Heywood's 1546 proverb 'Enough is as good as a feast', my host rounded on me, pronouncing that anyone who would not eat to excess should not be writing a book about feasts.

---

1 'Better to write about laughter than tears, For laughter is the essence of mankind' – François Rabelais; 'Man is a laughing animal' – Aristotle. And Ecclesiastes also states: 'A feast is made for laughter.' Umberto Eco's thriller *The Name of the Rose* was based around the divine nature of laughter.

Giuco della Signora Gola (The Game of Mistress Greedy), Italian satirical cartoon, 1699. In contrast to the elegant banquet at Casa Nani (see first plates section), this unruly affair nevertheless sums up the word 'feast' for many people.

Perhaps he had a point: the proverb has a sanctimonious ring that jars with the spirit of feasting. On the other hand, in different circumstances it is absolutely right: the chapter on feasting in adversity has many poignant examples.

There is no simple way to define a feast because so much is due to the state of mind of the participants. Or participant. For example, can you have a solitary feast? Some would say no, but two Roman epicures clearly thought otherwise. Lucullus, a general renowned for his lavish feasts, saw no reason to temper his eating simply because he happened to be without guests, so when his cook provided merely a reasonable dinner, he bellowed, 'Today Lucullus dines with Lucullus!' and sent him back to prepare something more splendid. And Apicius[2] chose to feast alone for his last meal. Discovering that he had eaten his way through a large fortune and reduced it to a small one, Apicius was not prepared to compromise on the matter of his food and ordered the most luxurious banquet that Rome could provide. To quote Alexis Soyer's version of the event: 'On that solemn occasion, though there were enough culinary *chefs d'oeuvre* to delight an immense number of epicures, he only invited himself. "Sublime idea!" he ejaculated; "after

2 Apicius was credited with producing the definitive collection of Roman recipes, though it is more likely to be the work of several authors.

dining like two Vitelliuses, or several Luculluses, to die in the midst of plenty!" Thereupon he swallowed poison and was found dead at the head of his table.' But these are exceptions; most would agree that conviviality is a vital element of the feast.

There is no doubt that politics alters our perception of when and what makes a feast suitable. A warring society run by absolute monarchs is more likely to express its invincibility by laying on an elaborate display, no matter how hungry the majority of its subjects might be. The wildly extravagant coronation of Bokassa, self-proclaimed Emperor of the Central African Republic, was based on that of Napoleon Bonaparte and was shocking only because it took place in 1977. Two hundred years earlier, it would have been considered normal. Indeed, in cultures where the monarch was regarded as divine, it was expected that he should be provided with both quality and quantity – failure to nurture the king appropriately might anger the gods and lead to a famine. The notion of a queen riding round the streets on a bicycle, or that of a future queen having a modest four-course wedding breakfast in solidarity with the rationed post-war nation[3] – both laudable today – would have been incomprehensible, indeed despised, in many earlier societies.

Holding a feast to enhance power or social standing has not disappeared, even though nowadays many are held ostensibly for charity. The spectacular feasts enjoyed by city guilds always included political bargaining with the guest of honour, as well as performing the role of reinforcing solidarity amongst the guild members – being part of a recognisable group is no less important now than it ever was. Indeed, feasting is an important way of ensuring that cultural traditions survive. Social and cultural groups can be identified through their feasts since it is usually the case that certain food combinations, along with some other traditions, now largely superseded in everyday life, are kept alive through these special events. To paraphrase Brillat-Savarin: 'Tell me how you feast and I will tell you where you are from.' How many British people eat a rich spicy steamed pudding bursting with plumped fruit and nuts, bound with breadcrumbs and flaming with brandy – a

---

3 Gabriel Tschumi, chef to the royal household, pointed out with regret the diminution of royal wedding breakfasts over the three generations of his working life. At the beginning of the twentieth century, a wedding breakfast would have at least sixteen courses; that of Lady Elizabeth Bowes-Lyon to the Duke of York in 1923 had reduced to eight courses and lasted about an hour; Queen Elizabeth II's to Prince Philip had four courses and lasted little more than twenty minutes.

glorious medieval relic – except at Christmas? Look at the ritual feast of Passover, at American Thanksgiving, or at the festival of Diwali. Look at Iranian No Rooz and countless other new-year celebrations. Every culture has its own feasts that confirm its identity, and whose food is a source of comfort or, to an exile, of longing. One country's table manners, however, can be the opposite of another's and travellers never cease to marvel at other countries' eating habits. Occasionally it leads to confusion and discomfort. A Bavarian pastor told me how, as part of international reconciliations after the Second World War, he was host to a group of Japanese. Since food was scarce, the meal featured dumplings heavily, in all senses, and every time the Japanese visitors had managed to empty their plates, the pastor's wife pressed them to more. Every time, to their hosts' mounting incredulity (for the Bavarians were large and the Japanese were not), the Japanese accepted with alacrity, though it became clear that some discomfort was being suffered. It never occurred to either party to question the other's mealtime conventions.

Feasts may equally be an escape from or rejection of social norms: after the Restoration of Charles II in 1660, the anti-monarchist Calves' Head Club apparently held a covert feast every 30 January (the anniversary of Charles I's beheading). They prepared a dinner at which a cod's head represented Charles Stuart; a pike, tyranny; a boar's head, the king preying on his subjects; and calves' heads prepared in a whole variety of ways represented the king's head and his supporters. Copious toasts of defiance were drunk, after which the revellers wrapped one of the calves' heads in a bloody cloth and ceremonially flung it onto a bonfire in the courtyard. There will always be those who use a feast to shock and who revel in their guests' discomfort. If all the tales about Roman emperors are to be believed,[4] their guests suffered a string of indignities such as having their air-filled cushions deflated during the meal, or eating their way through trick food made from anything from pork to pearls, or sampling a succession of rare and eclectic dishes, convinced that they would be murdered at the end of the evening. But if feasts are used to control and manipulate, they are also used to placate. Samuel Pepys's observation, 'Strange to see how a good dinner and feasting reconciles everybody', will find echoes throughout the

---

4 They shouldn't be: many were fabricated by those wishing to illustrate how degenerate the Romans had become, even though quite enough were true to have made the point anyway.

book. Sometimes we do love to behave badly, and in recognising man's innate need to let off steam, religions and states often condone unruly behaviour: the Bacchanals, Saturnalia, the Feast of Fools, Twelfth Night and Carnival are all good Rabelaisian examples. In complete contrast were some Greek symposia and the Zoroastrians' silent feasts, both models of philosophical restraint.

And so it continues. There are superstitious feasts connected with fertility and the annual cycle of food production, there are feasts of mutual benefit where people are lured to carry out some communal task by the promise of a generous feast, often on the tacit understanding that both work and reward would be reciprocated. The gathering-in of a harvest is one example, building a house could be another. Rites of passage are used as opportunities for feasting in all societies. Thanksgiving is offered for many reasons from the harvesting of crops to the end of a war or the return of a long-lost relative.

Sometimes feasts come about as a result of a glut – of fruit, fish, fungi or some other perishable treat – or are based around an ingredient, like Elizabethan venison feasts or the turtle feasts so popular in the nineteenth century. Sometimes the aim is to encourage: one of the most spectacular medieval feasts, the Feast of the Pheasant given by the Duke of Burgundy in 1454, was given to promote the idea of a crusade against the Turks. And the world's largest banquet was given in Paris in 1900 to revive flagging republican spirits. Émil Loubet entertained France's 22,695 mayors in a huge marquee in the Tuileries Gardens with beef 'Bellevue', a terrine of Rouen duck, chicken from Bresse, and ballottine of pheasant (note the focus on meat in this description, another common feast element). The waiters used bicycles to serve the seven kilometres of tables and the chief supervisor used an early automobile to move about. This event was meant to evoke General Lafayette's Festival of Federation held in 1790 on the anniversary of the Fall of the Bastille when a series of 'endless tables' was set up in the park and representatives from all the provinces were invited to a continuous feast of fraternity.

A feast can occur for no other reason than generosity. Plenty of tales from the Middle East describe feasts of Arab hospitality with dozens of delicious dishes and sweetmeats, perhaps an entire herd of camels, produced to entertain a complete stranger. These feasts are examples of true open-handedness, where food and entertainment are given without counting the cost or expecting anything in return, in this world at any rate. The willingness to give generously to a complete stranger is integral to Islamic culture: 'If there is anything that resembles being a deity it is feeding people', and a guest is considered a gift from God.[5]

The enjoyment of giving pleasure must have prompted many a private feast; it has certainly been the motive for the feasts I have staged for my friends over the years (see chapter 28, for example). But, as will be seen in other chapters, I discovered as well that capturing people's imagination through a feast can be a useful educational tool; I found also that accepting a brief to design a feast for somebody else to mount imposes an interesting working discipline, since the exciting element of risk which is a hallmark of all my own creative activities had to be tempered by a fail-safe, though none the less pleasurable, formula.

There are infinite ways of having a feast and I do not pretend that this collection is comprehensive. I have selected events that interest me and which I hope produce a sat- isfying coverage of the subject – I ask for- giveness of those who find my omissions leave them hungry. One obvious gap is intoxication, though it is  not entirely absent from the text. However, the nuances that make thoughts and feelings profound, arousing or hilarious to the intoxicated are usually lost on those not similarly imbued. Likewise, that food and eroticism are connected is axiomatic if not a cliché, and the subject has been amply covered elsewhere. Some aspects of the feast, such as music, can never be given sufficient prominence in written descriptions yet music and musicians play their part. Indeed, much social and feast- ing history that would otherwise have been lost was passed down orally through ballads sung by troubadours and their successors. And therein lies the endless fascination of feasts. From whatever viewpoint they are regarded – theatre, food, drink, costume, music, perfume, etc., there is a lifetime's worth of discovery to be made. But a line has

---

5 I discovered this thirty years ago in Morocco where we gratefully accepted an evening meal and a bed for the night in an ancient house with keyhole doorways, offered by a complete stranger who had shown us round the ancient town of Moulay Idriss – an extraordinarily touching experience.

to be drawn somewhere; I reluctantly draw mine here in the hope that these extraordinary feats of human effort, imagination and generosity will inspire some members of our slightly insipid society to take courage and start planning a feast – the ultimate transient art. As one of Captain Scott's party put it (albeit in rather different circumstances since he was relishing his food in Antarctic conditions), 'This is the most satisfying stuff imaginable.'

2

Paradise: the origin of feasts

Pleasures may be divided into six classes, to wit, food, drink, clothes, sex, scent and sound. Of these the noblest and most consequential is food.

MUHAMMAD IBN AL-HASAN AL-KATIB AL-BAGHDADI

In the beginning there was Paradise, and *paradisi* – a Persian word – was a beautiful pleasure park irrigated with clear mountain water, for all the world like an intricately knotted silk Persian carpet spangled with thousands of tiny flowers and populated by lively gazelles. A thousand years later this Zoroastrian vision of gardens with cool fountains was revived during the European Renaissance, and in 1689 Sir John Chardin wrote wistfully: 'There is such an exquisite Beauty in the Air of Persia, that I can neither forget it my self, nor forbear mentioning it to every body: One would swear that the Heavens were more sublimely elevated, and tinctur'd with quite another Colour there, than they are in our thick and dreary European Climates.'

The Persians' legendary delight in indulgence impressed and seduced those who experienced it. A succession of conquests from Greeks, Arabs, Mongols and Turks changed their borders, their religion, and their centre of power, but invariably each conquering culture assimilated the indigenous Persian culture, finding it more congenial than its own. As well as this, all the caravans bearing silks and spices from the Far East to the West passed through Persia. Trading went both ways: the Tang emperors of the eighth and ninth centuries were apparently very partial to Persian cakes. And so, although Persia had her share of successful warriors, her lasting influence on a very large part of the world has been through pleasure, especially that of food and feasting, but also those of polo, chess, falconry, wine-drinking and smoking, to name a few. Because of this flow, many elements of the East that are considered exotic – 'Arabian' Nights with their genies and magic carpets; whirling dancing dervishes, 'Turkish' delight, and harems; orange flowers, perfumed musk and ambergris; the Magi

9

following their bright star; jewel-encrusted swords, hookahs, rose-water and saffron rice – are all in fact of Persian origin. Zoroaster's theory of 'hot' and 'cold' foods, which he worked out in the seventh century BC, was a hundred years ahead of both Hippocrates' system of 'humours' – adopted throughout Europe – and the Daoist 'yin and yang' philosophy that still exists in Chinese communities.[1] Much later, the Crusades into the Middle East created a crucial conduit for such luxurious ingredients as spices, saffron, almonds and sugar, especially if made into marzipan. It is no exaggeration to say that Persia profoundly influenced the culinary and feasting traditions of at least a third of the world.

Few written records of ancient Persia survived, so it is from the ancient Greeks and Romans that we first read about her reputation for good living. Herodotus, a Greek traveller of the fifth century BC, came from a country where food and wine were consumed in moderation. He noted the Persians' richly equipped table and was clearly impressed by the quantity of food: 'The richer Persians cause an ox, a horse, a camel, and an ass to be baked whole and so served up to them . . . They eat little solid fare but abundance of dessert, which is set on a table a few dishes at a time; it is this which makes them say that "the Greeks when they eat, leave off hungry, having nothing worth mention served up to them after the meats." . . . They are very fond of wine and drink it in large quantities.' When Alexander the Great was campaigning in Persia a century later he sent back to Greece pomegranates (still used as a fertility symbol at weddings), saffron, pistachios and yoghurt, not to mention lemons, which permeated most Mediterranean countries' cuisines.[2]

After the conquest of Persia by Muslim Arabs in the seventh century, the Islamic Abbasid court swiftly absorbed its predecessors' most enjoyable lifestyle, adding the Arabs' desert culture of open hospitality and also the fascinating (to Europeans) habit of belching roundly after a meal, but forbidding the use of alcohol (not very successfully, judging from numerous subsequent accounts, in particular the poetry of Omar Khayyám, which is full of exhortations to enjoy life, and wine, to the

---

1 There is not necessarily a direct connection between these three; each is slightly different. I merely mention that Zoroaster was the first. Persia itself did not emerge until about 550 BC, but its rulers adopted Zoroastrianism. Incidentally, there is some dispute as to whether the yin/yang philosophy is Daoist.
2 It is because of the Greeks that we call Persia Persia and not Iran, as it should be called. Persia (Fars) is merely one province of the larger country of Iran and has been so for over two thousand years; but however incorrect, many modern Iranians still prefer the word Persia.

full). The Arabs also brought an ornate language of food. 'She dazzles the eyes of the beholders with her light, and shows you the light of the full moon even before the evening has arrived' sounds like a line from a love poem, but the subject is actually a dish of rice pudding. Many writers extolled the virtues of leisurely eating: 'When you sit at the table with your brothers, sit long,' wrote one Shi'ite imam, 'for it is a time that is not counted against you as part of your ordained lifespan.' Generously, the Arabs redistributed Persia's cuisine throughout the many lands they conquered.

Islamic pressure on the indigenous Zoroastrians led to many fleeing eastwards to India, taking their customs and cuisine with them. Saffron had already spread from Persia to India around 500 BC, and Buddhist monks there soon used it to dye their robes. The Persians were conquered by nomadic Turkic-speaking Mongoloid tribes who arrived from the steppes of central Asia around the eleventh century. When the Mongols subsequently extended their control to India, they took Persian luxuries with them; these were the basis of the fabulous Moghul court culture. Culinary influences took the form of dishes like biryani and pilau, the tandoori method of cooking, nan bread, tikka, and spice mixtures like garam masala – all considered Indian now, but all of Persian origin. The Mongols also took Persian food to northern China in the thirteenth century where they introduced milk, butter and lamb; to this day, northerners have a predilection for mutton which is generally disliked in the rest of China, where dairy produce is also virtually unknown. The widely travelled family of rice-based dishes known variously as pilaff, pilau and even, arguably, paella, are all versions of the Persian word for one of their most important festive dishes, *polow* – a description of which appears later in the chapter – and *pi-low* still exists as a dish of Persian origin in Xinjiang, which borders with Afghanistan, once part of Iran.

The use of sugar in Europe also emanated from Persia[3] where they had perfected the technique of boiling juice from the crushed cane; the method had already reached Tang dynasty China in the ninth century.

---

3 A characteristic of Persian cuisine is the mixture of sweet with sour. One of her great celebratory *polows* is called 'jewelled rice' and features large sugar crystals scattered over its sparkling mixture of rice, fruit and nuts. A ninth-century Arab also dreams of 'white rice with melted butter and white sugar' being 'a dish not of this world'. Sweetness in savoury dishes was popular throughout medieval Europe and in places never quite died out. In a transit camp after the Second World War, Primo Levi noted the Hungarian cooks serving 'fiery goulashes, and enormous portions of spaghetti with parsley, overcooked and crazily sugared'.

Initially known in medieval Europe only as a costly medicine, it evolved into an essential part of any banquet worthy of the name. It came via the routes already mentioned and also from Arab conquests in North Africa, and from there into Spain where the Moors planted sugar cane as well as saffron, bitter oranges and almonds – another Persian staple necessary for thickening sauces and making marzipan. Long before they were used further north, marzipan and sugar sculpture played a central role in Arab feasts, especially enjoyed after the day's fasting during Ramadan. Nasir-i-Chosrau, a Persian travelling in Egypt in the eleventh century, reported that the sultan had a whole tree made of sugar; this was only a small part of the 73,300 kilos he used during Ramadan. The caliph al-Zahir had seven huge palaces and 157 figures made out of sugar; a later one ordered a whole sugar mosque and then invited the poor in to eat it after the celebrations.

Sir John Chardin describes several typical seventeenth-century Persian entertainments. There are marked similarities between Chardin's accounts and the European medieval entertainments described in chapter 3, but rather than Europe influencing Persian habits, it was the reverse. Persian customs had changed little for hundreds of years. Talking of their clothing, Chardin wrote: 'If the Wisdom of one Nation appears in a constant Custom for their Dress, as has been said, the Persians ought to be mightily commended for their Prudence; for they never alter in their Dress . . . I have seen some Cloaths that Tamerlain [born 1336] wore, which they keep in the Treasury at Ispahan; they are cut just in the same Manner as those that are made at this time of Day, without the least difference.'

Guests at a feast were greeted with heady perfumes. Chardin describes going to a wedding feast where he was greeted by having half a pint of rose-water sprinkled over him followed by a similar quantity of saffron-coloured water, so that not only was he doubly perfumed, but his vest was brightly stained as well. Next, his arms and body were rubbed over with oils perfumed with ambergris and labdanum (a pungent resin from cistus leaves), and finally a garland of jasmine blossom was put around his neck. The perfuming ritual was provided by the women of the household since the guests, naturally, were all male.

A grand feast would begin in the morning. When royalty was entertained, the streets were 'finely gravell'd, and one Side thereof was covered with Brocards [of gold and silver] and Silks spread, and the other was strewn with Flowers.'[4] The whole length of the way was lined with noblemen's servants holding out expensive presents: bales of wool, silk and cloth of gold, whole services made of gold, silver and china; exquisitely tooled trappings for horses, and gold and silver coins. All this was showered at the shah's feet before he was led into a secluded courtyard where a white marble basin trickled out cool water. The whole floor of the great hall was covered with rich tapestries and cushions worked out of the finest coloured silks and golden thread. In the centre of the floor was a huge square marble basin with four fountains tinkling their cool music. On each of the four sides of the basin were four perfuming pots, 'of an extraordinary Bigness, finely embellish'd with Vermillion guilt, between eight little square Boxes of Ivory, adorn'd with Gold enamell'd, and full of Sweets and Perfumes. The whole Hall was covered with large Basons of Sweet-meats, and round the Basons were scented Waters, Bottles of Essences, Liquors, Wine and Brandy of several Sorts.'

Despite his English knighthood, Chardin was the son of a Parisian jeweller who became court jeweller to Charles II after fleeing France to escape the persecution of the Huguenots, so his admiration was more than that of a mere bedazzled layman. Chardin had returned to Persia with some stupendously costly jewels that the shah had commissioned him to procure; running through his account are increasingly frustrated comments on the Persians' love of prevarication when doing business. However, during one distraction he was permitted to see the shah's tableware, and even his practised eye found the service (four thousand pieces, made entirely of fine gold and precious stones) 'incredible, the vast Quantity, and the Value of this Plate; there are cups so large, that one cannot hold them in one Hand when they are full ... What seem'd most Royal to me, was a Dozen of Spoons a Foot long, and large in Proportion made, to drink Broth out of, and other Liquors; the Bowl of the Spoon was of Gold enamel'd, the handle was covered with Rubies, the end was a large Diamond of about six Carats.'

Grand entertainments were not rushed. To start with, sweetmeats were brought round: marzipans, sherbets, biscuits and cakes both tart

---

4 This is remarkably similar to Froissart's fourteenth-century description on p. 24. Chardin commends the Persians' skill in making gold and silver cloth by drawing down the wire and twisting it with silk, 'the best and smoothest that can be imagined ... they last for Ever, as it were, and the Gold and Silver does not wear off while the Work lasts, and keeps still its Colour and brightness.'

and sweet, some flavoured and perfumed with costly spices like saffron. While this was being enjoyed, heady incense swirled around, women dancers waited to entertain, and musicians sang epic poems. Much later, C. J. Wills, a nineteenth-century English doctor, described the singer at a Persian feast: 'He put his hand to the side of his mouth to increase the sound, his face became crimson with his efforts, the muscles and veins stood out in relief on his neck, and his eyes nearly started from their sockets. He frequently paused to take breath, and ceased amid a round of applause.' After this, some time might be spent in resting or walking in the gardens, or perhaps in some archery or inspecting the stables or, if the guest was the shah, in allowing him to indulge in the delights of the host's seraglio.

The best description of the food at a Persian feast comes from an occasion, recorded by Chardin, when the French ambassador and his retinue arrived at Isfahan in 1672 and were entertained by the shah's officers. A golden tablecloth, or *sofreh,* was spread on the floor, and on it were placed several different kinds of bread, the excellent quality of which met with Chardin's approval. This done, servants brought in 'eleven Basons of that sort of Food called Pilau, which is Rice bak'd with Meat: There was of it, of all Colours and of all sorts of Tastes, with Sugar, with the Juice of Pomgranates, the Juice of Citrons, and with Saffron: Each Dish weigh'd above Fourscore Pounds, and had alone been sufficient to satisfy the whole Assembly.' The first four dishes each contained twelve fowls in the rice, the next four had whole lamb each, and the last three had mutton; to accompany these vast pilaus came four huge flat dishes, each one so large and heavy that it was necessary for the diners to help the porters to unload them. 'One of them was full of Eggs made into a Pudding; another of Soop with Herbs; another was fill'd with Herbage and Hash'd Meat; and the last with fry'd Fish. All this being serv'd apon the Table, a Porringer was set before each Person ... fill'd with Sherbet of a tartish sweet Taste,[5] and a Plate of Winter and Summer Sallets.' The Frenchmen who were used to the opulence of Persia ate heartily at the feast, but the newcomers 'fed apon the Admiration of the Magnificence of this Service, which was all of fine Gold, and which (for certain) was worth above a Million'. Many visitors to Persia had been impressed by these

---

5 So far, this is the earliest example I have found of a diner describing the flavour of his food rather than just its ingredients; Chardin has recognised the 'tartish sweet taste' typical of Persian cooking. But he was, after all, French.

huge silver and gold chargers overflowing with luscious meats. A feast for the shah would normally be expected to be more lavish, and indeed at one time it used to be, but Abbas the Great, who was shah from 1588 to 1629, discovered the extent of waste and deceit involved in laying on such a banquet and ordered an upper limit on what could be spent on ingredients for entertaining the shah. There was no limit to the gifts and other trappings, though.

And so the shah passed the whole day and most of the night at the feast eating and drinking and enjoying the pastimes laid on for him. No entertainment for the shah of Persia was complete without 'the Diversion of an artificial Firework', so the darkness of the garden lit up with crackling showers of colour. The shah was fond of sport, in particular of drawing the longbow and other trials of strength. Naturally his favourites praised him on the strength of his arm, and 'he took so much Pleasure in those Commendations, that to convince 'em the more how much he deserved them, he took some Cups of Gold enamel'd of the thickness of a Crown-piece [about 2 mm], and squeezing them with one Hand, would make the Sides meet. This is almost Incredible; but this Prince really has the Shape and Presence of as strong a man as any is. He was carry'd away about the break of Day, not being able to Ride or Walk, through Weariness and Merry-making.'

3

The golden age: medieval feasting

. . . whispering from her towers the last enchantments of the Middle Age.
MATTHEW ARNOLD

Most people, when asked to imagine a feast or a banquet, conjure up images of the spectacular entertainments that took place during the late medieval and Renaissance era throughout Europe. This golden age lasts approximately five hundred years, from the late twelfth century until the end of the seventeenth century. Before then, during the Dark Ages, the people who carved Saxon churches and made intricate Celtic jewels probably feasted well; but there are so few records of this period that any speculation about their feasts has to remain just that. However, their entertainments may have been less elaborate than later medieval feasts since writings of the period indicate that the mortal sin of gluttony was a serious concern. The Venerable Bede, writing in the eighth century, commends King Oswald for giving his Easter feast – complete with its silver serving dish – to the poor waiting at the hall door. After the Norman conquest of 1066, the style of feasting in England began to reflect the influence of French court behaviour and food. This in turn was influenced, via the Crusades, by Middle Eastern civilisations whose use of exotic spices, nuts, fruit, vinegars, sugar and rose-water in cooking gradually filtered up to northern Europe.

The golden age can be divided loosely into two parts, the earlier covering the late medieval period and the later starting some time in the fifteenth century with the changes gradually spreading out from what is commonly known as the Renaissance. This chapter covers the first period. During that long time-span it is notable how little the food changed at feasts and banquets. We have seen more changes to our eating habits in the last forty years than occurred during those five hundred. There was a gradual evolution in the emphasis on different courses and how they were presented, which is discussed elsewhere, but it is fair to say that if you were to serve seventeenth-century guests,

The Banquet at Casa Nani. Pietro Longhi. This elegant banquet was laid on for Clemente Augusto, Elector Archbishop of Cologne in September 1755.

RIGHT *Preparations for a banquet.* c.180–90 AD. Fragment of a Roman mosaic pavement from Carthage.

15thC Persian miniature showing the jewel-like Persian gardens in which many banquets were held.

Two 15thC versions of *Histoire du Grand Alexandre* show all the accoutrements of a medieval feast. ABOVE *How the noble King Alexander was poisoned* exemplifies an important preoccupation of the period. BELOW *Wishing over a peacock*: guests were invited to express their wishes over a peacock served up in full plumage.

OPPOSITE *Queen Isabel's entry into Paris in 1389.* Anonymous painter from Bruges, c.1470. The procession was important since it allowed ordinary people to admire the splendour of their rulers.

La requeste con
templation z plai
sance de treshaut
et noble prince
mon tres cher seigneur z maistre
Guy de chastillon conte de blois
seigneur dauesnes de chymay
et de beaumont z seigneur ane
et de la gode ¶ Ie Iehan froi
sart prebstre et chappelain a mon

tres cher seigneur dessus nome
et pour le tampe de lore tresorier
et chanonne de chymay et de lille
en flandres me suis de nouuel
resueillie et entre dedens ma for
ge pour ouurer et forgier en la
haulte et noble matiere de la
quelle du tampe passe ie me
suis ensonne Laquelle traitte
et propose les fais et aduenues

Charles V of France entertains Emperor Charles IV of Bohemia, Twelfth Night, 1378. From Grandes Chroniques de France. Battles against the Saracens were an enduring theme for a 'soteltie'; this one involved both a ship and a castle.

Masquerade at a French court feast. Anonymous painter from Bruges, c.1470, in *Chronicles of Froissart.* The dreadful accident where the king's nobles are set alight (see p.35).

(see p.35)

NEXT PAGE TOP *The Meat Stall.* Pieter Aertsen, 1551. Symbols of Christian piety, crossed herrings draw the eye to a Biblical scene (the flight from Egypt) in the background. Such simplicity contrasts with the fatty meat, puddings, sausages and creamy curds which have for centuries been connected with feast days, luxury, gluttony, excess, and therefore desirability.

LEFT *Animals awaiting slaughter for a feast.* Roman mosaic, Tunisia, 3rdC. AD. To the Romans, the words 'feast' and 'meat' were almost synonymous; meat also played an important sacrificial role.

RIGHT *Prize fatstock.* Anonymous, English school, c.1820. Many naïve paintings of this period betray their owners' desire for animals that bulged with fat.

almost anywhere in Europe, with the food from a thirteenth-century feast they would find the dishes familiar. Only the style of presentation would have changed significantly.

The elements that characterised medieval spectacles were the chivalrous pageantry epitomised by jousting tournaments, the humour, much of which seems unsophisticated and repetitive to us, the rituals surrounding the serving and carving of a grand feast, and the comparative lack of tableware. Grand events during and after the Renaissance were characterised by the symmetrical placing of dozens of dishes to completely cover the dining table, the theatrical performances commissioned for great festivals, and most notably the separation of the final dessert course. A 'banquet' eventually came to mean only the dessert course and was sometimes offered as an event in its own right without the rest of the meal. But the similarities between medieval and post-Renaissance feasts are as great as the differences.

The most impressive medieval feasts live on in legend just as their hosts intended, yet when we read snippets like Holinshed's 'At this vast and extravagant entertainment ... the number of minstrels, the richness and variety of the dresses, and the crowds of guests that graced this festival were astonishing. The number of dishes served up on this occasion, we are told, amounted to thirty thousand', or 'such was the sumptuousness of that banquet, that the meates which were brought from the table, would sufficiently have served up ten thousand men', they are so far away from anything we know of today that it is difficult for us to understand just what went into one of these extraordinary events. With so many dishes, was the food delicious, or as primitive as we are led to believe? How did they manage such large-scale catering, and what were these feasts for?

The earliest surviving English cookery book, *The Forme of Cury*, was written about 1390 by King Richard II's cook, who describes his sovereign as 'the best and royallest of all Christian kings'; and well he might, for the young king was an enthusiastic entertainer – indeed it was necessary to bring in statutes to regulate his extravagance. The word cury, meaning food preparation, is interesting in itself;[1] it is common in early cookery books: John Russell's description in 1460 of

---

[1] Many English words connected with eating and dining came over with the Norman conquest, e.g., beef, mutton, pork, venison, supplanting in culinary contexts the Anglo-Saxon agricultural words ox, sheep, pig, deer. Cury (variously spelled curee, curie, curry and kewery) has the same derivation as cure, both in the sense of preserving and of restoring health or of caring for people (hence also curate).

cooks 'with their newe conceytes, choppynge, stampynge, and gryn-dynge many new curies' has a familiar ring.

Early recipes are difficult to understand since quantities and methods are sketchy and many of the words are unfamiliar to the modern cook. In order to interpret them it is necessary to combine the skills of linguist, hunter, botanist, butcher and cook with an ability to recognise dishes and cooking methods from other countries, but that is not to say that the resulting dishes were not appetising. If you took a modern recipe and removed all the quantities and most of the explanation, it would appear just as puzzling.[2] Many medieval dishes taste unfamiliar, but we are at least more willing to try the cuisine of other cultures than were the nineteenth-century writers who took one look at medieval recipes and pronounced them disgusting slops. We should also remember that we are discussing food for special occasions here, not everyday food which undoubtedly did have severe shortcomings at times.

Here is an example of a very popular medieval dish from *The Forme of Cury*; it is one of several versions of the same recipe. Blancmanger – 'white eating', with a variety of spellings including blomanger and mangar blanc – was a delicacy served up at feasts and weddings, and given to mothers after childbirth and to invalids. A typical medieval food, the meat is sweetened and the dish coloured, although this one is less spicy than many meat dishes.

For to make Blomanger
Do Ris in water al nyzt and apon the morwe wasch nem wel and do hem upon the fyre for to they breke and nozt for to muche and tak Brann of Caponis sodyn and wel ydraw and smal and tak almaund mylk and boyle it wel wyth ris and wan it is yboyld do the flesch therein so that it be charghaunt and do thereto a god party of sugure and wan it ys dressyd forth in dischis straw theron blaunche Pouder and strike theron Almaundys fryed wyt wyte grece and serve yt forthe.

Roughly translated, it directs you to cook rice (a more luxurious version might use almonds) in water all night. The next day rinse it thoroughly

---

2 This recipe for 'Grilled cod with garlic mash, and rocket & walnut purée' is from a smart book of modern chef's recipes, which I have rewritten in the style of the authentic fifteenth-century recipe above: 'Tak rokyt and braynuttys smal y-scredde and myng them wel wyth rawe oyl; and tak potatys and do them in fayre water, and when they are y-sodde hew and medle altogeder smal and cast thereto powder pepyr and salt and garlec smal mynced and fair buttur a grete quantite; and tak codys and do fle hym and gredyl hym uproun ynowe and so serue yt forthe.'

and dry it over a fire to separate the grains. Then take some stewed capon (chicken) meat and chop it finely. Add almond milk to the rice and bring it to the boil, then add the meat (some versions include eggs and cream as well) and pound it all to a paste, adding plenty of sugar. Turn the paste into a dish and dredge it with white powder (ground almonds, for example) and decorate with fried almonds. On fast days a version was made with fish instead of the poultry. Sometimes blanc-manger was coloured golden with saffron (in which case it became mangar jaune), or 'de-parted' into other colours by dredging it with powdered dried flowers or sanders, and decorated with cloves or blades of mace or perhaps studded with ruby-red pomegranate seeds – I passed by a bush of ripening fruits near a château in south-west France recently and wondered if they were descendants of a medieval plant. Virtually identical blancmanger recipes can be found in seventeenth-century cookery books. Unfortunately, in nineteenth-century Britain this delicate dish degenerated via an almond and rosewater jelly into the meatless arrowroot-based curd we know today as blancmange. The original dish came from the Middle East via Spain and France and lives on abroad. A relic of menjar blanc made from eggs, almonds, chicken stock, sugar, saffron, cinnamon and powdered biscuit exists in Ibiza as the local equivalent to Christmas pudding. Similarly, someone I met at a dinner described a curious pale meat dish he had eaten in Turkey. It was sweetened, with the chicken so well pounded that it stuck to his teeth; I recognised it immediately.

Records of feasts go back much further than cookery books, and to get an idea of the atmosphere at a medieval feast it is worth remembering the background of the people who took part. Sir John Froissart's *Chronicles*, written in the fourteenth century, consists of page after page of fighting. Sometimes it is surprisingly chivalrous and courteous, sometimes shockingly brutal in its vengeance. He vividly describes sieges, negotiations and the woes of captured crusaders: 'They were nothing there at their ease: the heat of the country and diet sore changed them; for they had been used before to sweet and delicate meats and drinks . . .' Interspersing these calamities are the feasts and tournaments staged by people who, fabulously wealthy though they were, were not immune from famine and disease and who display universal human concerns, loyalties, irritations and delights. There was a huge gap between the top level of society and everyone else. Although poor people had their own ways of celebrating, the nearest they would get to the magical feasts of the nobility would be incredulous descriptions and the remnants of the meals which were either distributed amongst the servants or left in the alms-boxes afterwards.

These spectacles were a combination of chivalrous hospitality and the aggressive display of wealth and power expected of kings and noblemen. Chivalry is a concept at the heart of medieval life. The word comes from *chevalier*, as does the word cavalry: the chevaliers were the mounted elite of the army, and of society too. A 'verray parfit gentil knight', whilst battling with impossible tasks set by his pure and idealised lady, strove to attain the goals of perfect valour, courtesy, generosity, and swordsmanship without yielding to the temptations that would inevitably beset him. A knight who reneged on a promise was a social outcast: one of the many battles Froissart described was a skirmish between England and Scotland, after which the captured knights were allowed a few weeks' grace to settle their affairs at home (even indulging in some jousting *en route*) in the knowledge that they could be trusted to return to captivity at the agreed time. These qualities – those of the archetypal Christian – were epitomised by the courts of King Arthur and Charlemagne, both of whom inspired quantities of romantic legends.

Although feasts are mentioned, contemporary accounts rarely describe the food; it appears that their authors did not consider food particularly noteworthy (or perhaps they feared that any allusion to it might be construed as gluttony), but if medieval food preparation did conform to a routine and food really changed so little, then it was probably thought unnecessary to spell it out in detail – readers would know what to expect. More importantly, the meals at medieval feasts were just one element of a much larger event which often went on for days, entertaining hundreds if not thousands of people. These occasions sometimes left writers lost for words: '. . . we cannot help fancying ourselves transported into the fabled regions of romance, or the in-chanted land of fairy revelry' or 'if its fame were rehearsed, the reader would perhaps doubt of the truth thereof', writes Holinshed. Feasts were given in between entertainments but were often eclipsed by the pageantry and the gifts, the music and jousting, the story-tellers and jesters, the costumes and the dazzling treasures on display. Preparations could take months of planning, including the ordering of wine and the forward purchase of animals for slaughter. Meat and poultry was one item that did sometimes merit a mention. To people for whom meat was the ultimate food, the variety must have been gratifying, even to those used to such fare. The inventory for the great feast given in Yorkshire at Cawood for the enthronement of George Neville, Archbishop of York, in September 1465 lists the following:

Oxen, one hundred and foure.

Wild Bull, six.

Muttons, one thousand.

Veales, three hundred and foure.

Porkes, three hundred and foure.

Swannes, foure hundred.

Geese, five thousand.

Capons, seven thousand.

Piggs, three thousand.

Plovers, foure hundred.

Quails, one hundred dozen.

Fowles called Rayes, two hundred dozen.

Peacocks, foure hundred.

Mallards and Teales, foure thousand.

Cranes, two hundred and foure.

Kidds, two hundred and foure

Chickens, three thousand.

Pigeons, foure thousand.

Conyes [rabbits], foure thousand.

Bytternes, two hundred.

Hernshawes [young herons], foure hundred.

Pheasants, two hundred.

Partridge, five hundred.

Woodcocks, foure hundred.

Curlews, one hundred.

Egritts, one thousand.

Staggs, Bucks, and Roes, five hundred and four.

Pasties of Venison cold, one hundred and three.

Pasties of Venison hot, one thousand five hundred.

Give or take the odd crane, that is 41,833 items of meat and poultry, an impressive amount to have amassed; sixty-two cooks directing five hundred and fifteen scullions and kitcheners were needed to cope with it. Judging by contemporary pictures you could have bathed in the

cauldrons used for cooking such banquets; some required ropes and pulleys to tilt them without toppling them over. The French writer Monteil's description of a fourteenth-century French kitchen gives us a good sense of the atmosphere:

Field kitchen and *Manhandling a cooking pot.* Bartolomeo Scappi *Opera*, 1570. Later illustrations, but they show how vast quantities of food were produced, both in kitchens and in temporary situations.

The chimney-pieces are no less than twelve feet in length. One man would not have strength sufficient to use the tongs or the shovels; the andirons [firedogs] do not weigh less than a hundred pounds; the trivets forty pounds; copper saucepans of forty pounds are common, as are spits of eleven and twelve pounds. One roast [course] is composed of one, two, or three calves, two three or four sheep, plus game, venison and poultry. The boiling of the saucepans, the exhalations from the grease, render the atmosphere so fat, so thick, that it is only necessary to breathe in it to feed. A person would not dare enter one of these kitchens on the eve of a fast day, for fear, as it were, of breaking his fast.

A great deal of effort went into making the dishes look as well as taste good; many spices also served as colourings. As well as meat and poultry, the Cawood inventory mentions lots to drink and a little fish, including 'porpisses and seales, twelve', and side dishes like 'Parted dishes of Ielly, three thousand. Plain dishes of Ielly, three thousand. Cold tarts, one hundred and three. Hot custards, two thousand. Cold custards, three thousand. Of all kindes of sweet meates, abundance.' 'Abundance' in this case meant around thirteen thousand. Recipes from *The Forme of Cury* make it possible to imagine the flavours; the hot custards sound delicious.

By taking an otherwise meticulous description and adding the missing feast details from other accounts, we can piece together the battery of sensations that assaulted the late medieval reveller. Sir John Froissart's account of the spectacles that young King Charles VI laid on in Paris in 1389 to celebrate the first entry of his new Queen Isabel makes a good example. Hundreds of guests and thousands of spectators watched the processions, pageants, jousting and other entertainments from Sunday till Friday. These were interspersed by several feasts at which spectators were kept at bay with wooden barriers guarded by sergeants and ushers.

The queen arrived with her retinue of ladies carried in litters or riding side-saddle, attended by dukes, lords and burgesses on horseback. They were watched by a huge throng of the people of Paris. At such occasions the streets were usually strewn with sweet-smelling herbs and flowers since even in June the ground would be dirty, but in this case the ground was covered with cloths of silk and camlet,[3] and all the houses were hung with woven tapestries, 'in such plenty as though such cloths should cost nothing'. Along the route various tableaux had been staged to welcome Isabel. These were elaborate constructions: the first one was decorated with banners of shining golden suns and the arms of France to portray the heavens full of stars. Inside were young children dressed like angels singing sweetly. To represent Christ there was a small child who was absorbed in 'a little mill made of a great nut'; presumably this toy was a diversion to keep him from fidgeting. The next scene was a fountain draped with blue cloth decorated with fleurs-de-lys, out of which spewed great streams of red and white wine that was offered to everyone in the procession by pretty girls who sang songs as they went. After this refreshment, the cavalcade arrived at a

---

3 Camel-hair cloth.

tableau of a castle and watched a short play about crusaders at war with the Saracens, always a popular theme since the players could enjoy a thoroughgoing fight and the onlookers could feel patriotic; this pageant was 'well regarded'. The procession made its way past a tableau of the Holy Trinity in which singing angels produced a rich crown of precious stones for the queen, and then past a small stage made out of tapestries with 'men playing upon organs, right sweetly'. The last spectacle was a sturdily made castle with a cast of allegorical figures and a tour de force of a courtyard which was full of real trees. Living in this urban paradise were hares, rabbits and wild birds, but according to Froissart the reason these unfortunate creatures stayed put was that whenever they tried to escape, the crowds outside frightened them back into the haven of the courtyard. And so the procession continued, with other diversions along the way, including what may be the earliest description of a tightrope-walker who 'with two brenning candles in his hands issued out of a little stage that he had made on the height of Our Lady's tower, and singing he went upon the cord all along the great street, so that all that saw him had marvel how it might be'. Finally the Queen arrived at the church of Our Lady and was invested with her crown after she had made some costly gifts of her own to the church. After some more exchanges of gifts and dancing at the palace of Paris they retired.

The next day King Charles laid on a feast. Colour and pageantry extended into the medieval banqueting hall, making it far more than just a sumptuous meal. Three hundred years earlier, William the Conqueror's son William Rufus had built Westminster Hall in London as 'a theatre of modern revelry'. He held a great feast to celebrate its completion, deciding afterwards that it wasn't nearly big enough: 'but a bedchamber in comparison of that I minde to make'. Such halls were huge and were designed to inspire awe. Walls and columns were gilded or brightly painted inside and out with stripes and chevrons, sometimes even with frescoes, and often the host sat under an ornate canopy. If the walls were not painted, the usher, as for Archbishop Neville's feast, 'must see that the Hall be trimmed in every poynt and that the cloth of estate be hanged in the Hall and that the Quyshions of estate be set in order apon the benche, being of fine sylke, or Cloth of Gold.' Now that the paint has long worn away, we imagine medieval buildings were always sombre grey stone and should be left that way; indeed the citizens of Stirling were outraged when the castle banqueting hall was recently restored to its former gilded glory. 'Garish and tasteless,' complained local papers as the offending gold roof gleamed down from the castle rock. But a glance at medieval tapestries in any museum will confirm the glowing colours of that period.

Clothes were showy too: plumed hats and embroidered silks shimmered with golden threads; plenty of paintings and illustrated manuscripts survive to show how spectacular were the costumes of this period – on the occasion of Isabel's entry into Paris, King Charles' surcoat was of brilliant scarlet trimmed with white ermine. The carvers and cup-bearers were equally colourful since they were themselves noblemen. Decoration and colour extended to the food as well. Costly ingredients like saffron or gold leaf were used to 'endore' pies and tarts; nuts and chopped candied fruit added pinpoints of colour and texture. Pounded herbs gave green, spices and flowers gave other colours: for example sanders, a species of sandalwood (not the scented kind), makes a vivid orangey red if you grind it up and steep it in liquid. Various shades of brown came from burnt toast or any other caramelised food – we still use this for gravy browning today. Cooked blood gives a dense black (as in black pudding) which could be contrasted with white snippets of lard or some other coloured item. Sometimes open tarts were made in heraldic shapes, each partition filled with a different coloured food. 'To make a Spinage tart of three colours, green, yellow and white', and 'Tart stuff that carries his colour black', run the recipe titles.

Amongst all the colour and noise, the rituals of preparing and serving the medieval high table[4] were spectacles in themselves. First of all a buffet, or sideboard, would be covered with rich cloths to display the costliest examples of silver and gold plate; King Charles' was apparently greatly coveted – that, of course, being the whole point. Some banqueting halls had permanent dining tables but many erected trestles. In Paris, the very large marble table in the hall was made longer by a great plank of oak four inches thick. The top table was laid with several fine linen cloths carefully folded to produce neat creases. These creases, so commonly seen in contemporary paintings, were repeated in wood carvings on walls and furniture and are called linenfold pattern. On top there might also be layers of runners or napkins which could be

---

4 The high-table format still survives at conferences, weddings and formal banquets and some university colleges.

removed as they became soiled. Linen cloths were valuable items and often only the top table would have so many layers, so it was necessary for lesser mortals to learn how to conduct themselves properly at table in order to minimise the amount of detritus and splashing of food. Keeping the cloths clean was not particularly easy when food was eaten with fingers, spoon and knife. Wynkyn de Worde[5] conjures up a world very different to the courtly ritual at the top table. He warns against scratching and picking away at various unsavoury parts of the anatomy, guddling with unwiped fingers in the pies for gobbets of food, slurping wine with greasy lips, wiping soiled fingers on the tablecloth and clothing, and spitting on the floor. But everyday eating habits should not be confused with a splendid banquet where everyone would be on their best behaviour. Having said this, what was then acceptable in polite society may not be nowadays: although many restaurants in France still allow patrons' dogs to sit under the table, I doubt if they would permit them to run around on top like the Duke of Berry's little dogs did. Before forks were used, the polite way to bring food to your mouth was with the thumb and first two fingers, leaving the unsullied little finger to dip into the salt. It has been suggested that the gesture – long regarded as affected – of raising your little finger while holding a cup in polite company is a relic of that custom.

On the pristine cloth, stacks of bread cut into square 'trenchers' were placed ready to eat off. These trenchers served as disposable plates and must have saved a lot of work in the kitchen – offcuts would have been used to thicken sauces and baking coarse trencher bread would involve far less work than washing-up when water had to be heated over the busy fire. The soiled trenchers, soaked in nutritious gravy, were put in the alms-box with other leftovers to be collected by poor people. Bread trenchers were used in Britain until well into the fifteenth century, when they were replaced, first by wood and pewter and then by china. Fine bread was cut for eating: the top table was given a roll or the superior 'upper crust' of *pandemain* because the bottom of a large loaf becomes hard when baked on the floor of a bread oven. The king's knife and spoon would be wiped, assayed for poison, kissed, placed on the table and the whole setting covered with a napkin. A great salt cellar would be placed by the king; these were

---

5 Wynkyn de Worde's *Boke of Kervynge* was written in 1513 and is typical of many etiquette books of the period.

splendid examples of silversmithing and objects of great prestige. On the continent they were made like little ships (called *nefs*), sometimes from a nautilus shell with gold or silver sails, and set on wheels so that they could be pushed along the table. King Charles' *nef* contained his spoon, knife, a tiny fork and his poison-detector. Less elevated company sat 'below the salt'.

Everything the king or a great lord ate and drank had to be checked or assayed for poison by a trusted knight. It was an act of great responsibility and people were rightly anxious about it; failure could carry a high price. Just how much food poisoning was deliberate must remain a subject of speculation because even though people's natural immunity against bacteria would have been formidable compared to ours, the use of untinned copper and bronze pans alone could have produced some unpleasant toxins. Some years after our feast, Froissart describes a flurry of anxiety amongst the nobility when the king became seriously ill. Sir Helion of Neilhac, the squire who had last served him a drink, was summoned. "'Sir," quoth he, "here is Robert Tanques and I, we took the say [assay] in the presence of the king." "That is true," quoth Robert of Tanques, "ye need not doubt therein nor have any suspiciousness, for as yet there is the same wine in the flagons, whereof we will drink and assay before you."' The squires were exonerated and the king eventually recovered. Various objects were used to assay food and utensils; in some courts everything was wiped with bread which had to be eaten by a servant; some courts used other things in the belief that they would either detect poison or else render it harmless. Charles' poison-detector was a 'serpent's tongue' (actually a shark's tooth), but 'unicorn horns' (really narwhal tusks), agate, rhino horn and bezoar stones (bezoar comes from the Persian meaning Conqueror of Poison; these 'stones' were supposedly made by deer, see p. 105) were all used.[6] A poisonous liquid was supposed to effervesce and be rendered safe when poured into a rhino-horn cup, and indeed an alkaloid would react with keratin, the substance of horn. Alkaloids might also have corroded 'unicorn horn', bezoar and sharks' teeth since these organic materials are marked quite easily, but it is difficult to imagine how an inert stone like polished agate could have detected much. Scented water used for the ceremonial washing of hands was

---

6 Rhino-horn cups were mainly used as detectors in the Middle and Far East. Agate was supposed to change colour on contact with poison.

also assayed before being brought to table; this ritual was offered before the meal and again before the final dessert course.

The feast was divided into courses with the number of dishes per course increasing according to importance; three courses was the usual but at great feasts like that of 1389 in Paris many more might be served. In 1466, during the Wars of the Roses in England, a party of Bohemian lords was impressed by a dinner of fifty courses given them by Edward IV; shortly afterwards the Earl of Warwick (known as the Kingmaker) outclassed his king by entertaining the party with sixty courses – an intentionally threatening message. Warwick had a reputation for generous hospitality; in London he 'held such an house that six oxen were eaten at breakfast, and every tavern was full of his meat, for those who had any acquaintance in that house he should have as much sod [stew] and rost as he might carry on a long dagger.' Warwick was brother to Archbishop Neville, whose spectacular feast at Cawood was another pointed signal to the king. Whatever the number of courses, all but the last were rather similar. The king and highest nobles were offered the widest choice, others what their rank accorded, just like Chinese banquets of that period. This explains why at Archbishop Neville's feast we see listed thousands of chickens, geese and various other items yet only four hundred swans and peacocks, these two prized items being reserved for the superior tables.

Froissart dismisses King Charles' feast in three words, 'great and noble', but the first course would have had soup followed by an impressive selection, similar to Neville's list, of roasted meats, poultry, game meats and game birds (some of these birds being extinct today). The roasted meats (or fish if it was a fast day) were interspersed with a number of other dishes which could be fish or 'made dishes' such as pies, fricassés, vegetable purées or 'porrays', savoury or sweet jellies, custards and tarts. Meat and poultry was classed either as 'greater' or 'lesser' according to both size and status, beef and most game being classed as 'greater'. In Italy at this time some game animals were roasted whole and covered in gold leaf before being sent to table to be carved.

Carving was a chivalrous skill carried out at table by a nobleman. He would be expected to know that a bird was held in the left hand and carved with the right, and that there was a correct term to describe how to carve each creature. Several books describe exactly how each creature should be dismembered before being sauced and offered to

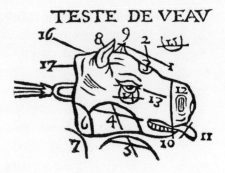

How to carve a calf's head. 15th century diagram. Carving was a skilful accomplishment which men of noble birth acquired in order to serve at the royal feast table.

eat. John Russell's *Boke of Nurture* written about 1460 is one of the earliest. Some terms sound comical if not brutal: 'tame that crab, a slut to kerve … unlace that coney … unjoint that bittern … display that crane … mince that plover.' 'Thigh that woodcock' before you 'Raise his legs as a hen, and dight his brain.' To 'unbrace' a mallard you 'Raise up the pinion and the leg, but take them not off. Raise the merry thought [i.e. the wishbone] from the breast, and lace it down on each side with your knife, bending to and fro likeways.' Watching a skilled carver at work, with his flashing knife deftly transforming the meat into a neat pile of slices, would be a fine spectacle, especially if it had been an Italian gilded roast. Such prowess with the carving knife would be intended to impress a nobleman's dexterity on his king. It was also the carver's duty to sauce the meat. Medieval sauces were generally sharp, spicy and brightly coloured, thickened with bread or ground almonds rather than cream or eggs. The bright green vinegary mint sauce we serve with roast lamb is a typical, albeit simplified, remnant that clearly displays its Middle Eastern origin.

Certain creatures were reserved for royalty or great noblemen; some still are. Porpoises and sturgeon, swans and peacocks were all highly prized so it is likely they would have featured at Charles' feast. A favourite piece of showmanship was either a swan, peacock or pheasant which had been skinned then roasted and then sewn back into its plumage, the head and tail being secured with a skewer or rod to hold them in place. The beak and peacock's comb would be gilded and a golden collar or garland placed round its neck. Sometimes a piece of cloth soaked in spirits would be put in its beak and lit so that it appeared to be breathing fire as it was carried in. These apparitions were so popular that if a freshly roasted bird was not available there would be a huge gilded pie with a dried stuffed bird sitting on top. Nowadays we make do with china terrine dishes with hares or hens moulded onto the lids. My own attempt at reconstructing a swan is described in chapter 28.

The second and subsequent courses would be similar except that the meat or fish tended to be stewed rather than roasted, and often served with frumenty. Frumenty is made from slowly simmered whole wheat or oats and was a universal favourite: the medieval equivalent of 'chips with everything'. 'Fatt venesoun with frumenty hit is a gay plesewre, your souerayne to serve,' writes Russell. There would also be a number of pies – some of them huge – elaborately decorated and gilded. These could conveniently be made in advance which would ease pressure on the kitchens. Their strong pastry crusts were so thick as to be inedible but fulfilled the same role as a casserole (a robust hot-water crust is impervious to juices) and, like casseroles, their lids were removed to reveal the hot liquid contents: a mixture of meat, fish and fruits made exotic with spices and given zest by adding wine or verjus (the acid juice of unripe grapes or apples). The 'mincemeat' we use for making pies at Christmastime gives some indication of the flavour combinations in those dishes, as does Middle Eastern food. Open tarts were filled, quiche-like, with savoury or sweet egg mixtures, usually brightly coloured. The numbers of eggs used in some medieval inventories are impressive: eleven thousand for one of Richard II's feasts in 1387, thirty-nine thousand for the coronation of Pope Clement VI in 1342. Sadly, the logistics of supplying such quantities are lost to us. Offering a variety of dishes was important, not only because it gave a generous impression but also because medieval people were advised to eat different types of food according to their 'humour' or disposition. Fresh fruit was regarded with suspicion as it was thought to induce diarrhoea and fevers. Given that the Black Death had swept through Europe only forty years before Charles VI's feast and was to recur several times, such caution was understandable, if unfortunate.

After several courses of meat and fish came the dessert or 'voidée', both words indicating the 'unserving' or emptying of the table, when hands were washed and a fresh cloth was placed on the table. A remnant of this ritual still happens in restaurants when your table is completely cleared and all the crumbs are swept off the cloth before the dessert. Dessert always included thin crisp wafers, which were endlessly popular. They were made from a rich batter of egg yolks, cream, rose-water, flour and sugar pressed between iron tongs hot enough to cook but not to burn; wafers were meant to be an elegant white. Spices such as caraway seeds were chewed to aid digestion and sometimes turned into comfits by coating them in sugar, and a spiced, sweetened wine called hippocras was universal. Sweetmeats became increasingly elaborate from the fifteenth century onwards, but in medieval times sugar was an expensive medicine and its role at a feast was as a digestive. The voidée always finished the meal and the host would retire afterwards. In actual fact, at King Charles' feast there were so many spectators that one of the tables 'was by reason of the press overthrown to the earth and the ladies caused suddenly to rise without order, and sore chafed with the press and heat that was in the palace'. A door was thrown open to allow in fresh air, but the party was over: the court departed without its dessert that day. They would have made up for it at one of the other feasts over the next four days, however, perhaps after the jousting tournaments or when the 'ladies and the king and the lords danced and revelled all that night, near hand till it was day in the morning'.

The reason Froissart gave so little account of the feast was that he wanted to focus on the 'pastimes that were made between the messes', which clearly interested him more. Entertaining your guests was just as important as feeding them and a whole variety of diversions would be on offer, extending the spectacle of serving the meal. Music was everywhere, as the fourteenth-century poem *Sir Gawain and the Green Knight*[7] describes:

> The first course comes with a burst of trumpets
> Whose banners hung from them in brilliant colours.
> And now a clatter of kettledrums, a chiffing of fifes:
> Wild music that ricochets off walls and rafters;
> And the listeners' hearts leap with the lively notes.

Minstrels and jesters (the two roles were often combined) wandered among the guests singing and playing gentle tunes on their lutes. At the Feast of the Pheasant, given by Philip, Duke of Burgundy in 1454

---

7 *Sir Gawain and the Green Knight* is an oddity because Sir Gawain almost succumbs to the trials set him in the form of the seductive wife of his host. Indeed some scholars consider the poem to be a satire. Although he passes the test and his life is spared, Gawain considers he has failed the code of chivalry and bitterly regrets his near-misdeed. The poem, however, contains some vivid descriptions of medieval feasting and hunting episodes.

to inspire a last desperate crusade to liberate Constantinople from the Turks, a huge pie was brought in, revealing a group of musicians when its crust was cracked. The organiser of the feast, Olivier de la Marche, entered on an elephant to sing a moving falsetto song about the captive Eastern Church. Minstrels were an important constituent of the medieval feast, travelling round Europe and being often handsomely rewarded for their talents. Much history would have been lost to us had not their songs kept it alive. A jester or fool, as well as telling stories and jokes, could use his wit to defuse a potentially awkward situation and his services, too, were well recompensed, both with money and privileges. Shakespeare's fool in *Twelfth Night* is far from an idiot; instead he manipulates the other characters like puppets. Mummers and people dressed as 'wild men' could appear at almost any stage of the proceedings.

Froissart's 'pastimes' were known variously as sotelties or subtleties, or if on a large scale, pageants. The word soteltie combines various Old French words: *sot*, a fool; *sot-l'y-laisse*, a satirical dialogue; and *subtil*, ingenious, skilful, crafty. The meaning of the word subtle has slightly altered over the centuries; nowadays we would not use it to describe these exuberant entertainments. In France they were called *entremets* (*mets* means course) since they came between the courses; the equivalent of a pageant was an *entremets mouvant*. Sotelties and pageants took many forms, their aim being to surprise and impress the guests with the skill and ingenuity of the household; often they delivered a message. Early sotelties were usually inedible, made of hard pastry which was gilded or painted, and sometimes bore written messages which were read out to those too far away to see. Later sotelties were made from sugar which was worked into a malleable form and made into translucent (and edible) goblets and plates;[8] these were greatly enjoyed, if not by the top table then at least by the spectators afterwards. Pageants depicted all sorts of exploits, the greater part being military though later ones used allegorical images of classical figures to enact messages that could be flattering or threatening, depending on the target audience. Some of these contraptions were huge: ships, whales, garrisons with soldiers, even elephants like Olivier de la Marche's, were constructed and wheeled into the hall accompanied by musicians and actors.

8 See chapter 16 for details.

For a grand feast, the kitchens coped with the tabletop pastry constructions whereas carpenters, painters and sculptors were brought in weeks in advance to construct the larger efforts. These were the same anonymous craftsmen that carved fantastic gargoyles and playful wooden misericords in churches, who painted quirky miniature scenes round the edges of illuminated manuscripts and whose imagination clearly ran riot at times; showing off was encouraged. Some entertainments bore serious messages: battles between Saracens and Christians such as Queen Isabel saw during her procession were perennial favourites throughout the crusades; other accounts mention sotelties of a hen with her chicks or, more obviously, 'a wyf in childbed', both of which might raise a blush at a wedding feast. For a coronation an allegorical display of peace, harmony and justice might be a suitable theme, or even the combining of two countries' flags to indicate the new monarch's intentions. But the spirit of carnival lurked around these creations, and sometimes inside them; mechanical peacocks strut over the tablecloth, live songbirds are wrapped up into table napkins, powdered poppies are slipped into a neighbour's wine cup 'to make White Wine Red at Table', and quicksilver is placed inside a chicken to make it leap about in the dish. Richard Warner, in *Antiquitates Culinariae*, describes a feast at which, while the guests were happily engaged in their meal, 'a Zany or Jester suddenly entered the room, and springing over the heads of the astonished guests, plunged himself into the quivering custard, to the unspeakable amusement of those who were far enough from the tumbler not to be bespattered by this active gambol.' All kinds of creatures appear to have been baked into pies: live snakes or frogs wriggled out as well as the birds of nursery rhyme – even an unfortunate dwarf called Jeffrey Hudson, who was served up to his queen inside a cold pie. These pies were baked with a filling of bran or some other meal which was emptied out after the paste had cooked. If the pie was a large one, it was easy enough to pop the birds (or dwarf) in and replace the lid, which was heavy enough to stay in place. If not, a hole was made in the base, the bran emptied out, and the birds or frogs stuffed inside from underneath. Such pies were opened by running a knife vertically round the inside edge of the crust, freeing the lid which was then lifted off with pastry 'handles'.

Fire was an exciting addition to the spectacle; peacocks breathing fire have already been mentioned. Distillation, like so many other elements of the medieval feast, arrived via the Moors and by the fourteenth century flambéing food was all part of the showmanship, along with the carving displays at table; today's flaming Christmas pudding remains with us almost unchanged from those times. If you wonder if anything ever went amiss with these ambitious events, I can tell you that it did. Returning to Froissart's chronicles, he mentions not only how the mishap with the ladies' table brought about by the spectators' enthusiasm for the 'pastime' caused displeasure to the new queen, but also describes a much more unfortunate incident that happened five years later.

In 1394, a marriage was to take place at court between one of the king's knights and one of the queen's gentlewomen, so great festivities were planned. The king laid on a feast and asked Hugonin de Guisay, one of his squires, to 'make some pastime'. De Guisay decided to stage a mummery of wild men which the king and some of his friends would enact. Wild men (sometimes referred to as wodewoses or woodhouses) were a popular diversion. Completely disguised by hairy coverings, the wild men would arrive, dance or gambol with the company, and often leave without anyone knowing who they were or where they came from, evoking the pagan strangeness of the Green Man. De Guisay made six costumes out of linen cloth covered with pitch embedded with flax to look like hair. The king and five knights secretly dressed up 'and when they were thus arrayed in these said coats and sewed fast in them, they seemed like wild wodehouses full of hair from the top of the head to the sole of the foot. This devise pleased well the King and was well content with the squire for it.' The usher was advised that when the wodehouses arrived to dance, all the torchbearers were to stand at the back of the hall. All went to plan, the ladies being suitably intrigued, particularly the Duchess of Berry who drew the disguised king away from his companions and insisted he should not escape until she found out who he was. So great was the mystery that the Duke of Orleans, who had arrived late and not heard the instruction to keep torchbearers out of the way, grabbed one of the torches to get a better look and accidentally set the pitch alight. One knight, Nantouillet, remembered there was a buttery nearby where they rinsed pans; he rushed out and threw himself into the water, saving his life. The king was saved by his flirtatious duchess, who threw the train of her gown over him to protect him from the fire and then discovered whom she had saved. The other four, including Hugonin de Guisay, died from their burns. 'Thus the feast of this marriage brake up in heaviness.'

Medieval feasting, with its use of vivid colour, robust spicy flavours, heraldic music, showmanship and not-so-subtle entertainments, was gradually superseded as a result of Renaissance influences that crept up through Europe from Italy from the fifteenth century. In northern parts of Europe the older traditions survived well into the sixteenth century; they were typified by occasions like the Field of the Cloth of Gold in 1520 which, as an event held jointly by France and England, was a display of almost unrivalled brilliance but one that set aside modern trends in favour of tried and tested medieval splendour.

4

Competitive feasts: disconcerting elements

There is no enemy like food
INDIAN PROVERB

Seeking, gaining and holding onto power has been responsible for many spectacular feasts. Kings, armies, craft guilds, social climbers and politicians have all staged attempts to out-feast each other. Sometimes an extravagant feast is provoked by a challenge or an insult. In Damon Runyon's short story 'A Piece of Pie', published in 1956, Miss Violette Shumberger (who has 'a face the size of a town clock and enough chins for a fire escape . . . and a laugh that is so hearty it knocks the whipped cream off an order of strawberry shortcake on a table fifty feet away') defeats her male eating-competition challenger with psychological warfare as much as with her gustatory prowess. On the other hand Alasdair Crotach, eighth chief of the Clan MacLeod, was piqued by a condescending Sassenach remark. On a visit to the Palace of Holyrood in 1538, MacLeod had been much impressed by King James V's magnificent silverware, his abundantly loaded table, the brilliant candlelight and the costly court clothing. Noticing his appreciation, a Lowland nobleman commented that MacLeod would not, of course, be able to produce anything on Skye to compare with such a table, such costumes and such candlesticks. MacLeod was actually a cultured and intellectual man and resented this remark. In riposte he said, 'But sir, you are mistaken; on Skye I have a greater hall, a finer table, and more precious candleholders by far than any you see before you here.' Overhearing MacLeod's remark, the king promised that he would visit Skye the following summer to see for himself.

And so he did. In 1539 King James sailed with a band of jovial lords and ladies up to Dunvegan, where MacLeod welcomed them with a troop of horses and carried the party right up to the top of Healaval Mhor, the nearest of two flat-topped mountains now known as MacLeod's Tables. By this time dusk was falling and as they reached the summit, which is indeed like a flat tabletop, the visitors saw hundreds of devoted clansmen circling the 'table' with blazing torches. 'Here, sire, is my hall', said Macleod. 'Its walls are great mountains, its floor the mighty deep, its roof the canopy of heaven. My table is two thousand feet high and here bearing lighted torches are my priceless sconces and your faithful servants.' The king was delighted by the gesture and, as befits a good story, the Lowland lords were duly struck dumb.[1] History does not record what they ate up there, but the clan was well known for its hospitality, one visitor writing, 'The six nights I remained in Dunvegan, it was not a show of hospitality I met with there, but a plentiful feast ... The family were placed around, under the protection of their great chief, raised by his prosperity and by respect for his warlike feats, now enjoying the company of his friends at the feast, amidst the sounds of harps, overflowing goblets and happy youths.' Given the date and the venue, the likelihood is that it would have been a meaty late medieval style of feast featuring much roasted venison and game birds, with fish from the bountiful waters round Skye and baskets of bread and wine brought up in panniers. One can only hope that the flaming torches kept the midges at bay.

MacLeod's event was a type of competitive feast, though he probably hoped for royal favours of the political kind rather than any sort of reciprocal feast. Truly competitive feats of one-upmanship require that each occasion should become grander than the last. Such events have the ultimate result of bankrupting one of the parties, in terms of either wealth or prestige. Nevertheless, they crop up all over the place. There is the *mucaqara*, an Arabic duel of extravagant camel-slaughtering after which the meat is given away, the donor hoping for legendary status. Abd al-Muttalib, the Prophet's grandfather, slaughtered far more camels than the people of Mecca could eat, boasting, 'We feed until the birds eat what is left, while the hands of other hosts tremble.' In Indonesia some islanders held competitive feasts whose main ingredient was ever-increasing amounts of pork, each event a provocation

---

1 Perhaps James remembered his father, James IV, who had himself been goaded into providing a feast in response to an implied insult. When a party of French visited him in the Scottish Borders in the winter, they commented that he would be unlikely to be able to provide a sumptuous feast of local produce. The next night they were regaled with fresh salmon and trout from the rivers, shellfish from the coast, game of all sorts, plus beef and mutton in plenty from the surrounding hills. But for dessert in a Scottish winter? A train of servants brought in covered dishes and set them in front of the guests. The lifted lids revealed gold nuggets panned from the local river, a gesture that charmed James' visitors.

to the host's rival, who spent months if not years building up the resources to outdo his challenger. In twelfth-century Japan, wealthy aristocrats and samurai held competitive tea-tasting parties called *tocha* which could last for three days. The tea was tasted blind and the participants laid bets on which variety was being served. More and more costly possessions were wagered until it was decided that such activity seriously threatened the country's wealth, and in consequence *tocha* were banned.

Sumptuary laws like this crop up from time to time in relation to feasting; even monarchs were not exempt. The Reverend Richard Warner described the court of Richard II of England as a place where 'magnificence and prodigality of royal entertainments rose to their greatest heights'. It was for this enthusiastic young king that the earliest known English cookery book was written (see p. 17) and his feasting became so costly that a statute was passed to curb his expenditure. During one year no fewer than seven of these sumptuary laws were passed, so clearly Richard was not especially keen to assist in the economies. Sumptuary laws were also used to reinforce social position: for example, what one could eat at official banquets in sixteenth-century Hungary was minutely regulated by ordinance of the Free Cities. The number of guests and servants and musicians was also designated. People were separated into three categories: first came officials, noblemen and patricians; next were members of the Council of the Hundred; and lastly all other citizens. The first group could be served ten courses at a wedding, the second one eight and the third six. This last group could not be served pâté or torte either. Every plate above the allowed number drew a fine of two *forints* (florins). Similarly, the Florentine *Pragmatica* of 1356 sought to curtail excessive rivalry at banquets and weddings by fining anyone who served more than three courses at a wedding (though it has to be said that since fruit, vegetables and cheese were exempted, and a roast could be stuffed with a great many other creatures, some pretty sumptuous meals were concocted within these rules). The Venetian Republic was more specific: in 1516 a decree stated that 'at each meal not more than one course of roast meat and one of boiled may be served, nor may these courses contain more than three types of meat or fowl'. Spot checks on the kitchens by officials helped to curb the over-enthusiastic chef. Venetian gondolas had already been regulated a hundred years earlier. They used to be brilliantly decorated, each owner vying with his rivals to make his boat the grandest, the most gilded, the most intricately painted, the most gorgeously draped. Again, this was deemed a waste of resources and so it was forbidden to paint gondolas anything other than black, which is what they remain to this day.

Serious competitive feasts contain more than an element of aggression. At such events the host aims to outdo and ultimately vanquish his opponent, and so the enjoyment of the feast is tainted with anxiety: a free lunch must be paid for in the end. The most famous competitive feasts of all were the 'potlatches' held by the Kwakiutl people of British Columbia in the second half of the nineteenth century. Originally these affairs were much like any other peoples', with gifts exchanged and special food eaten; but they changed when the Hudson's Bay Company moved into the area, bringing with it not only monetary wealth but also diseases that disrupted local hierarchies and led to a jostling for power. As a result the Kwakiutl social structure became unsettled, and chiefs felt it necessary to hold increasingly preposterous feasts in order to be seen as the highest-ranking. Potlatches could be held for various reasons, the naming of a son, marriages and funerals being among the most common. Once a feast had been given, the principal guest had to reciprocate with interest, which could be considerable. Large reciprocal feasts could take up to ten years to prepare, and in the meantime the prospective host would hold a series of minor potlatches, using the gifts from the original event to spawn an accumulation of returns with interest. In this way his 'wealth' grew large enough to meet his obligation to the major potlatch. This could be viewed as a perfect example of capitalism, with inherently useless possessions or events being used to acquire more of the same in order to increase real power and possessions. But wealth cannot be augmented indefinitely; someone ultimately has to pay, and each potlatching series would end by somebody being unable to better his rival and as a consequence being bankrupted, both socially and in terms of physical wealth.

The atmosphere of these events does not conform to most peoples' idea of a feast, since they were occasions at which the host made his guests feel ill at ease. The food at some potlatches was remarkable for being not only expensive but also for being intended to disgust. At the beginning of the twentieth century, the ethnologist Franz Boas recorded many accounts of Kwakiutl feasting behaviour. The most prestigious feasts either used quantities of expensive eulachon oil[2] mixed with a species of cranberry known as viburnum berries, or else, at a seal feast, long strips of blubber.

> ... They cut the blubber length-wise. When there are more than a hundred seals, they cut it spirally, in this way: so that it is one long strip of blubber [see diagram p. 42]. This is done when two rival chiefs try to give great seal-feasts to outdo each other. Two chiefs of one tribe do this; and the long strip is given to the speaker of the rival chief. A whole length of blubber is coiled into the feast-dish. Then they pour olachen oil on it, and place it in front of the speaker. Then he arises, takes one end of the blubber, and puts it around his neck. He bites off the blubber from the singed skin and swallows it. If he is an expert at bolting it, he eats almost three fathoms[3] of blubber. If he is not an expert he cannot eat more than one-half of a fathom. Then he gives up. Then the speaker of the chief just promises a seal-feast.

Once the blubber-swallowers had managed their feat they slipped out behind the house to vomit, 'for it really makes one feel squeamish', and then washed themselves in hot water and urine.

The oil and berries were used not only to display wealth and to make the guests feel sick but also to create an unsettling ambience. Another account describes a salal-berry and crab-apple feast: 'When a chief wishes to give a very great feast, when he gets angry with another chief, he buys many boxes of crabapples ... Generally they have ten boxes ... and if a chief is very angry he may get twenty ...' The crab-apples are mixed with eulachon oil and 'the young men build up the fire with the dead cedarwood to make the guests feel uneasy.' The oil and crab-apples are then 'accidentally' thrown onto the fire and a skirmish ensues in which the guests try to put out their host's fire with blankets while the host's family pour oil on to keep it alight, making sure that some gets spilled onto the guests and causing considerable damage in the process. 'All the tribes go to bed early; for they do not know what the chief is planning, and they are afraid of the feast of the salal-berry cakes and crabapples and oil, if there is much of it, because it makes one feel squeamish. Therefore all the chiefs and common people are afraid of it; but there is no way of not going to the feast

---

2 The eulachon is an oily fish also known as candlefish. It contains so much oil that, once dried, it can be stuck into the earth and lit like a candle.
3 Three fathoms is eighteen feet or 5.5 metres.

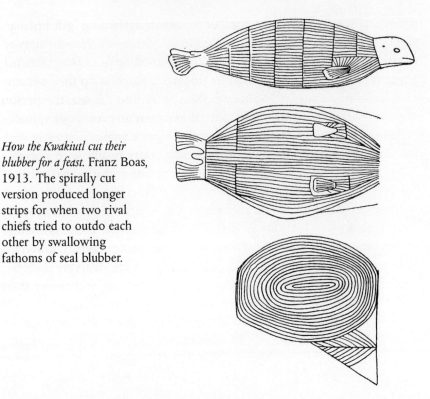

How the Kwakiutl cut their blubber for a feast. Franz Boas, 1913. The spirally cut version produced longer strips for when two rival chiefs tried to outdo each other by swallowing fathoms of seal blubber.

because they would be laughed at by the numaym [people] of the host.' The description ends with someone trying 'to put out the fire with seven canoes, and he had oil poured on his face by the great host ... Besides, he put on four hundred blankets. The house was nearly burned ... This is the worst thing that chiefs do when they get really angry, and at such a time the house dishes[4] are scorched by fire.'

The blankets referred to were Hudson's Bay Company blankets, which were given away by the hundred, sometimes the thousand, as the common currency of potlatches; contemporary photographs show bales of them stacked up ready to be given away. Other gifts (jewellery, sewing machines, oil-boxes, canoes, and especially the painted slabs of copper which were family heirlooms) were evaluated in terms of blankets'-worth. The interesting thing about the 'coppers' is that although of limited intrinsic worth, each time one was extravagantly given away it became more valuable, its additional kudos being ex-

---

4 House dishes were made of wood and held the oil and berries. They were treasured objects belonging to each family.

pressed at the feast in the telling of its ever-lengthening 'gift history'. Coppers acquired heroic names such as *Making-the-House-Empty-of-Blankets*, *About-Whose-Possession-All-Are-Quarrelling* or *Making-Satiated*. Sometimes coppers were burnt or smashed; patched up they became priceless objects, and if one was thrown away into the sea, the person at whom the gesture was directed had to destroy an even more valuable copper or lose face. The concept of an object's value increasing with the amount of times it is given away contrasts nicely with potlatch capitalism; a manifestation, perhaps, of ancient and modern cultures combining in these extraordinary events.

Eventually the Canadian government feared a breakdown in social order; potlatches, like *tochas* and colourful Venetian gondolas before them, were outlawed, though attempts at regulation were ignored for many decades. It would appear that the overseers of many societies have difficulty coping with uncontrolled expression and prefer their citizens to abide by the adage 'Enough is as good as a feast'.

5

King Midas' last feast

Not all that tempts your wand'ring eyes
And heedless hearts, is lawful prize;
Nor all that glisters, gold.

THOMAS GRAY, 1748

Every child has heard the cautionary tale of King Midas who loved riches so much that he wished for everything he touched to turn to gold. When his wish was granted, legend has it that not only all his food turned to gold, condemning him to starvation, but also his beloved daughter, which broke his heart.

Midas was an Iron Age king of Phrygia who ruled in what is now central Turkey around 700 BC. In 1957 a team of archaeologists from the University of Pennsylvania uncovered a fabulous burial site just west of Ankara which, from the richness of its trappings and the remains of an ancient palace nearby, they deduced must have been the tomb of King Mita, or Midas. Owing to the dry climate the exquisitely inlaid wooden furniture and rich indigo and brown cloth was astonishingly well preserved, as were 157 intricately decorated drinking vessels. But perhaps most remarkable of all was that the remains of a funeral meal that had been prepared some 2,700 years ago were sufficiently well preserved for samples to be carefully collected by the archaeologists who found them. Nineteen-fifties' techniques for analysing food were too primitive to be able to conclude anything meaningful, but by 2001 a molecular archaeologist and a chef were able to work together to decode and recreate Midas' feast. Patrick McGovern extracted the residues with solvents and all the individual components were separated out and then analysed using infrared spectrometry.[1] From this he was able to deduce the ingredients and, with the help of the chef, even the method of cooking the funeral feast. It would seem that an aromatic stew had been made out of lamb (or

---

1 There is still some of each sample left for future scientists to examine.

possibly goat) which had been roasted over a wood fire before being boned out and simmered with herbs and spices such as fennel, star anise and perhaps some sort of peppery herb, since pepper itself would probably not have been introduced to ancient Phrygia. Some kind of lentil-like pulse added bulk and it was moistened with honey, wine and olive oil. This sounds similar to Mycenaean and Roman recipes: pungent mixtures that used honey to sweeten and contrast with the sour and spicy elements.

Using these archaeological findings, McGovern and Pat Horowitz (chef at the university museum) created the Midas Touch Banquet for 150 people, and with archaeologist Daphne Derven a similar one was created in California for 125 people. First of all the guests were offered a Turkish *meze* platter including rocket, goat cheese, asparagus sprues, fresh figs and a vinaigrette with pounded sour cherries. *Dolmades* were made of vine leaves stuffed with chicken and currants;[2] There was also flat bread as found in the tomb, served with a garbanzo (chickpea) and olive spread made by pounding together garlic, garbanzo beans, olives, lemons and sesame tahini. Then came the aromatic fire-roasted lamb and lentil stew, spicy with fennel, anise, cumin, celery seed and fresh herbs. There were sweetmeats too: delicious little tartlets were filled with caramelised fennel and served with boiled-down pomegranate juice and *pekmez* (a raisin and honey syrup); dried apricots were topped with sheep's-milk cheese and pistachio nuts; and there was a goat's-milk and honey dessert. Unable to resist the glister of gold, and because it was thought that it would be expected, the Philadelphia chef produced some 'Midas-touched' white chocolate truffles. (The California banquet aimed at stricter purity of interpretation, and disapproved of the truffles because chocolate is not at all authentic – cocoa beans were not to reach Europe for well over two thousand years.) The truffles were dabbed with little pieces of gold leaf, but actually there was not a single piece of gold found in King Midas' tomb (the lustrous drinking vessels were made of bronze), giving the lie to the legend that King Midas had starved to death from turning everything he touched into gold.[3] The most golden thing was found in the drinking vessels, which contained clusters of sparkling crystals – the remains of a liquor. The

---

2 The word currants is an ancient corruption of Corinth. Old recipes call for raisins of Corinth or sometimes corince.
3 In fact he lived to be between sixty and sixty-five years old, which was well above the usual life expectancy for the period.

chemical-residue analysis revealed that it had been an alcoholic drink made from honey, barley and grapes – an amalgam of mead, wine and beer.[4] This curiosity was recreated for the feast by a small brewery in Delaware which made King Midas Touch from yellow Muscat grapes, lightly toasted two-row barley malt, thyme, honey, and saffron for its colour and subtle aroma. Daphne Derven described what for her was one of the highlights, when Midas' drinking bowl with its sparkling crystals of gold elixir was passed round the table for each of the guests to hold. 'For just a moment, we held in our hands the residue (carefully sealed and protected of course) of a feast held two thousand seven hundred years ago – it was a golden moment!'

---

4 Homer, a contemporary, describes in both the *Iliad* and the *Odyssey* a drink made from wine, barley meal and honey, which sounds similar except for the curious addition of goat's cheese. An early form of flavoured drinking yoghurt, perhaps.

6

Ingredients of the feast: fish

How foolish is man to believe that abstaining from flesh, and eating fish, which is so much more delicate and delicious, constitutes fasting.

NAPOLEON BONAPARTE, 1817

Although in most cultures meat is regarded as the cornerstone of a feast, nevertheless fish play an important part in the history of celebrating; indeed they provide the festival food for many who never eat meat. Eating fish is often bound up with symbolic meanings, and they appear in numerous shimmering guises at feasts and festivities both in art and in life.

The ancient Athenians were passionately fond of fish, to the disapproval of moralists like Plato. Nevertheless, or perhaps as a result, Attic comedies frequently included innuendoes about fish and loose morals. At that time meat, food of gods and heroes, was sacrificed and then distributed scrupulously fairly, which meant that it was anybody's guess as to which part they would be allocated. Not only was it charged with religious connotations, but sacrificial meat was usually boiled without seasoning: plain fare even by Greek standards. Fish, on the other hand, were not sacrificed and so could be enjoyed in many different fashions. Fish was luxurious, decadent, and greedily coveted.[1] Philoxenes of Cythera summed up the Greek attitude when his doctor told him that he was about to die from eating too much of a particularly delicious fish. Accepting this prognosis, Philoxenes' first thought was for his meal, replying, 'So be it then, but I may as well finish the rest before I go.'

To the early Romans, in contrast, the very fact that fish were wild and not controlled meant that they were not highly regarded; they were a nation of agriculturalists and meat-eaters. Wealthy Romans

---

1 In an attempt to prevent prices from rising, fishmongers in Athens were forbidden to sit down until they had sold all their stock.

Athenian fish platter. The centre of this striking dish has a well in it, presumably for holding a dipping sauce.

only embraced fish culture with enthusiasm once they were satisfied that fish could be accommodated into their lifestyle of conspicuous consumption. (The often quoted Trimalchio's feast – a first-century satire[2] – contains no fish because the host is a social climber and doesn't yet know about the luxury of fish; he serves pork.) It became fashionable to keep tame fish in cleverly constructed salt-water ponds as a status symbol, and fiercely competitive bidding between wealthy Roman gourmands at the fish auctions recalls the potlatch culture, in which being seen to outdo a rival is essential. If a host could make it known what an exorbitant price he had paid, then so much the better: sometimes a whole fish was weighed at table in front of the guests to reinforce the message.

The serving of a whole enormous fish, elaborately decorated and displayed on a costly platter, was an object of admiration at a Roman banquet just as the gilded peacock was to medieval diners. The emperor Elagabalus[3] served his fish in a blue sauce so that they looked

---

2 The author, Petronius, was a companion of Nero's and director of the pleasures at the imperial court. Something clearly went wrong with the relationship, however, because he committed suicide in AD 65 to avoid being killed by Nero. Such was life in Rome.

3 Also known as Heliogabalus (AD 218–22), this depraved emperor is also famous for teasing his guests. Amongst a string of legendary practical jokes, he is supposed to have served up grains of gold mixed into the peas, not to mention amethysts, rubies, ground-up pearls, even preserved spiders, in other dishes. The guests were allowed to keep these treasures which would presumably compensate them for their broken

as though they were still in the sea. He also served a showy dish made from just the internal organs and barbels of red mullet,[4] which meant wasting all the rest of these outrageously expensive fish. And there are many other accounts of similar extravagance.

Muraenae (a kind of eel, sometimes translated as lampreys and sometimes as moray eels) were huge favourites as party food; indeed they were the first fish recorded in Latin literature as being used for celebrations. The Greeks and Egyptians also shared this devotion, which verged on worship. No doubt their impressive size helped; some classical accounts seem scarcely credible, but as late as 1786 a sea eel weighing 27 kilos (60 lb) was caught in the Elbe. *Muraenae* were also kept as pets: one Roman lady decorated hers with golden earrings,[5] others gave them pearl necklaces and the plutocrat Crassus wept, went into mourning and built a monument when his beloved eel died. Such soft-heartedness sits strangely with a race better remembered for its cruelty. Most, however, fattened their eels to eat, for they were a luscious delicacy. Julius Caesar ordered six thousand at the public feast he provided on his triumphal return from defeating the Gauls. Eels responded well to good feeding – they had voracious appetites. Some thrived on marinated veal, others had a more sinister diet. Vedius Pollio, a friend of the Emperor Augustus, was supposed to have chopped up the bodies of offending slaves and fed them to his eels, both to make them more succulent and also to provide amusement as he watched his erstwhile servants being demolished; no doubt it made a change from watching people being torn to pieces in the amphitheatre. Finally, a slave who had been clumsy enough to break a glass vase managed to escape before he could be thrown into the pool. He reached Augustus who was so moved by the tale that he ordered all Pollio's vases to be smashed and used to fill in his pool. The slave was given his freedom.

Red mullet were also the object of obsessive devotion; slaves must have lived in perpetual fear of inadvertently harming a fish. But although some wealthy Romans seemed genuinely distressed if any harm came to their favourites, it may simply have been because of their monetary value (small fortunes were paid at auction for red

teeth. Elagabalus had other interesting vices. Most famously, he had himself operated on so that he could enjoy the life of a hermaphrodite.

4 The barbel is the bearded part round its mouth; there is also a large genus of the carp family called barbels, including the coarse fish of that name well known to European anglers.

5 Eels don't have ears, so they must have resembled people who sport eyebrow and navel rings.

mullet) – ultimately the creatures were not spared a cruel dispatch in the name of gastronomy, as Seneca relates. He tells us that the flesh of mullet was regarded as tainted unless it died right in front of the person who was going to eat it, presumably because the freshest fish is the best. So banquet guests were provided with a glass cooking vessel containing a red mullet whose skin apparently went through a glorious spectrum of colours as it expired, 'giving pleasure to the eyes as well as to the other senses'.[6] Red mullet were amongst the most esteemed sea fish when they came back into fashion during the Renaissance and are still highly regarded throughout the Mediterranean.

Carp is another celebratory fish used in many cultures. For both Chinese and Japanese it is a symbol of good health and longevity as carp live to a great age, so huge, brightly coloured paper fish are a familiar sight at many festivals. Chinese New Year is the traditional time to serve a whole golden carp; the head represents a good beginning to the year, the tail a good ending and anything golden is auspicious. A goldfish swimming in a bowl is one of the items found on the table at No Rooz, Persian New Year. This little fish is not there to be eaten but symbolises freshness, a vital element in Persia's pre-Islamic Zoroastrian past. As a symbol of fertility and plenty, fish crop up at a number of Jewish festivals. Ashkenazi Jews serve a carp with its head on at Rosh Hashanah to represent being at the head and not the tail of life. It is possible that the custom of serving it at New Year came from China, for carp have been associated with Eastern Europe since Jewish traders brought them back via the silk routes in the seventeenth century. Their importers managed to transport them alive in tanks and also learned the technology of rearing them. A few years ago we saw them still being sold live from tanks in the markets of Moravia at Christmastime.

For obvious reasons, foods with lots of seeds or eggs are used as fertility symbols, and fish, with their large shoals and thousands of eggs at spawning, are well suited. They play a part in the traditional marriage customs of West Bengal where, as part of a Hindu bride's dowry, her family provides a centrepiece in the form of a beautifully decorated carp painted with vermilion and oil, presented on a fresh banana leaf, offering a colourful vision of silvery pink, brilliant red and dark green. When the newly-weds arrive at the groom's family home after the

---

6 The dorado is also supposed to display an iridescent range of colours as it dies. Seneca's story is reminiscent of present-day diners in Japan shaving off paper-thin slices from a lobster served still alive, freshness being more important than the lobster's suffering.

marriage ceremony, the bride sometimes brings with her two small live fish which are released into the family fishpond to breed and multiply. In the West, salmon (smoked, or poached and served whole) is one of the most popular choices for a modern wedding breakfast.

In the Christian world fish is the emblem of Christ.[7] As well as this, for hundreds of years fish formed a major part of the Christian diet because of the great many fast days when, as well as eating less, people had to abstain altogether from meat, eggs and dairy products. Meat was thought to stimulate lust, whereas fish were considered cooling and therefore conducive to piety because they helped people to subdue their passions and overcome temptation. So fish appear in various forms symbolising Christianity, purity and innocence. The crossed herrings often displayed in Dutch still-life and genre paintings are invariably a Christian reference. However, confusingly, a fish and some forms of shellfish were also used as a sign of promiscuity or of a brothel. Sometimes both symbols are present in the same painting, representing Christian purity alongside the temptation of the flesh. If a man offers a woman something as obvious as an eel or other elongated fish, or if a woman offers a fish to a man with an enigmatic smile, then this is indicative of lewd intent. Similarly, closed oysters displayed in the proximity of a woman can denote virtue or virginity whereas opened oysters represent the opposite. But equally, in many still lifes of banquets and meals where oysters lie opened ready to eat, there is no concealed meaning; it all depends on the context.

It is difficult for most of us to imagine quite how integral to everyday Christian life replacing meat with fish was (at least for those fortunate enough to have both). And though the purist may be puzzled by the apparent incongruity of hosting sumptuous feasts on fast days (for gluttony was as grievous a sin as lust), these should be viewed in the context of the accepted customs of the time: people genuinely believed that substituting fish for meat was necessary for the good of their souls. Anything up to half the days of the year were at certain times designated fast days, yet important guests still had to be entertained and impressed. One of the most famous fish-feast stories is that of the great Vatel, maître d'hôtel to the Prince of Condé, who committed suicide because only a meagre part of the fish he had ordered for a banquet for Louis

---

7 Because the Greek letters making up the word for fish – ICHTHVS – form an acronym of the initials of the words Iesous CHristos THeou (H)Uios Soter (Jesus Christ, Son of God, Saviour).

XIV had turned up. His reaction seems rather out of proportion until you realise that 27 April 1671 was a Friday and therefore a fast day. A skilled cook and his staff could improvise many things, but to prepare an elaborate banquet without fish on a fast day for the king and his sizeable retinue was clearly too daunting. '... I cannot survive this blow,' the distraught Vatel said; 'I have my honour and reputation to lose.' He went to his room, shut the door and ran on his sword. As his assistant de Gourville was hurriedly removing the body (tradition had it that the king should not stay where there had been a death), the rest of Vatel's large fish order started to arrive.

Enormous quantities of fish were needed to service fast days in Europe. Herring was one staple, salted and pickled in barrels or eaten fresh, smoked, or in Holland even raw, and fisheries round the north-eastern coasts of Britain exported their herring all over the world. Not universally loved, because people who couldn't afford variety became so weary of it in Lent, herring fed the lower orders at the feast and is there-fore rarely mentioned. Important though the herring trade was, it was cod that probably had the greater historical and political significance. The Hanseatic League, a medieval group of commodity merchants, rec-ognised the economic importance of the cod fleets by underwriting fishing communities during years when fishing was lean, and by the mid-sixteenth century cod accounted for two-thirds of all fish eaten in Eur-ope. Even when the Reformation released people from fasting, some countries continued to enforce fish days to protect their fishing fleets and with them their shipbuilding skills. Wind-dried into stockfish or served fresh as a centrepiece, cod still forms part of many festive winter meals in Scandinavia. Salt cod was traded by northern fishermen for the wine and oils of the south where, as *bacalao* or *morue*, it constitutes the 'fasting' feast on Christmas Eve in many European countries. Like many south-ern staple dishes, it has now become a fashionable luxury in northern cities. The cultural importance of cod was reflected in the furious cod wars fought between Britain and Iceland in the 1960s to safeguard that great British staple, the fish supper. Now, because of depleted fish stocks, there must be a moratorium on cod fishing to allow populations to recover; so fish-eaters who have chosen not to eat meat on moral and health grounds now find themselves with different dilemmas.[8]

---

8 At the time of writing there is about to be a moratorium on North Sea haddock fishing as well, and much oily fish has now been found to contain pesticides and heavy-metal residues.

Most celebratory fish is chosen because it is both delicious and big, but on a more modest scale Londoners in the nineteenth century greatly enjoyed special whitebait dinners down by the Thames when these tiny fish were in season. They provided the centrepiece for an annual Ministerial Fish Dinner during the Regency period – a convivial summer outing where the entire Cabinet sailed down the Thames in gilded ordnance barges to enjoy a fish feast of anything up to twenty-two courses at one of the many taverns at Greenwich or Blackwall. Besides a choice of soups and all manner of fried, minced, poached and roasted fish, not to mention the shimmering piles of crisp whitebait, there was another eagerly devoured treat: '*Les casseroles de green fat*' (it was quite usual in those days for menus to be a jumble of English and French). Green fat was the most coveted part of the edible turtle.[9] During the late eighteenth century traders had worked out how to bring over turtles alive in tanks from the West Indies so that they could be purchased as fresh as possible. They were such a popular delicacy that the Shakespeare tavern in Covent Garden always had fifty turtles on standby ready for the turtle feasts that were all the rage. Weighing up to 65 kilos (150 lb), a turtle could provide a feast for twenty-five people; the callipash – its decorative shell – was used as a serving dish, which probably explains why inlaid tortoiseshell furniture and jewellery was so fashionable at the time. Alexis Soyer's 1846 recipe for turtle soup involves four pages of detailed instructions starting with the decapitation of the turtle and its hanging overnight. It continues with eighty-six pounds of assorted meats to make ten gallons (about forty-five litres) of reduced stock, three pounds of butter and four of flour to make a roux, and is completed with the precious green fat (apparently best off the largest turtles). The spacious kitchens Soyer had recently redesigned for the Reform Club must have helped to cope with this culinary giant.

Whether fish were chosen as the centrepiece for certain extravagant occasions because it was a fast day, or whether the fish themselves excited the host, who can tell? Maybe both. But there have been some splendid examples of flamboyant fish functions. Several involve a repetitive theme; if there is a significance attached to this I have not heard of it. The first Earl of Carlisle, for example, was apparently famed

---

9 The ravenous crew of the *Essex* (whose disastrous voyage inspired the story of Moby-Dick) described turtle fat as tasting like good butter.

for his fish dinners at Henderskelfe[10] in the 1660s – perhaps these dinners were an example of Restoration exuberance. The guests would be ushered in to see the tables in the dining hall completely smothered in shimmering gold and silver plate displaying every conceivable species of fish prepared and decorated in countless different and delicious ways. In the seventeenth century it was normal to have the table completely covered in dishes so, apart from the lavishness of the display, this in itself would not be particularly remarkable. The unusual part was that there was no eating of this sumptuous spread; the guests just had to stand around admiring the extravagant spectacle, no doubt speculating as to its cost. When the food finally became cold and congealed the tables were cleared, the guests seated, and an exact replica of the display meal was served. The discarded first serving would almost certainly have been distributed amongst the many spectators hovering nearby who were not counted among the privileged seated guests.

Another tale of duplication is told in Alexandre Dumas' *Grand Dictionnaire de Cuisine* under the heading of 'sturgeon', and is a story typical of the eighteenth-century dining circle in which everyone took it in turn to produce a dinner to outclass his rivals. On this occasion the host was His Highness the Chancellor Cambacérès and among his fashionable guests was that wily political operator M. de Talleyrand, who would have been a useful person to impress since he made his way into so many important households. An inveterate schemer, Talleyrand was once described as 'a metre of *merde* in a silk stocking'.[11] The success of his delicate career owed much to his being a desirable guest with many a tale to tell; he must have been grateful for this one.

Cambacérès, who maintained that 'It is to a large extent by the table that one governs', was keen to impress. So his servant was sent out to find something suitable for the dinner and returned well pleased, for he had managed to buy two enormous sturgeon, one weighing 162 pounds and the other one 187 (72 and 83 kg respectively). The problem that now had to be solved was how to display and serve these two monsters to maximum effect without either fish being shown to the detriment of the other. Eventually a plan was hatched. Once all the guests were seated in anticipation of a special culinary treat, the door

---

10 Henderskelfe burnt down in 1693 and Vanbrugh's Castle Howard was built on the site afterwards.

11 In his favour, however, is the encouragement he gave to Antonin Carême, who left his household to work for the English Prince Regent whose subsequent coronation banquet is described in chapter 16.

to the dining room opened and a small procession appeared. Heading the spectacle were three musicians dressed up as chefs playing their violin and flutes. Following them was the head porter, bearing a halberd. Four footmen carrying torches escorted two kitchen assistants who between them carried a ladder on which was laid the smaller of the two vast sturgeon, exquisitely decorated with flowers and fresh leaves. Many of the guests, being well educated in the classics, would have appreciated this allusion to Athenaeus' *Dinner of the Sophists*, in which sturgeon 'crowned with garlands and accompanied by the sound of flutes' were brought to table by magnificently dressed slaves. Cambacérès' impressive apparition was carried round the table slowly enough to draw gasps of admiration from guests, some of whom forgot themselves enough to clamber onto their chairs for a better look and all of whom greatly anticipated this delicious treat.

When the procession had made its way round the table and everyone had been suitably impressed, it began to retreat to the kitchens prior to serving the huge fish. However, disaster struck on the way out as one of the assistants stumbled and the sturgeon slithered off, spewing its glorious flesh all over the floor with a crash. There was uproar as the disappointed guests saw their dinner in ruins before them. Only one person remained unperturbed. His Highness the Chancellor Cambacérès finally silenced the company's anguished cries by calmly ordering, 'Serve the other one.'

A second procession then emerged, identical to the first except that there were twice as many musicians, twice as many bearers and footmen and, of course, that the second fish was even larger and more beautifully decorated than the first. It was an outrageous trick to play – but how exquisite must the sturgeon have tasted, both to the relieved guests and to their satisfied host who knew his dining rivals would have a hard time trying to outclass him.

Other similar stories exist, and this casts doubts on the authenticity of any of them. An almost identical tale is told about the aptly named Cardinal Fesch, who had two fine turbot and some important clerics to impress, and indeed there exists a third version in which the joke is attributed to Talleyrand. Nevertheless, whether or not it was true, I thought the sturgeon story was marvellous and was inspired to use the concept as part of the entertainment for a New-Year feast; my version is described in chapter 28.

7

Chinese banquets:
an ancient food culture

If there is anything the Chinese are serious about, it is neither religion nor learning, but food.

LIN YUTANG, 1935

If the culture of ancient Persia can be said to have influenced most Western and Arabic feasts, Chinese banqueting can claim both an ancient history – arguably the oldest – and also a familiarity in most countries of the world owing to the great numbers of Chinese who left their homeland in the twentieth century, taking their cooking skills and their celebrations with them. Not a colonising nation outside her own vast territory, China assimilated new ingredients into her food culture over thousands of years from trading links and from invading armies that overthrew successive dynasties. This flow of delicious snippets did not fundamentally alter the Chinese way of cooking, however. It was merely absorbed into a tradition that has remained little changed for well over two thousand years; a banqueting tradition which progressed to become supremely refined, then stultified ('cast in something more solid than concrete' wrote Ken Hom of the last imperial dynasty), and finally emerged outside China in the late twentieth century as a vibrant and inclusive way of feasting.

In the 1920s, archaeologists discovered 500,000-year-old fragments of hominids in the Zhoukoudian caves in China. Other fossil bones left in the caves indicated that when Peking Man feasted, he relied largely on venison. Nowadays Peking duck rather than venison has become China's best known banqueting dish. The earliest records of Chinese culinary history go back as far as the Shang dynasty, which flourished from 1570 to 1045 BC.[1] Even at this early stage rice, great staple of the

---

1 All the Chinese dates cited are a bit approximate owing to the different method of calculation, but the Shang dynasty is roughly contemporary with the Bronze Age Mycenaean civilisation in Greece.

Chinese banquet, had already been cultivated for several centuries. These earliest of imperial banquets were in part religious rituals designed to display authority. Two thousand people were required to run the imperial food service and the importance of the banquet is demonstrated by the fact that one chef was elevated to the status of prime minister. During the immensely long period between then and now, dynasties came and went, borders expanded, new religions were adopted, journeys to other civilisations lengthened and agriculture improved. Each change brought its influences and while these refined and enlarged the country's cuisine, they did not essentially alter it.

It was during the sixth century BC that the twin strands of Daoism and Confucianism emerged, each lending its distinctive approach to Chinese food and cooking. Laozi, founder of Daoism, developed the holistic approach to food that remains central to the Chinese diet, through the mystic path or Dao (Way) of contemplative right-eousness. *Yin* and *yang* – the contrast and balance between hot and cool foods and their link to health – complemented this concept, as did the resurgence of interest in immortality. This began as a quiet worshipping of natural objects and developed into a quest for access to the Jade Islands of the immortals; absorbing certain food and liquids, especially some of the more exotic ones, was thought to help this process. These ways existed alongside Confucianism, which was more concerned with the ritual and practicalities of cooking, so that the method of preparing food in China came to be referred to as 'cut and cook'.[2] In his work *Lun Yu* Confucius emphasised that the discipline of ritual is a way of instilling virtue, and he laid down rules of etiquette and of how recipes should be followed. These ideas evolved into the state orthodoxy in matters to do with banqueting, and the notion that supernatural powers could be placated by the Son of Heaven paying public homage to the ancestors became crucial to imperial court life; indeed the honouring of ancestors remains a basic element of Chinese life today.

From about 200 BC the art of banqueting flourished, especially during the Han and Tang dynasties, which were regarded as eras of cultural flowering. As banquets became more sophisticated, so they became more ritualised as Han emperors reaffirmed the ancient belief

---

2 Five hundred years later, stir-frying and wok cooking are mentioned. Two thousand years later, all these cooking methods and the lively balance of ingredients, textures and flavours are still the essence of Chinese cuisine.

that the Son of Heaven could achieve longevity, even immortality.[3] Many of these sacrificial rites required the emperor to fast before preparing and offering food to the heavenly powers on behalf of his subjects in order to ensure a good harvest and good health. The entire court had to witness the Son of Heaven presiding over these stupendous and lengthy ritual banquets which, impressive and refined though they undoubtedly were, lacked a certain culinary spark. By the time of the Tang dynasty, health, food and drink had long been regarded as worthy subjects by writers of both verse and prose. Two complementary approaches to food in the eighth century are apparent from comparing the work *The Tea Classic* by the scholar Lu Yu – which propounded the Daoist view that tea bestowed immortality – with a poetic, though rather more down-to-earth, drinking poem by Wang Han:

> Beautiful grape wine glittering in a jade goblet;
> I was about to drink when the lute sounded, hastening me to mount my horse.
> If I should lie drunk on the battlefield beyond the Great Wall, please don't mock me,
> For how many warriors returned from these expeditions since the ancient days?

Culinary sparkle was added during the Song era, which is generally agreed to be the golden age of Chinese banquets. The Song dynasty lasted from around AD 907 to 1279 – roughly contemporary with the crusades in Europe and the Near East, though historians have suggested that in sophistication the Song banquets were nearer to those staged at Versailles in seventeenth-century France. One of the most splendid banquets took place in 1151 when the Emperor Gaozong was entertained by Prince Qinghe. Several of the vessels and table pieces were priceless Shang dynasty artefacts over two thousand years old, made from mother-of-pearl, jade, gold and silver – a veneration of antiquity that contrasted with Western attitudes at that time. Prince Qinghe's chamber was decorated with hangings of calligraphy and painted silk, with bronzes, jewels and intricately carved wood. Bales of luxurious silk cloth were given to the guests, who were entertained by fine music

---

3 Hence the jade burial suits and amulets of that period. Jade allegedly prevented the body from decay and bestowed immortality.

as they dined. Like most historical feasts, serving was according to rank. The Emperor Gaozong was offered thirty-two courses, each one consisting of dozens of dishes, while lower down the scale palace officials had eleven courses and third-rank officers were given seven dishes, a box of sweet deep-fried food and five flagons of wine. The emperor's meal started with a large selection of fresh and preserved fruits, with other choice items fried with honey to follow before the savoury dishes were reached, and almost certainly ended with soup – quite the reverse order from a Western meal. Seven hundred years later not much had changed; in 1863, John Gavin wrote to his mother in Edinburgh about a Chinese marriage feast: 'As in everything else, Chinamen begin at the wrong end[4] so we got dessert first, all sorts of fruit, sugar candy and stinking stuff which we had to take with chopsticks, then came the substantial dishes which we also had to eat with chopsticks.' The Emperor Gaozong was not served 'stinking stuff'; if one man's meat is another one's poison, official food-tasters made sure that imperial morsels were untainted. Gaozong's banquet continued with preserved meats, pickled foods, choice items threaded on skewers, dishes designed to increase a thirst for the plentiful wines provided, and ended with fifty individual items of sweet and savoury 'finishing food' which could have included little steamed dumplings filled with bean paste. Pears, apples, peaches, plums, apricots, prunes, oranges, grapes and pomegranates were all widely eaten during the Song dynasty, either fresh, or preserved in honey or dried. Even in those days, some of the ingredients for the banquet were brought hundreds of miles, kept fresh on ice. Prince Qinghe's feast for the Son of Heaven presented the fabulous wealth and resources of his vast country; and by the use of antique pieces to link China's illustrious past with its all-important present, Qinghe's compliment was completed.

By this time, though, feasts were not only the prerogative of the emperor and his court. Owing to the growth of wealth in Song China

---

4 Deh-ta Hsiung points out that the sequence of food is not the only aspect of Chinese life that is reversed: fasting is another example. 'To understand this, one has to look into the social history of China: vegetarianism existed long before the introduction of Buddhism into China, partly for economical and partly for health reasons. In the bad old days, the very poor could only afford to "feast" (eat meat) once a year – i.e., on New Year's Day, while the better-off felt that they should "fast" (eat vegetarian food without meat) at least once a year. So they decide to fast on New Year's Day to show respect to the Gods, because they have been feasting too often throughout the year, particularly on the New Year's Eve, when a grand feast would usually take place. So the "fasting" is not a precursor, but rather an "antidote" to a rich meal. Like everything else, we Chinese always do things the other way round to you Westerners.'

as well as new international trading opportunities, the merchant classes had become wealthy enough to hold their own banquets. Clearly they wanted to emulate the splendour of court affairs, but they were also interested in developing their own styles of dining which remain characteristic. Increasing urbanisation popularised restaurant entertaining; it took Europe another six hundred years to embrace the concept. The southern Song court was based near modern Shanghai in the rich valley of the Yangtze river, a lush region so perfect for growing vegetables and so richly endowed with both river fish and seafood that the normally reclusive Emperor Lu was moved to venture out from his vast palace compound to admire the sight of his city's thriving food markets. The area is still known as the Land of Fish and Rice, and these riches, combined with Buddhist influences, were responsible for the wealth of delicious vegetarian dishes still prevalent in Chinese food. Some people maintain this is why Chinese food is so healthy; others attribute it to the perfect balance of *yin* and *yang*, still others to the fact that, apart from a small enclave in the far north, where the brief hundred-year reign of the Mongols[5] left a legacy of butter and fermented milk, dairy foods are almost entirely absent.

The Ming emperors who came to power in 1368 were keen to restore their ancient culture after the Mongol interruption and, mindful of the colossal Shang kitchens, employed thousands of kitchen staff to restore their culinary tradition through spectacular feasts; records of the Imperial Banqueting Court show that the structure of religious and social order that had evolved over nearly three thousand years was back in place. Innovation, apart from the assimilation of some new ingredients that filtered through from the Americas after their discovery, was not to be a feature of the Chinese banquet. The Manchu or Qing, last of the imperial dynasties, who ruled from 1644 until the emperors were overthrown in 1912, were deeply absorbed in their country's cultural history and embraced its traditions, as is often the way with invasive newcomers keen to become respectable. Theirs was a period of consolidation and regimentation: it was the Manchu who imposed the wearing of a pigtail on all male Chinese, and the Manchu who kept China isolated. Britain's notorious conduct during the Opium Wars in the nineteenth century did nothing to convince Chinese rulers

---

5 The Northern Chinese also differ from the rest of China with their great predilection for mutton, another Mongol passion, and their preference for wheat, noodles and bread over rice.

of the benefits of opening up to the outside world; but by then the expansionist West had begun to breach China's armour of inscrutability, though it was a long time before travellers could venture far inland.

One change in eating habits, which happened by chance and had a lasting impact on Chinese banquets, occurred at the end of the seventeenth century when the Emperor Kangxi slipped out unseen to mingle with his people in the streets. Chancing upon bean curd (tofu), which until then had been dismissed as humble food suitable only for peasants, the emperor returned to Beijing and immediately ordered his chefs to make him some bean-curd dishes, raising its status for ever. Apart from the introduction of tofu, the old style prevailed in the banqueting hall: Manchu guests were graded like their predecessors and service was by rank, each with its entitlement to a certain number of dishes. Since such banquets could last for three days and involve anything up to three hundred dishes, the first day took the form of 'feasts for the eye': the food was apparently edible but not available for consumption. On the second and third day, more and more courses were added and this time they were eaten. The system did not meet with universal approval: eye feasts as opposed to 'mouth feasts' were vehemently condemned as profligate by the culinary writer Yuan Mei in 1792. An indication of the type of food offered to the top echelon is given by Harry Luke, a diplomat who in 1957 went to a banquet in Hong Kong for twenty visiting Chinese aficionados of the classical Manchu school of gastronomy. It was recognised as the most lavish display of the traditional cuisine of China since the fall of the dynasty in 1912.

> The repast, consisting of 32 main courses, began with a dish of subtle piquancy to whose principal ingredient 200 ducks contributed their tongues. A hundred large frogs were needed merely for the flavouring of the next. There followed, served in silver tureens, a delicacy known as 'Magnificent Evergreen': the kidneys of chickens enveloped in the lining of hand-picked bamboo shoots. Sucking pig and shark's fin soup, even though the soup took a fortnight to prepare, were mere banalities beside the 'Dragon's crystals' (composed of the internal organs of a dried rare Siberian fish marinated until they gleamed like precious stones) and the culminating *pièce de résistance* in the form of Bears' Paws. The paws had to be soaked for 10 days in cold water so that the

hairs could be pulled out one by one and the skin peeled off in such a manner as to avoid the slightest bruising of the flesh. Hot water might have acted more quickly but would, it appeared, have impaired the flavour.

With typically British disdain he notes: 'Such compositions of highly particularised appeal I must leave to others'.

Naturally, as in any absolutist regime where the monarch is a god in the eyes of his people, there was a huge difference between the everyday food of the peasant and that of the imperial court. Food has always been precious in China and her people have learned to make imaginative use of scant resources. While fantastic banquets were being held by the rich and powerful, the poor man's diet could be sparse and monotonous; this, like the cooking techniques, has not changed. Only a few years ago two film directors told me how thrilled they were at the opportunity to travel far into China's hinterland not long after it was opened up to visitors from the West. These two gastronomes were aghast to discover that for their entire holiday they were to eat boiled rice with very little to enliven it. All Chinese meals work on the basis of *fan* (some sort of bulky staple such as rice, noodles or dumplings) enriched with small amounts of *cai* (meat, fish and vegetable dishes); clearly the film-makers' meals consisted mainly of *fan*. But their trip did not include any major festivals; had there been any they would have found things different for, as Lin Yutang wrote about his country-men, 'If there is anything they are serious about, it is neither religion nor learning, but food.' Festival food is the conduit between the living and their ancestors: hungry ghosts are fed, and wandering spirits are welcomed to their empty space at the family feast at Dong Zhi, the winter solstice. The Chinese year is punctuated with festivals, each requiring a feast, though the greatest of all is New Year. Festivities last for about a fortnight, beginning with Little New Year when Zao Wang, the kitchen god, is sent up to heaven, his lips smeared with honey to sweeten his report on the family's behaviour. Once he has been welcomed back on New Year's Eve with food offerings and firecrackers and a new statue is settled into its niche in the kitchen, the most important feast of the Chinese year begins.

A New Year feast always has twelve special dishes to symbolise good luck. Certain colours are important too, particularly gold and red, so rich red sucking pig or dishes slowly cooked in soy to a deep crimson are popular; tiny golden kumquats or oranges will feature somewhere. There must also be some deep-fried food – probably crisp spring rolls[6] with a soft moist filling – a soup, which might be a voluptuous silky fish congee, and the three special meats: duck, pork and a whole carp, the Chinese fish of fortune. Everything is carefully prepared to include a satisfying combination of the five essential flavours along with contrasting textures and the right balance of *yin* and *yang*. Always one appreciates that here is a nation which has evolved a way of feasting that wastes nothing; so there may be fuzzy braised 'hundred leaves' (tripe)[7] in a dark rich gravy or bony chickens' feet with silky-soft cartilage to suck (since the Chinese love hyperbole, these are known as 'phoenix claws'), slithery steamed rice-flour cannelloni with plump prawns inside, carved carrot slices, steamed rice and fried rice, soft-fried noodles and crispy noodles, piquant dipping sauces, crispy ducks' feet, crunchy squid, braised abalone, glutinous sticky spare ribs, morsels of chicken steamed in delicately perfumed bamboo leaves, richly braised beef and dark, crunchy bitter greens. Sometimes a food is chosen for its name or meaning: for example *lung ha* (lobster) sounds in Chinese like 'dragon', which is a symbol of prosperity, *fat choy* (black moss) sounds like 'prosperity', *how shih* (dried oyster) means 'good deeds', pigs' tongues signify profit, and *yu* (fish) sounds the same as 'to spare', so it is served at the end to symbolise plenty for the coming year, which will be welcomed in the next day with a deafening battery of firecrackers.

---

6 These were originally a New Year speciality; New Year is also called Spring Festival since it marks the end of the winter.

7 This is reminiscent of the Scots word for tripe: monyplies meaning many folds, another French absorption.

8

Ingredients of the feast: meat

The lordliest food of the people of this world and of Paradise is meat.
THE PROPHET MUHAMMAD

No one knows exactly when, why or how man began to eat meat, but the phenomenon has been the subject of endless theories. Meat fascinates us, whether or not we choose to eat it, and in any discussion about the evolution of feasting it plays a pivotal role. Even in societies where feasts are held without meat, a statement – moral or religious – is usually implied by its exclusion. This is not to say that it is impossible to have a feast without meat – that would be absurd – merely that in most cultures meat is, and has been, the dominant feasting food, the one which represents luxury, enjoyment, riches, deliciousness and power. And fat: a word with many connotations.

Current thinking is that early humans started to eat meat in order to obtain the special fats present in bone marrow and brain tissue. These both contain high levels of the essential fatty acids necessary to build our brains and make our bodies function. Seafood and oily fish also provide them in abundance, and one theory suggests that we evolved from fish-eating hominids living by the seashore. Ignoring the fact that seals have not evolved such large brains despite having access to these essential fats, it seems that consumption of them played a significant part in humans' developing a large brain and thereby the capacity to evolve in the way they have. Procuring meat required cooperation between humans. Some theories offer the notion that sharing out meat after the kill was the starting-point for both feasting and the beginnings of social order. Since meat could not be preserved, it all had to be eaten at once; and if a hunt was successful after a period of hunger such a glut would have been relished all the more. And hierarchies, through which people learned their position in society, were formed by distributing choice parts amongst a large group. Universally, choice parts seem to have been the brain, tongue and bone marrow and it is still possible to see the preference for essential fats:

anyone watching one animal eating another will notice that the head is always eaten first; even ruminants sometimes eat small mammals and also eat the head before any other part. The liver and heart, rich in minerals, have long been the hunter's perk, and very recently a Latvian hunter described to me a current tradition where, after hunting elk but before dividing up the carcass, they saw the leg bones open. The raw marrow is mixed with salt, pepper and onion, served on bread and butter and shared amongst the hunting group with a celebratory shot of strong spirit. Although nowadays we are told of the dangers of eating fat, and many people wealthy enough to be able to discard it do so, it is still the case that the population as a whole craves fat, eagerly consuming it in the form of processed and fried foods, chocolates and snacks. As Jason Epstein wrote in the *New York Times*: 'McDonald's Pavlovian subjects see the arches, imagine the burning grease and sugary sodas, and billions of stomachs, bypassing the brain, propel their owners toward them. What McDonald's promises are enough calories from fat to sustain a daylong mammoth hunt and enough sugar for a quick sprint if you become the quarry.'

But concern about eating too much fat is a very recent development. For most of man's history, meat, and fatty meat in particular, has represented the pinnacle of luxury. Meat and milk animals such as cattle, goats and sheep were currency, and still are in many parts of the world. The fatted calf was killed to welcome home a prodigal son. To the ancient Greeks, whose diet was on the whole a simple one, roasted meat was the food of the gods and of heroes: the victorious Ajax is given a whole roasted ox. The Romans, being at once more agriculturally inclined and more far-reaching in their military conquests, were enthusiastic meat-eaters, especially at their very lavish banquets. Indeed, the name Italia has been said to come from the Greek *etalos* or Latin *vitulus*, both meaning a young cattle beast, and Roma to originate from *Rumia*, meaning city of the ruminants. It is the Trojan pig, though (served whole and stuffed with sausages and dozens of roasted songbirds), and huge silver platters of birds' tongues that epitomise the late Romans' meaty feasts. Very fat animals were the subject of admiration: Varro's *De Re Rustica*, written in the first century BC, describes a pig in Arcadia which was so fat that it could barely move; in fact 'a mouse had settled on its back with her young family, softly ensconced in the fat, where they fed at the expense of the careless animal'. As to whether the pig didn't notice its parasitic family or was simply unable to do anything about it, there is no comment.

Further south and east where pigs are forbidden food, sheep and camels provided feasting fare for Middle Eastern and other Islamic nations. The Arabs' renown for hospitality stems from examples like that of Hatim al-Ta'i, a pre-Islamic Bedouin poet who as a young man is said to have killed his father's whole herd of several hundred camels for a party of strangers. Not surprisingly the father was disgruntled but his son pointed out (rightly) that he had given his father immortal glory by the act, no doubt stressing that if there is anything that resembles being a deity, it is feeding people. Most Muslim feasts include as much meat as possible, sheep meat being preferred above all for entertaining. The cultural origin of this lies in the lamb Abraham sacrificed in place of his son. The Hari Raya Hagi, the Eid el-Kebir and the Kurban Bayram are all Muslim sacrifice festivals and are still the only times of the year when many people have a chance to eat large quantities of meat – after all, you can't kill less than a whole lamb. When people are not feasting, however, meat constitutes a modest part of the Middle Eastern diet; two seventeenth-century writers both believed that, in a hot climate, the eating of much meat was not desirable. Giacomo Castelvestro, explaining the Italian summer diet to his English patron, wrote: 'In this, the hottest of the seasons, we use far more fruit and vegetables ... than meat, which in the extreme heat seems quite nauseating.' Sir John Chardin (who was French) spent many years in the Middle East and although he firmly believed that a cool European climate was suited to eating a lot of meat, hot climates were different: 'The great Debauches in Meat and Drink are grievous to the Indians for the little while that they last; and this is the Reason that the English live there so little a while; the excessive eating of Beef, and the extravagant use of Brandy, Sugar and Dates, pulls 'em down in a little time. The variety of meats likewise carries off abundance of Europeans, or makes them droop away much.'

Both writers came from a temperate climate where meat assumed a particularly important role. The Celts and other northern races were regarded by southern civilisations as having coarse appetites: 'The barbarians only judge you to be a man if you can eat a mountain,' said Aristophanes. In other words, consuming heroic amounts of meat washed down with plenty of strong ale not only represented having a good time but indeed was necessary to prove one's superiority and manliness. If eating lots was good, eating too much was even better:

in one of the Icelandic sagas, Logi devours an enormous platter of meat plus all the bones and finally the platter itself, as a challenge. The Frankish Emperor Charlemagne recognised a 'vigorous strong soldier' in a man who stripped all the meat off the bones and then broke them to suck out the marrow.

So meat equates to strength, vigour, power. But it went deeper than that. The word meat was interchangeable with 'food' right through the Middle Ages,[1] a time when meat-eating was incorporated into Christian practice. Thus a meat day was also called a fat day and a feast day. The opposite was a fast day a lean day, a non-meat day. Meat, fat, feast signified opulence, abundance, deliciousness, desirability, joyousness; but also decadence. All were connected, not only because God had so ordained it but because people did actually want meat and fat (and possibly decadence) so much – 'herbs and fish' were scorned along with 'scum and vermin' as food for fasting and famines. The mythical Land of Cockayne, which was so popular in poetry and paintings of that period, is awash with never-ending supplies of luscious meaty, creamy and sugary foods (called milk-meats and sweetmeats) that vary only according to the comfort food of the country where the particular work was composed. One version seduces with a hundred cartloads of fat being pulled by goats, another with mountains of pasta smothered in cheese. It is no coincidence that bills of fare, especially for medieval feasts but for later ones also, are heavily weighted in favour of meat and poultry (the example on p. 21 is a good one) as well as the spices used to cook them – all the other choice things tend to be condensed into a few lines. Vegetables are barely mentioned until they appear in Italian books of the sixteenth century. In northern Europe, fast days were a particular trial since the replacement of meat, lard and dairy products with fish and oil frequently meant using dried, salted and sometimes rancid products: the expression 'as brown as oil' gives a depressing insight into the quality often suffered.[2] Even once

---

1 Therefore in accounts of people being offered meat, it could in some circumstances simply mean food. This use of the word continued beyond the Middle Ages: at his enthronement in 2003, the Archbishop of Canterbury quoted the seventeenth-century poet George Herbert, whose feast day coincided with the occasion: 'You must sit down, says Love, and taste my meat. So I did sit down and eat.' Similarly, until recently, beef was used as a generic term for meat in Scotland. Elderly people still sometimes ask me for 'some of your venison beef'.

2 Some paintings by members of the Bruegel family show cripples deformed by rickets, caused by the lack of vitamin D. This is present in fats and oils but can become denatured when these are stale. So brown oil was rightly despised.

the Reformation released many Protestant Europeans from the strictures of fasting (so that, for example, Dutch people gratefully dressed their salads with melted butter instead of oil), plenty of others still yearned for fat either because of fasting rules or from simple poverty. Le Jeune, writing in 1634, quotes a French peasant saying, 'If I were a king I would drink nothing but fat.' Not beer, not wine, but fat.

Apart from the fat element of meat, there was a segregation of the flesh of mammals from that of birds. For one thing, poultry was sometimes considered to be 'not meat' for the purposes of Christian fasting and this distinction seems to have become absorbed into Western culture. Until recently, birds, both domestic and wild, were sold by the 'fishmonger, poultry and game dealer' rather than by the butcher, and I have always been interested by people who decide not to eat meat but yet feel that poultry is somehow in a different category and is therefore acceptable. Perhaps because poultry is regarded as less 'noble', or perhaps simply because of its paler colour, as an alternative to red meat it has gone in and out of fashion. While the aristocracy spent much of its time hunting, red meat was favoured: the more, the larger and the fattier the merrier. Spanish conquistadors arriving in South America were treated to great feasts, but their accounts were disparaging owing to the lack of 'proper' meat; instead of the beef, mutton and game which constituted feasting meats to the Spanish, their hosts offered huge quantities of poultry. But once the descendants of these chivalrous hunters became physically removed from the forests (many of which in any case were severely depleted so that there was less game to chase), favouring civic politics or studying the arts and sciences in preference to galloping off to hunt with the king, lusty red meats were considered by some to be savage fare. To the cultured Renaissance mind, the white meat of poultry was more civilised, better suited to spiritual learning. There was a notion in the fifteenth century that the further away from the earth a food was, the better would be its flavour; therefore where meat was concerned, birds were best. In rural areas, flocks of geese were reared for their golden fat to frizzle at the Martinmas feast. *Menus oiseaux* (which included thrushes, blackbirds, nightingales, sparrows, buntings, finches, quail, ortolans, woodcock and snipe all cooked gently in fat like a dainty version of today's *confit de canard*) were very popular at that time in France, whereas the delicate flavour of a pheasant was considered the ultimate gastronomic treat in Italy.[3]

Britons also enjoyed a great variety of birds and lesser game beasts and included them in their feasting menus, but for serious feasts this nation of grass-growers remained wedded to mutton, venison and, above all, beef – visitors to England had often commented favourably on its excellent quality. A significant turning point in its production was when, from the seventeenth century onwards, improved cereals and, more importantly, brassicas made it easier to over-winter cattle and to keep them in condition for the table. This had the effect of reducing the number of deer kept in parks – well-nourished cattle produced fat and creamy milk and so were preferred. By the eighteenth century, there were more domestic animals in England than in any other country and the 'Roast Beef of Old England' had become an institution. Like the ancient Greeks, British people preferred their meat plain, considering it good enough to need little enhancement other than maturation to improve the flavour. The Reverend Richard Warner wrote in 1791: 'In our climate we seem to have little real occasion for the exertions of the cook. The great improvements in agriculture which have taken place in this country, enable us to fatten our cattle in every season of the year, and, temperate as our climate is, we can also keep our meat, till it is sufficiently tender for the stomach to receive it, without the aid of those tricks which the abuse of cookery has intro-duced ... It is, here, the art of spoiling good meat.'

In this climate was spawned the Sublime Society of Beefsteaks, the best-known of several beefsteak clubs. The motto of the society was 'Beef and Liberty', a very eighteenth-century sentiment. It was founded in 1735, and the twenty-four 'jolly old Steakers of England' met together at the rooms of Henry Rich, a celebrated harlequin at Covent Garden Theatre, to enjoy their slabs of dressed beef. Walter Arnold, last secretary to the society, wrote a history of it in 1871 and describes how, after a few changes of venue due to fires, the society settled in a suite of rooms at the Lyceum Theatre; there the original gridiron rescued from the Covent Garden fire formed a ceiling ornament. When dinner was announced at five o'clock, an enormous grating in the form of a gridiron opened up in the dining room,

---

3 Much later, in *La Physiologie du goût*, published in 1825, Brillat-Savarin also rated pheasant highly but this was because of the extraordinary enhancement of flavour gained by hanging it. Indeed he was responsible for the French word for hanging meat: *faisandage*.

connecting it with the kitchens. Over this gridiron were written the lines:

> If it were done when 'tis done, then 'twere well
> It were done quickly

And here the Sublime Society lived and dined on beefsteaks. The accompaniments were simple (baked potatoes, Spanish onions raw or fried, beetroot and chopped shallot) because the steaks were the only thing that really mattered. 'Beef-steaks! Such was the food – served hot and hot, and passed from cook to serving-man through the gridiron . . . You heard them hissing – you saw the white-clad cook turning them with his tongs – the hot pewter plate was before you . . . and at the close, when you wanted an extra excitement to induce you to eat one solitary mouthful more, you would aid in demolishing the last "shallotted steak", and join in the strife for possession of the final morsel that remained.'

A steak from the centre of the rump (in which lurked, supposedly, a certain 'fifth essence') could weigh 500 grams (a good pound), and the eleventh Duke of Norfolk was said to have eaten fifteen at one sitting; for a member to eat three or four in an evening was not unusual. In 1833 the Ettrick Shepherd, the poet James Hogg, was a guest at the society and described his meal.

> . . . what glorious beef-steaks! They do not come up all at once, as we get them in Scotland – no, nor half-a-dozen times; but up they come at long intervals, thick, and tender, and hot as fire. And during these intervals they sit drinking their port, and breaking their wicked wit on each other, so that every time a service of new steaks came up, we fell to them with much the same zest as at the beginning. The dinner, I think, would last from two to three hours, and was a perfect treat – a feast without alloy . . . O, it is a joyous Club!

Exciting as this succession of beefsteaks clearly was, the roasting of an ox arouses an even greater fervour. Roasting an entire animal carcass arouses primitive excitement, not only because of the quantity of meat but also, I suspect, because it involves controlling a huge fire. Nearly two hundred years after the event, people still talk about the whole ox roasted on the river Thames when it froze in 1812, and a spit-roast is still a popular spectacle at weddings and large celebrations, though nowadays a smaller creature is usual. A fine sixteenth-century Hungarian description of a whole ox, stuffed and spit-roasted over a wood fire built underneath it, comes from George Lang. The ox was prepared with the head, horns and feet left on; these were covered in wet rags to protect them from the fire and the feet were tucked up and secured to the shoulder blades. The stuffing consisted of a quail larded with bacon and placed inside a capon which was placed in the stomach of a lamb, 'and the lamb was nestled inside the calf. Good enough – let 'er go! Now the calf was crammed into the stomach of the ox. The poor ox never imagined it would sometime be so pregnant.' It sounds like a nest of Russian dolls. When the fire had been lit and ladles prepared to baste the ox with lard and 'boiling salt' (presumably this means brine, which would have given it a delicious crisp crust), the animal was cooked for four hours before being pronounced done.[4] Somehow – it would be fascinating to know how – they contrived to get the ox from

Roasting an ox over the fire. Nineteenth century engraving. The cook is basting the carcass with brine or juices, and two men are required to turn the spit.

---

4 The chronicler of this account was clearly not a practical cook. Having roasted whole sheep, deer and wild boar, I can confirm that four hours is nowhere near long enough to roast an entire ox, even before it had been stuffed with four other beasts. Although it would be smaller than modern breeds, eighteen hours would have been nearer the mark, and the fire would have needed constant supervision.

the fire onto the table whole, in a sitting position, whereupon many hundreds of black-handled knives were stuck into it, 'making it look like a quilled beast of prehistory'.

Much later, Alexis Soyer gives us an account of the first attempt to roast a whole ox by gas for a banquet that he prepared for a thousand and fifty members of the Royal Agricultural Society of England when it held its annual meeting at Exeter in 1850. In actual fact Soyer cooked a baron and saddleback (i.e. no forequarter) rather than a whole ox. Nevertheless these weighed 240 kilos (535 lb), and Soyer was given permission to roast the meat in Exeter Castle yard since sceptics foresaw a 'Pandemonium conflagration'. However,

> to the surprise of every one, a few bricks, without mortar, and a few sheets of iron, forming a temporary covering to a space six feet six inches in length, and three feet three inches in width, were the only apparatus, with two hundred and sixteen very small jets of gas coming through pipes half-an-inch in diameter. It was hardly credited that such a monster joint could be properly done by such means; however incredulity soon vanished on seeing it frizzling and steaming away; and after eight hours' roasting it was thoroughly dressed, at a cost of less than five shillings for gas.

Once it had cooled down it was carried by eight men through the streets of Exeter accompanied by a band playing 'The Roast Beef of Old England', and followed by 'thousands of the incredulous of the previous day'. Soyer had designed a Grand Triumphal Arch seventeen feet high festooned with swans, geese, ducks, barnyard fowl and pigeons displayed along with ox, calves', rams' and stags' heads and two whole lambs, all still in their plumage or skin. A profusion of corn sheaves, fruit and vegetables included all the usual things from asparagus to sea-kale, but also (a testament to Victorian glasshouses) 'pine apples, citrons, cherries, grapes, melons, peaches, apricots, green-gages ... – all being the production of the county – and surmounted by various implements of agriculture. There was also an elegant jug, ornamented with flowers, filled with clotted cream. On the top of the huge piece of beef, was placed a black pig's head, weighing eighty pounds when killed.' Sadly, there is no picture of this gruesome vision. The thousand and fifty farmers tucked into Soyer's 'Baron of Beef à la Magna Charta', along with 528 other substantial meat dishes, 198 dishes

Carving the Baron of Beef for The Lord Mayor's Banquet, Illustrated London News,
November 1847: 'The November pageantry of The Lord of the City is the last of
a host of similar things which the value of time and the increase of business and
population have made impossible.'

of hot potatoes, 198 salad dishes, 264 fruit tarts and 33 Exeter puddings
(a rich concoction of lemon, eggs, rum, cream, sponge cake, ratafias,
sago and suet), presumably served with the clotted cream.

Soyer's account is typical of its period; the farmers' obvious relish of
large quantities of meaty foods reminds us of Charles Dickens' exuberant descriptions, particularly in *The Pickwick Papers*. And, like much of
Dickens' writing, Soyer's innovatory cooking method highlights the
contrast between the bucolic and the industrial. Whereas only thirty-
five years previously twelve blacksmiths had cooked a similar-sized
roast of beef over their wood-fuelled forge fire to celebrate Britain's
victory in the Peninsular War, by 1850 Soyer is enthusing about his neat
gas jets.

Agricultural improvements were supplemented by the Victorians'
enthusiasm for importing novelty species.[5] In a section entitled 'The

5 See the menu at the end of chapter 18.

New Venison', Mrs Beeton poses the question of why, since fallow deer are a species 'acclimatised' to English deer parks, other species should not also be tried. She then describes how some 'spirited noblemen' introduced small herds of eland[6] to their parks. In 1859 Viscount Hill of Hawkestone Park had one killed. 'The noble beast was thus described:– He weighed 1,176 lbs as he dropped; huge as a short-horn, but with bone not half the size; active as a deer, stately in all his paces, perfect in form, bright in colour, with a vast dewlap, and strong sculptured horn.' The carcass 'lays on fat with as great a facility as a true short-horn; while in texture and flavour it is infinitely superior . . . the fat firm and white . . . It was tried in every fashion, – braised brisket, roasted ribs, broiled steaks, filet sauté, boiled aitchbone &c., – and in all, gave evidence of the fact, that a new meat of surpassing value had been added to the products of the English park.'

For the next hundred years, farmers were encouraged to produce larger and fattier cattle in increasing numbers to feed a rapidly rising population whose affluence demanded meat more often than before. Since grain seems to fatten beef quicker than grass, agriculture responded accordingly until during the 1960s nutritionists realised that serious health problems were emerging. Just as the human body has not evolved fast enough to cope with a recently changed fat structure, so the human psyche, despite three decades of being told that animal fat is harmful, refuses to end its love affair with fat. And rightly so, for some fats are still essential for body and brain development. It is feeding cattle on grain which delivers the high-speed energy that alters the proportions of saturated to unsaturated fat and renders fat harmful. Grass is far less easy to digest (hence the ruminant's system of multiple stomachs) and so delivers its nourishment more slowly, allowing the beneficial ratio of fats to emerge. Unimproved and wild animals still have the best ratios, but cattle reared exclusively on grass will return to levels close to those of their wild ancestors. So the jolly old Steakers of England – 'les rosbifs' – may continue to feast on the fat of the land.

---

6 In thinking that eland and other antelopes are kinds of deer, Mrs Beeton made the same mistake as many others have since. Antelopes are in fact bovids, like cattle, so it is not surprising that the lush English pasture produced an eland carcass as fatty as a shorthorn cattle beast.

9

Feasting in adversity: enhancing the ordinary

If life deals you nothing but lemons, make lemonade.

JEWISH PROVERB

The word feast normally conjures up extravagant quantities of sumptuous food and an illustrious gathering of people. Yet there are times when an otherwise insignificant meal needs to be taken in context. During the research for this book I asked many people what their most memorable feast had been, and I was struck by how many of them recalled an occasion on which they had been in some sort of hardship that had clearly heightened the enjoyment of a frugal meal, elevating its status in their estimation. In my view these modest, sometimes solitary and touchingly personal experiences are rightly regarded as feasts.

Hunger is the spur to appetite which helps us to relish food; literature is full of accounts of hungry people's preoccupations. Sometimes they are discerning, sometimes, as Virginia Woolf describes, they display 'the indiscriminate greed of a hungry appetite, that crams itself with toffee and beef and tarts and vinegar and champagne all in one gulp.' At the extreme, those in concentration camps during the Second World War recall being so preoccupied with survival that they could think and talk and dream of little else than food. But it is something in addition to hunger alone, some special extra attribute, that lifts these moments above the rest. For the Italian writer Primo Levi, imprisoned in Auschwitz, the pivotal occasion happened after the camp was abandoned by the Germans in 1945. He searched the empty buildings with some friends and found some potatoes and a stove which they brought back to their hut. When they managed to light the stove their fellow prisoners suddenly proffered some precious slices of bread in gratitude, an unheard of gesture until then since it had been a case of everyone looking after himself. This apparently simple act of sharing food, 'the first human gesture that occurred among us' as Levi called it, was the significant moment that marked the return from pure self-interest to humanity and hope for the future.

When people are starving their bodies crave the nutrients they lack. This was evident during Captain Scott's Antarctic expeditions when the team's diaries reveal a frequent and disproportionate preoccupation with their rations. In their dreams they feasted on carbohydrates: 'Night after night,' Apsley Cherry-Garrard recalled, 'I bought big buns and chocolate at a stall on the island platform at Hatfield station, but always woke before I got a mouthful to my lips; some companions who were not so highly strung were more fortunate, and ate their phantom meals.' Paradise in those snowy wastes was sugar-based: 'I wanted peaches and syrup – badly. We had them at the hut, sweeter and more luscious than you can imagine. And we have been without sugar for a month. Yes, especially the syrup.' And for Christmas dinner in 1911: '. . . we had a pretty good tuck-in . . . It consisted of a good fat hoosh with pony meat and ground biscuit; a chocolate hoosh made of water, cocoa, sugar, biscuit, raisins, and thickened with a spoonful of arrow-root. (This is the most satisfying stuff imaginable.) Then came 2½ square inches of plum-duff each, and a good mug of cocoa washed down the whole. In addition to this we had four caramels each and four squares of crystallised ginger.'

Similarly at the other end of the twentieth century Mike Stroud describes his trek to the North Pole with Sir Ranulph Fiennes. They underestimated the amount of food needed, so that towards the end they were walking on half rations and losing more weight than they had anticipated. The more ravenous they became, the more food featured in their daily diaries as a sort of fantasy fulfilment. Eventually Fiennes started to write the menu which he imagined eating when he got home. This feast grew and grew and grew, the dozens of courses occupying page after page of his diary. Unfortunately the reality often turns out to be a grave disappointment: once the body has become unused to fat and sugar the longed-for fantasy can be sickening instead.

Certain circumstances will enhance the flavour of otherwise ordinary fare. Think of the exciting taste of forbidden food: the squashed sausage roll and blackened marshmallow hoarded by a child for a secret midnight feast. Think of how appetite transforms the simple into the sublime: I shall never forget the look of near-ecstasy on a man's face when, answering my question about his most vivid feasting memory, he described eating his last piece of bread while out hill-walking on his own. Like Fiennes and Stroud he had underestimated the amount of food to take, and by the last day there remained only a slightly mouldy and rather stale piece of caraway-seed bread that had to be slowly chewed, but the bursts of flavour intermittently exploding from the caraway seeds were clearly a remarkable sensation which he remembered with infectious delight.

Sometimes the situation is reversed, and the right ambience can prompt the return of a lost appetite; then the food acquires a special piquancy. This happened to a friend of mine who had been in hospital for seven weeks and found that his cancer treatment left him unable to bear eating anything. One day he rang up from his sterile ward to say that he could come out of hospital for a couple of hours and would like to visit. When he arrived he seemed delighted to be in normal and familiar surroundings once more and, settling himself down at the kitchen table, astonished me by asking first if he could have some beer and then proceeding to roll a cigarette to go with it. Two hours came and went. When I squeezed some fresh oranges for his wife, the zesty smell prompted Tim to ask if he could have a glass of juice as well, and then another, and then a bowl of soup, and then another. We watched this defiant freedom feast with exultation, not daring to break the fragile spell that could mark the beginning of a recovery. The next day he ate eight chips.

The Hungarian writer George Lang also remembers flavours intensified by relief from an anxiety: 'perhaps one of the sweetest experiences I ever had ... with the taste I can still recall'. As a small child he had been inadvertently left at his kindergarten for several hours and concluded he must have been abandoned. When his father eventually arrived he bought a gingerbread man and some honey bread for his son on the way home – clearly an effective treat, since Lang remembers the sweet taste of those breads rather than any resentment.

Unexpected kindness can raise plain food to the level of a feast and leave a lasting impression. In the book *Life as We Have Known It* (a 1930s collection of reminiscences of working women, mainly talking about conditions in the nineteenth century), a Mrs Burrows remembers a particularly cold winter's day in the Lincolnshire fens when at the age of eight she had left school to work for fourteen hours a day with a gang of children in the open fields '... followed by an old man carrying a whip which he did not forget to use'. Numbed with cold, they prepared to sit down under a hedge to eat their cold dinner and drink their cold tea when

> ... we saw the shepherd's wife coming towards us and she said, 'Bring these children into my house and let them eat their dinner there.' We went into that very small two-roomed cottage, and when we got into the largest room there was not standing room for us all, but this woman's heart was large, even if her house was small, and so she put her few chairs and table out into the garden, and then we all sat down in a ring on the floor. She then placed in our midst a very large pan of boiled potatoes, and bade us help ourselves. Truly, although I have attended scores of grand parties and banquets since that time, not one of them has seemed half as good to me as that meal did ... She was one of the plainest women I ever knew, in fact she was what the world would call ugly,

but Mrs Burrows decided she must have been an angel in disguise.

A warm welcome made simple food and drink taste especially delicious for Laurence Sterne too. In *A Sentimental Journey*, written in 1774 and possibly based on the author's own experiences in France, the narrator's horse loses two shoes on the stony road; so he walks into a peasant's farmhouse and finds a family consisting of an elderly man and his wife with five or six sons and sons-in-law, and their various wives,

> and a joyous genealogy out of 'em. They were all sitting down together to their lentil-soup; a large wheaten loaf in the middle of the table; and a flaggon of wine at each end of it promised joy through the stages of the repast – 'twas a feast of love.
>
> The old man rose up to meet me, and with a respectful cordiality would have me sit down at the table ... so I sat down at once like a son of the family; and to invest myself in the character as speedily as I could, I instantly borrowed the old man's knife, and taking up the loaf, cut myself a hearty luncheon; and as I did it, I saw a testimony in every eye, not only of an honest welcome, but of a welcome mixed with thanks that I had not seemed to doubt it.
>
> Was it this; or tell me, Nature, what else it was which made this morsel so sweet – and to what magic I owe it, that the draught I took

of their flaggon was so delicious with it, that they remain upon my palate to this hour?

Clearly the humane act of sharing and the feeling of joy at being included are important to us, the more so when it happens with strangers.

Those lucky enough to have experienced a close family will not fail to empathise with Charles Dickens' classic description of the Cratchit family's modest Christmas dinner in *A Christmas Carol*. The loving understanding that the best possible has been done in the circumstances is more important than the offering itself and this appreciation manifests itself in fulsome praise. After the Cratchits' rather small goose has been applauded and then polished off, the pudding is brought in, smelling slightly of laundry since it had been cooked in the copper clothes-boiler. It was a wonderful pudding. 'Bob Cratchit said, and calmly too, that he regarded it as the greatest success achieved by Mrs Cratchit since their marriage. Mrs Cratchit said that now the weight was off her mind, she would confess she had had her doubts about the quantity of flour. Everybody had something to say about it, but nobody said or thought it was at all a small pudding for a large family. It would have been flat heresy to do so. Any Cratchit would have blushed to hint at such a thing.' Small wonder that Ebenezer Scrooge's grudging heart finally melted.

Despite their poverty, many families tried to keep up appearances even though it meant eating virtual meals. George Lang writes about a Hungarian sculptor called Amerigo Tot whose whole family would sometimes sit under a big tree in the yard where the neighbours could observe them but could not see that in fact they were ladling nothing into their soup plates from the tureen; this pretence was enacted so that no one would think they were starving. The Jewish writer Claudia Roden wrote in similar vein about her grandparents sharpening the carving knife ostentatiously on the doorstep even when there was no roast to carve; a family feast in their neighbours' minds only.

Impending poverty can also provoke extravagant gestures, improvident though these may be. When it is clear that circumstances are about to reach rock bottom, people are often prompted to have a last fling, a metaphorical shaking of the fist at the higher powers waiting to crush them. Isabel Rutherford told me of a feast she laid on when her world had crumbled about her. Unbeknownst to her she had been made a Lloyd's 'name' and was to be bankrupted for life by the consequences, losing her home, her husband (who ran off) and everything else except her children and £87. Realising that things could not get any worse, she spent the £87 on champagne and then alerted her friends, giving them a map reference with instructions to rendezvous in a remote and beautiful meadow next to a stream high up in the Cheviot Hills. Sheep had neatly cropped the grass, a rickety ping-pong table was quickly painted to look like marble, a pair of silver-plated candelabra was produced, and the tinkling of the stream provided music. A freshly caught salmon, a pheasant or two and a mountain of fruit materialised in the dusk along with cutlery, plates, glasses, and the splendidly attired guests who still talk about this extraordinary banquet. Isabel's unquenchable nature helped her to struggle back, though it took many difficult years.

Those who always have plenty can at times feel uncomfortable knowing that others cannot enjoy their luxurious banquets. Sometimes they act on their scruples. Karl, last ruler of the Austro-Hungarian empire, when being crowned king of Hungary in 1916 thoughtfully acknowledged his subjects' distressed situation due to the First World War. He made his coronation feast an occasion which, for all the right reasons, meant that the food did not leave a delicious taste in the mouths of his illustrious guests. Coming right at the end of centuries of truly lavish feasting in Europe, this was one of the last opportunities for a display of royal grandeur, although the new king could not know that within a few years his entire empire would cease to exist.

But to the feast. After the usual array of distinguished guests had assembled in the beautifully decorated castle at Buda they were led in a procession to the dining room. When the royal couple arrived the ancient medieval ritual of hand-washing took place. They pulled off their gloves, and a few drops of water were carefully poured over their hands into a ceremonial basin and then dabbed off with fine towels. They were then seated at the high table.

Their meal was served by a long procession of the highest-ranking noblemen in Hungary. They bore nineteen courses in all, each one presented on a magnificent gold platter. The feast started with 'the roast of homage' and went on with a pheasant dressed in all its plumage (both remnants of medieval feasting), some goose-liver pâté with truffles, chicken à la reine, assorted poultry in a salad, a venison pâté with truffles, ham, quails in jelly, a stuffed roast sirloin of venison, roasted pork, spit-roasted duck, turkey 'roasted in a medieval manner', a young roasted rooster, mountain trout, a fruit jelly from Tokay, assorted pastries, bonbons, fruit, and finally 'a homage basket for the crown prince', who was only four at the time. This magnificent sweet-basket was specially created by the pastry chef out of marzipan and spun sugar and was filled with the prince's favourite sweets. It is note-worthy that roasted meat predominates in this menu, indicating its high status. It is also interesting that beef is absent, making this meal clearly distinct from a British feast.

Such luxury seems out of place in this chapter but there is a twist to this story. Each of the noblemen in that magnificent procession of dishes presented his golden platter with a bow to the king and queen, and then one after the other simply carried on marching out of the dining room. Nobody was given anything to eat. History doesn't record whether the crown prince got any of his basket of sweets but it is assumed not, because as these were disappearing out of the door the new king rose to his feet and in the stunned silence raised a crystal goblet of Tokay wine to make a toast: 'Long live our country.' After a moment's silence came the response: 'Long live the king.' The guns outside sounded a salute and the coronation banquet was over. As soon as the food reached the kitchens it was transferred to a nearby hospital to feed badly wounded victims of the war. At what should have been the greatest feast of his life, the king gives away his food and fasts instead as a symbol of the responsible ruler he hopes to be, an act of sympathy for his beleaguered subjects.

The notion of a king being subservient to his subjects was not a new one (another example is described on page 93), but I wondered if the following event could possibly have nurtured Karl's idea. Only fourteen years earlier, King Edward VII's coronation had been postponed for six weeks because he had appendicitis. This was only announced the evening before the ceremony, and by that time the kitchen staff at Buckingham Palace had prepared the greater part of a sumptuous banquet since several of the dishes took many days to prepare. The staff listened to the news in silence. Whatever was to be done with the food for 250 illustrious guests?

Some things could be stored: the caviar and 2,500 quails were kept on ice and the claret and liqueur jellies were poured into 250 magnum champagne bottles which were conveniently available. But there still remained huge amounts that would not keep. The palace regularly used to pass on items of broken or spoilt food to charities, but the royal chef Gabriel Tschumi realised that this was something rather different:

> ... six or seven courses from the coronation banquet of a King – and from all the many charities it was hard to choose one which could be relied on to handle the position of the food fairly and discreetly. Finally we stored the food in hampers for the Sisters of the Poor, and, without any explanation of how it came to be passed on, gave it to them to distribute to poor families around Whitechapel and the East End.
>
> It was sad to think we would never know how the dishes we had laboured over for more than a fortnight had been received ... But on June 26th, the date the banquet was to have been held, it was the poor of Whitechapel and not foreign kings, princes and diplomats who had the *Consommé de faisan aux quenelles, Côtelettes de bécassines à la Souvaroff* and many other dishes created by the Royal Chef and his staff to grace the King's coronation.

The banquet from hell

Everything in a pig is good. What ingratitude has permitted his name to become a form of opprobrium?

Is there a woman, no matter how pretty she may be, who can equal ... Arles sausage, that delicacy which makes the person of the pig so valuable and so precious?

ALEXANDRE-BALTHAZAR-LAURENT GRIMOD DE
LA REYNIÈRE

Those quotations give the impression that Grimod de La Reynière approved of pigs, or at least the delicious things that *charcutiers* make out of them. They were written shortly after the French Revolution of 1793, a period when Grimod was in a state of poverty following a legal battle over his late father's estate and was therefore unable to enjoy the high standard of dining he had become accustomed to. Alexandre-Balthazar-Laurent Grimod de La Reynière was the son of an extremely wealthy *fermier général*.[1] Unfortunately, young Grimod was born with deformed hands (one was a webbed pincer, the other like a bird's claw, both requiring false hands to be fitted). In order to quash any suggestion of hereditary deformity, his parents let it be known that their son had been mauled by a pig; an unconvincing story that did little to endear them to their son, who thenceforth harboured a grudge against both parents and pigs which was to last for many years.

Grimod de La Reynière had a varied and eccentric life, starting as a lawyer and including spells as *enfant terrible*, drama critic, founder of the Jury Dégustateur[2] and several dining clubs, and author of the

---

1 The *fermiers généraux* were up-market tax collectors and hated for it. Grimod's father Laurent was not interested in being a tax collector – he was wealthy enough anyway. A self-effacing man, he preferred to paint and to live quietly, loathing above all thunderstorms, to avoid which he would block himself into a basement vault with a mattress soaked in oil. He did, however, uphold the family's reputation for being gourmands and for one meal was said to have eaten only the oysters of seven fat turkeys.

2 The Jury Dégustateur was a club (which included the Marquis de Sade amongst its occasional members) that judged the merits of various *traiteurs* and restaurants in Paris. Reputations were won and lost as a result. The jury met 465 times in total, until Grimod moved out of Paris to his country home in 1813.

Almanachs des Gourmands and the *Manuel des Amphitryons*.[3] He was extremely knowledgeable about the regional food of France, largely as a result of his travels following his expulsion from Paris by his parents from 1786 until the death of his father in 1794 during the height of the Terror. In his early years Grimod was known for his revolutionary views: he would invite a candlemaker's boy to his meals in preference to military noblemen and preferred to do his own food shopping, which was regarded as highly rebellious at the time. Naturally he despised his parents' unearned wealth (though was not averse to making use of it), his mother's noble lineage and in particular her blatant adultery. However, his political views shifted to the right during the Revolution and consequently he was always on the wrong side of the political fence, always making jibes against the authority in power, and constantly reaping the rewards.

Bibliothèque d'un Gourmand, and *Les audiences d'un Gourmand*, from *Almanachs des Gourmands*, 1803–1812, by the eccentric Grimod de La Reynière.

3 Amphitryon: someone who gives good dinners.

Amongst many contributing factors to the Grimod parents' ban-ishment of their infuriating son was a banquet he gave in 1783 in honour of his new mistress, a part-time actress called Madame de Nozoyl. (She came to the event dressed as a man and continued to embarrass Grimod's family for as long as the relationship lasted.) The dinner caused such a stir in Paris, and so many accounts were subsequently discussed, embellished and written about it that the reality is a little blurred – even the invitations became so desirable that many were forged (the Dauphin insisted on having one for his collection, and it is now in the Bibliothèque Nationale). These invitations had the appear-ance of a summons to a funeral feast, the first V being illuminated with a funeral bier complete with cross and flanked by candles. The word-ing ran:

> You are invited to take part in the collation-supper[4] of M. Alexandre-Balthazar-Laurent Grimod de La Reynière, Esquire, Advocate at the Parliament, Member of the Academy of the Arcades in Rome, free Associate of the Museum of Paris, and Editor of the Dramatic section of the Neuchâtel Journal; which will take place at his residence on the Champs-Elysées, in the Parish of Magdeleine de la Ville-l'Évêque, on the first day of February 1783.
>
> Every effort will be made to receive you according to your merits, and without daring to suggest that you will be completely satisfied, we assure you that from this day forward you will not want for oil or pork. [In minute handwriting someone has added here, 'M. De La Reynière's forebears were charcutiers, and he seeks to humiliate the arrogance of his father and mother.']
>
> We assemble at half-past nine for our supper at ten.
>
> You are firmly requested to bring neither Dog nor Valet, since the service will be provided by ad hoc service.[5]

This intriguing invitation was sent to seventeen main guests and a further three hundred spectators. When the guests arrived they were confronted by two armoured guards who checked their invitations and asked, 'Are you for Monsieur de La Reynière, the People's Bloodsucker

---

4 This indicates that it was not to be a full-blown dinner but rather a series of smaller dishes. It did seem to be served in courses, though, so must have been reasonably substantial. One can only hope it was, since the event took so long.

5 'Servantes ad hoc': the phrase refers to small tables or trolleys provided for the guests to serve themselves.

[referring to the tax-collector father], or for his son, Defender of Widows and Orphans?' Once sorted and divested of their arms, decorations and dogs, they were met by someone dressed up as the Chevalier de Bayard (a heroic medieval knight) who showed them into a gloomy room where a 'judge' noted the merits of each guest on official paper. When everyone had arrived, Grimod appeared in his advocate's robes and led them into a pitch-black room. After a few uncomfortable moments, two doors opened onto a room completely draped in black and lit *à l'antique* by 365 tapers. A choirboy stood at each corner of the room wafting funeral incense and in the centre of the table stood a funeral catafalque. A railing guarded by two halberdiers partitioned off the spectators. Grimod's father was not among them since he had retreated to the country home at La Reynière after being told there would be a firework display, though some accounts say that his mother made an appearance with her lover and that his uncle was present and rather rudely treated by the halberdiers.

Grimod profoundly disliked being waited on by valets so the food was presented on trolleys for the guests to help themselves. The exact dishes are not recorded since they seem to have been eclipsed by the host's conduct, the main thrust of which was to make the diners feel acutely embarrassed and to humiliate his parents, in particular his father. Grimod concocted a story that his great-grandfather had been a pushy pork-butcher who made his money supplying the army (he wasn't and didn't: Antoine Grimod was the son of a wealthy notary in Lyons). But for reasons of his own, young Grimod insisted this was so, and the first course of the supper consisted entirely of pork dishes. When it was finished, he asked his guests how they had enjoyed their meat and explained that it had been supplied by a cousin (it wasn't) and that he would be obliged if in future his guests would purchase their pork from his shop. Everything in the next course was cooked in oil, and the supplier, another cousin according to Grimod, was also commended to the guests. This course was apparently a jibe at Grimod *père*'s mildly eccentric habit of using oil to protect himself from thunderstorms. Coffee and liqueurs were taken in a separate room where the company was entertained with a lantern show and a display of electrical experiments given by an Italian scientist. The spectators behind the rails were given refreshments to sustain them while they watched the host reviling his parentage and making a few rude remarks about some of them as well. This performance lasted until seven o'clock the next morning, by which time many guests had fallen asleep and others had attempted to leave in fury, only to find themselves locked in. They threatened to have Grimod locked up in a madhouse.

The reason for the appearance of pork and oil at the banquet is explained, but why the funeral setting? Some have suggested it was to mark the death of a certain Mademoiselle Quinault whom Grimod had admired, but far more likely is the explanation offered by the late Phyllis Bober: that 1 February was the harbinger of Lent, and that entertainments dressed up as *memento mori* had been a popular carnival diversion since the Renaissance. In fact she traces the tradition right back to a similarly uncomfortable feast staged by the Roman Emperor Domitian. Grimod was a well-educated man who, with his fascination for the macabre, would have been familiar with such historical accounts; his would not be the first banquet or the last to be inspired by earlier events. Parallels can also be drawn with Petronius's satirical literary feast staged by the parvenu Trimalchio who, knowing no better, served only pork instead of the more fashionable fish at his banquet.

The Emperor Domitian was one of the more unpleasant Roman rulers, prone to executing people on a whim. His was a triumphal banquet to celebrate those who had died in a recent war and there are clear parallels between it and Grimod's: his guests were instructed to arrive at night without their servants; the event took place in a black-draped room; slabs shaped like gravestones were set beside each guest, illuminated with small lamps of the type found in tombs. Naked boys painted black came and danced like ghosts in front of the diners, and then a banquet of the sort of food served at funerals, but entirely black, was served up to them.[6] Whilst the terrified guests ate this, their host held forth on the subject of death and slaughter, leading most of them to conclude that they were to be the next victims, such was Domitian's bloodthirsty reputation. Each guest was dispatched back to his home with a strange slave, but no sooner had he started to relax after the ordeal, than word came that a messenger had arrived from the emperor. Thinking that the reprieve had been only temporary, he discovered to his relief that the messenger had in fact brought him gifts from the banquet: the gravestone nameplates turned out to have been made of silver; the dishes used at the dinner were also of costly

---

6 One version of Grimod's feast has him using servant girls, saying that their hair served as napkins for greasy fingers 'in the Roman fashion'.

La Chanson de Mort, Florentine, 16th century. A *memento mori* was often used in masquerades during *carnevale*.

materials; and a painted dancing boy now appeared washed and ready to work for his new master.

There are several Renaissance accounts of black banquets and carnival processions featuring the 'dance of death' which may also have drawn on Domitian's hellish feast. In the entry for Piero di Cosimo, Vasari's *Lives of the Artists* mentions a masquerade which, 'through its novelty and terror . . . filled the whole city with fear and marvel together . . . for even as in the matter of food bitter things sometimes give marvellous delight to the human palate, so do horrible things in such pastimes, if only they be carried out with judgement and art'. Carnival hell-banquets were served in classical settings of a black-draped Hades, with devils offering food on fire-shovels and screaming wretches providing off-stage sound effects. The food and wine was exquisite, though, even allowing for its repulsive presentation: containers made to look like toads, scorpions, spiders and lizards revealed delicious creations made out of larks and thrushes. At Lorenzo Strozzi's black banquet of 1519 in Rome, the Venetian ambassador Marino Sanuto describes edible table decorations shaped like skulls and containing roast pheasant, a centrepiece of 'bones' containing sausages, and desserts featuring *ossi dei morti* (bones of the dead) made out of marzipan.

In 1813, thirty years after his infamous dinner, Grimod de La Reynière bought the *seigneurie* of Villiers-sur-Orge just south of Paris. Grimod was fifty-five by then, and had just succeeded in marrying his long-term mistress, another actress called Adélaïde Feuchère. He had wound up the Jury Dégustateur and retired. Less than a month later, his friends were dismayed to receive news of his death and the notification of his funeral. A gratifying number of people, including many chefs and literary figures, assembled at the house where the coffin stood between two rows of torches. As they were discussing the merits of their erstwhile eccentric friend, the inner doors burst open to reveal a splendid feast (for it was the dinner hour), laid out on a black-draped table with a coffin in the middle. The room was lit with a thousand candles and Grimod himself sat waiting for his guests. As the mourners approached the table, a place was set for them and, according to one account, a small coffin bore each diner's name. The meal lasted well into the night: a test of friendship indeed.

And the pigs? Accounts of Grimod's eccentricities merge into each other. Was he still reviling his parents at this mock funeral meal by having charcuterie designs woven into the curtains, and by setting the table with cutlery whose ivory handles were carved in the form of pigs? Such details would certainly have appealed to a man interested in theatre, but we cannot be sure. What is true is that Grimod remained fascinated by pigs. He kept a good number at Villiers-sur-Orge and spoke to and referred to them as humans: a note accompanying some *boudins* which he sent to his wife in Paris reads, 'This is to give you a sample of the young man who was dispatched yesterday, early so I would not hear him screaming.' But according to the writer Monselet he owned a pet pig which had its own servant and mattress and which was given the place of honour at table on special occasions. Alexandre-Balthazar-Laurent Grimod de La Reynière lived to be seventy-nine and died moments after drinking a glass of water.

II

Feasting and fasting: Mardi Gras

There is more simplicity in the man who eats caviar on impulse
than in the man who eats grape-nuts on principle.

G. K. CHESTERTON

It may seem strange to include fasting in a book about feasts, but
fasting plays an integral and opposite role in the story of feasting. Fasts
have been imposed by many cultures as a fair method of sharing scant
resources. Until recently everyone was, to a greater or lesser extent,
aware of human vulnerability to famine and disease – even kings
and noblemen were not immune – so occasions for celebrating were
enhanced by the knowledge that life is precarious and must be lived to
the full. People who live in fear of hunger usually bolt as much food as
possible when the opportunity arises, so it is no great surprise that
in most accounts of feasts, the quantity is stressed above all other
attributes.

Fasting plays an important role in feasting inasmuch as any experience is better appreciated through an encounter with its opposite. In
order to cherish company we must have known loneliness, to savour
triumph we must have had failure, and without suffering hunger or
bad food we can never truly comprehend the concept of a feast. In
affluent and secure societies where eating is increasingly divorced from
sustenance and religious fasting is hardly practised, a significant part of
the population has never been confronted with this contrast. Everyday
food is presented as a treat, indulgence is encouraged, snacking replaces
spaced-out meals so that real hunger is unknown, and boredom sets
in.[1] In circumstances where people are sated with food, fasting can be
a way of rejecting corrupted values, a purification. I was interested to
discover how many people feel repulsed by mass over-indulgence at
occasions like Christmas and prefer to fast instead; like-wise, some

---

1 This is a situation reminiscent of the later Roman Empire, where ever more exotic and preposterous
culinary creations were required to make any impression on its jaded diners.

90

wealthy Chinese people fast at New Year, traditionally a time of feasting. Equally, vegetarianism in societies with sufficient food can be regarded as a form of perpetual fast, a purification process which rejects the concept of killing animals for food; indeed the Church at one time regarded vegetarianism as heresy since Christian doctrine required people to eat meat on feast days (if it was available, that is). Those that refused were seen to be rejecting God's gift of the feast and setting themselves apart from the pleasure shared by their companions.

In the course of a total fast, while the body is cleansed and hunger eventually diminishes, spiritual senses become heightened. During a long fast a state of euphoria can be reached, similar to that felt after a migraine; the spirit becomes nourished as the body starves, raising the question of whether the reverse is also true. The state of euphoria achieved by fasting has also been likened to sexual ecstasy, sometimes heightened by other self-imposed discomforts such as the hair shirts and self-flagellation beloved of some fanatic religious cults. As well as purifying, a deliberate fast requires submission and self-control. Sometimes this is an individual's own decision, sometimes it is the control imposed by society or religion over its subjects. Lord Byron's bingeing ('when I *do* dine, I gorge like an Arab or a Boa snake') and fanatical fasting were a good example of someone attempting, not always successfully, to control and then atone for his bodily excesses: 'I should not so much mind a little accession of flesh – my bones can well bear it. But the worst is, the devil always came with it, till I starve him out, – and I will not be the slave of any appetite.' But he was.[2]

Against this background, it becomes clear why so many feasts were preceded by a fast: the most obvious reward is contrast. The perfume and flavours of an evening meal during Ramadan are all the more appreciated after a day's total fast, and a harvest festival used to celebrate the end of an anxious period when the previous year's stores might have run worryingly low; indeed fasting before seed-sowing or harvest occurs in many cultures as a way of imitating nature's rhythms of scarcity and plenty. Eighteenth-century colonial travellers in America described the indigenous Creek people of Florida celebrating

---

2 In her paper 'Was Byron Anorexic?' published in *World Medicine* in 1980, Wilma Paterson claimed that Byron suffered from anorexia nervosa, an assertion which was not accepted in academic circles until some fifteen years later when it was resurrected to provide useful material for others' lectures and papers.

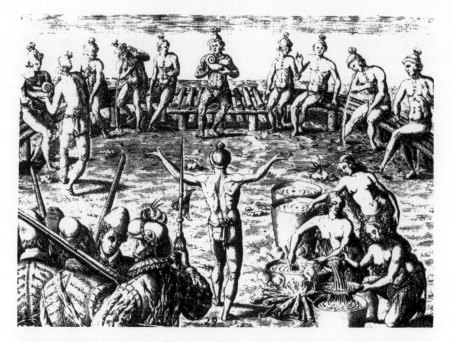

Boskita: ritual purging of the Florida Creek people during a fast. Theodore de Bry, 1592. The women brew a black purgative for the men to drink during their purification ceremonies before celebrating the corn harvest.

the Green Corn ceremony which marked their new year. They were not allowed to eat any corn from April until the harvest was ready in August. Once the corn was ripe they would fast for three days, during which time they brewed a powerful black purgative out of *Ilex vomitoria*, a variety of holly. After this *boskita*, or cleansing process, all past crimes were absolved and the new year could begin once more with a feast of freshly harvested corn.

The Christian Church's greatest spiritual feast – Easter – is preceded by Lent, the longest period of fasting in its calendar: forty days, in memory of Jesus' time spent in the wilderness. The word comes from the old English word for spring: *lencten*. Because spring was the time when food resources were at their lowest ebb (meat salted down for the winter would be scarce and fresh crops had yet to grow), a fast imposed on the whole society was a device whereby an authority – in this case the Church – could make sure that rich and poor shared the available resources. Fasting used to be regarded as an important communal activity that bound society together; it was pointed out that although rich people should not eat too much food on a fast day, nevertheless plenty should still be served at table so that the poor could benefit from the giving of alms afterwards – charity being also a Christian obligation. Indeed, during the fifteenth century the Duke of Ferrara used to hold charitable feasts at the end of Lent, on Maundy Thursday, where he and his sons would personally serve a magnificent banquet to a roomful of the local poor. The top table consisted of a priest and twelve paupers in imitation of the Last Supper, and afterwards the duke's family ceremonially washed their guests' feet, the humbled duke assuming the role of Christ.[3]

It is easy to forget how much a part of Christian life fast days were: at some periods there were as many as there were feast days, since Wednesdays, Fridays, Saturdays, all of Lent and all of Advent were fast days. Nowadays, observing even a Lenten fast is a personal choice for lay people; instead of grumbling companionably whilst observing a universally imposed order, each individual has to decide for himself and usually bears the constraint alone. For medieval Christians, fasting varied greatly in its severity. Sometimes it meant refraining from any food for part or all of the day, but usually (though not always) simply a reduction in quantity. Gluttony was regarded as a serious sin because inevitably it led to lust. Abstinence, which went along with fasting, meant cutting out certain types of food and the two concepts became so closely associated that to most lay people, fast days (sometimes referred to as non-meat or lean days) involved simply abstaining from certain foods. These always included meat, eggs, dairy products and at certain times wine. During a fast, Christians were also supposed to abstain from sexual intercourse.[4] The strictness with which these rules were enforced fluctuated according to current fashion and the Church's confidence that it was successfully overcoming paganism or rival religions. At many periods dispensations were available that could include pregnant women, invalids, old people, beggars and several other categories.

A great deal of medieval thought and argument went into exactly what constituted 'meat' or 'not meat'. It is well known that many monasteries were founded on productive salmon rivers. It is equally

---

3 Cynics would say that this was really an act of self-aggrandisement since the public were encouraged to witness the spectacle, the whole affair being calculated to exalt the duke and the d'Este dynasty.

4 This was not just a Christian practice; the Creek People also refrained from intercourse during their *boskita*.

well known that a diet of salmon can pall, as does endless salt fish, so that imaginative ruses for altering the definition of non-meat were legion. All sorts of explanations were proffered for the substitutions. Barnacle geese and some other water fowl were acceptable because they had scaly webbed feet and lived and supposedly gave birth (apparently without mating) in the water, and were therefore considered neither meat nor lust-inducing. The same reasoning meant beavers' tails were also allowable.[5] In 1658 Edward Topsell wrote:

> ... the tail of this beast is most strange of all, in that it cometh nearest to the nature of fishes, being without hair, and covered over with a skin like the scales of a fish, it being like a soal ... they are accounted a very delicate dish, for being dressed they eat like Barbles: they are used by the Lotharians and Savoyans for meat allowed to be eaten on fish-days, although the body that beareth them be flesh and unclean for food ... it is certain that the tail and forefeet tast very sweet, from whence came the Proverbe, *That sweet is that fish, which is not fish at all.*

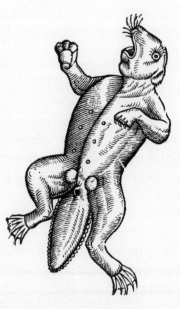

Beaver, Edward Topsell, 1658. Topsell describes the culinary qualities of the beaver's tail for eating on fasting days.

---

5 At least this is what one reads, but could that perhaps have been a coded message connected with abstaining from (or rather allowing) sexual intercourse?

In similar vein fully grown rabbit foetuses were explained away as not meat – perhaps fluids in the womb made them into a kind of water creature. In any case some medieval French monasteries bred rabbits specifically to enliven their fast days.[6] Some prelates regarded all poultry as allowable since they are not quadrupeds. In the thirteenth century St Thomas Aquinas worried that gluttony might tempt good Christians from proper abstinence, but even so he declared chicken could be eaten on fast days as he pronounced it to be of aquatic origin. He certainly thought long and hard about such things; once as a guest of Louis IX of France he was so absorbed in his theories that, oblivious of the horrified looks of the courtiers, he ate a whole lamprey which had been prepared for the royal table. '*Consummatum est,*' he said regretfully when he had finished.

The combination of fasting with torments such as cold, lack of sleep and skin diseases must have meant that many medieval monks not destined to become saints spent much of their time dreaming of bodily satisfaction in the same way that starving people become obsessed with thoughts of food. Perpetually lurching from feast to fast day resulted in overeating whenever it was permitted – some Benedictine monasteries had sixteen courses on feast days. This probably only served to upset the digestion and make fast days all the more uncomfortable. Small wonder that remedies for alleviating stomach cramps were common; a thirteenth-century suggestion from Albertus Magnus in his book of secrets, *In Secretum Secretorum*, recommends holding a young, pretty, innocent woman in your arms to warm the area and so ease the pain. This is the same cleric who suggested putting a blob of mercury inside a roast chicken for a joke: 'For seeing Quicksilver is hot, it moveth itself, and maketh it to leap and dance'[7] – just the sort of prank to appeal to Rabelais, who called Albertus Magnus 'that celebrated Jacobin friar'. As well as being a physician, Rabelais had been both a Franciscan friar and a Benedictine monk in his time, and saw no benefit to humanity in the miserable concept of the mortification of corrupt flesh. In his opinion, eating and drinking did more for the human soul.

Early cookery books often had two versions of a recipe, showing how to make it differently for feast and fast days. For those who could

---

6 Perhaps they got the idea from the Romans who bred hares in *leporaria* for their foetuses – a delicacy enjoyed in the same way as dormice.

7 Presumably it worked on the same principle as an artificial jumping bean.

afford it, fast-day versions of dishes requiring butter, eggs or cheese would substitute almonds. A costly luxury, they were ground to thicken sauces, steeped in water to produce almond milk, and made into curds to imitate cheese. This demonstrates people's attitude to enforced fasting: they put up with it because they had to, but used any legitimate excuse to ease the tedium; so that even if they were not allowed to feast in the religious sense, they could still celebrate or entertain and have a banquet. As John Taylor pointed out in 1630, 'Though a man eat fish till his guts crack, yet if he eats no flesh he fasts.' According to the Salerno School, whose teachings dominated the medieval European diet, all foods had certain attributes that could either aid or hinder a person's well-being by altering the person's 'humour' or disposition. This philosophy stems from the teachings of Hippocrates and was similar to Zoroastrian and Chinese attitudes to food, which held a dietary balance of 'hot' and 'cold' to be essential to health. Hippocrates' system was based on the four elements of fire, water, air and earth which manifest themselves in the human body as humours: black bile, phlegm, yellow bile and blood. Each humour had properties that were combinations of heat, cold, moisture and dryness, and people altered their diet to suit their individual disposition. Meat, being hot, was thought to encourage lust and other carnal desires whereas fish was thought to be cooling, purifying, helpful to piety and therefore suitable for fast days. This also explains why pregnant women were allowed to eat meat instead of fish on fast days since they were not supposed to eat too many cooling and watery foods (unfortunately fresh fruit came into this category).

We may find it ludicrous that anyone could believe that enjoying luxurious amounts of nutritious ingredients like fish and almonds could have any effect whatsoever in reducing lust, or that this could seriously constitute fasting; but to anyone brought up with those beliefs the concept of feasting on fasting foods was perfectly logical. Well, quite logical. More than one writer pointed out the anomaly of enforcing a diet of foods considered aphrodisiac while at the same time forbidding sexual intercourse. Rabelais the physician wrote: '. . . the most experienced physicians offer conclusive proof that in no other season of the year do men eat more aphrodisiac foods than in Lent. Think of all the white beans, kidney beans, chick-peas, onions, nuts, oysters, herrings . . . think of the countless salads made entirely of venereal herbs and fruits like rocket or colewort, nosesmart or peppergrass, tarragon, ginseng root, rampions, bellflowers, poppyseed, hopbuds, figs, raisins and rice!' He suggested it was a plot by the pope to foster the propagation of humankind, since people will always break imposed rules. This notion is echoed in Thomas Nashe's *Masque*,[8] which has Lent declaring: 'Children! I beget more (I maintain not their lawfulness) than Christmas and Shrovetide. O, the virtues of oysters, lobsters, sturgeon, anchovies and caviare!'

But I am not well qualified to point out flaws in medieval practices, because some years ago when we gave a wild-boar feast I made a beautiful vegetarian dish of slivers of vegetable swimming like fish in a crystal-clear 'pond' of delicious jelly made from vegetable stock. It was only later that someone asked if the gelling agent I had used was made from animal gelatine. Alas, I had overlooked this and it was. Nevertheless, that imitation fishpond would have been appreciated in medieval times, because people loved dishes disguised as something else; chefs with an aptitude for creating pseudo-meat dishes out of fish were greatly in demand. The fact that food was well spiced would certainly help to camouflage such different flavours. One popular culinary trick cited in many recipe books is a 'ham' made from salmon and white fish layered and moulded to look like fatty cured meat. To make this, one would probably have salted and smoked both kinds of fish, because all smoked foods taste rather similar, and afterwards poached them and then coloured the pink fish a deep red. Colouring food was second nature to medieval cooks; they would have used either alkanet (borage root) or sanders (red sandalwood)[9] to enhance the salmon. They could disguise the flavour of fish by adding herbs and spices normally used for bacon (sage and cloves, for example), and probably pounded the white fish with oil to give it a soft, fatty texture. The 'meat' and its simulated fat would be assembled in the shape of a hand of pork and the finished creation would be covered or served with sauces normally served with ham.[10]

---

8 Just as Rabelais spurned the strictures of Catholic fasting, so Nashe disliked Puritanism and wrote many attacks on the subject. His *Pierce Pennilesse, His Supplication to the Divvell* gives an interesting insight into the vices of sixteenth-century England and contains a lengthy description of the different types of drunkard – drunkenness being, his hero says, 'a sinne, that ever since we mixt ourselves with the Low-Countries, is counted honourable'.

9 Red sandalwood is not the same as that used for incense and perfume; it is odourless, and when shavings are steeped in liquid, they turn it a bright orangey red.

10 The disguising tradition lives on: many modern 'smoky bacon' snacks are made of synthetically flavoured and spiced potato or wheat starch and have little connection with real bacon. An existing relic of the medieval period are the *dulces* still made in the convents of Spain, Portugal and Brazil. *Dulces* are

Fast days were so much a part of everyday life that people rarely thought them remarkable enough to record; the occasional brief mention brings them vividly to life. Sir John Froissart, describing the siege of Ghent in 1382, tells of an added anxiety: 'And when the time of Lent came, then they were in great distress, for they had no Lenten stuff.' In Tudor times we hear that young James Basset is not very fond of fish; his tutor Guillaume le Gras, writing to James' mother Lady Lisle in a letter written in March 1537, writes '. . . we have received the sprats, for the which, Madame, I heartily thank you. I shall have good use of them for your son, who cannot accustom himself to the eating of fish: nevertheless, thanks be to God, he is in very good health this Lent.' On the other hand the French writer Montaigne relished fish. In 1588 he wrote in his essay 'On Experience': 'I am very fond of fish and have my fat days on the lean days and my feasts on the fast days.' Nearly two and a half centuries later Lord Byron, perpetually obsessed with his food, did not want to share a special treat even on a fast day. An extract from his Ravenna journal in 1821 reads: 'On dismounting, found Lieutenant E. just arrived from Faenza. Invited him to dine with me tomorrow. Did not invite him for today, because there was a small turbot (Friday, fast regularly and religiously) which I wanted to eat all myself. Ate it.'

So much for fasting; what of the feast? Carnival (to put away flesh) and Mardi Gras (Fat Tuesday) occur in the period leading up to Ash Wednesday, when Lenten fasting begins. Although I have pointed out that fasting usually precedes a feast, Mardi Gras is the great exception since it is a feast before a fast, a reversal typical of carnival. Its function was twofold: to allow people to let off steam and to give an opportunity for all forbidden food to be used up if it would not keep for six weeks. Naturally everyone made the most of the occasion, often buying in extra luxuries. The bizarre atmosphere of carnival feasting is reminiscent of food folklore such as the mythical Land of Cockayne, where dishes of custard, mountains of pasta and other delicious food tumbled all around and never ran out; as much food as possible was stuffed in as short a time as possible. During the Nuremberg carnivals of the sixteenth and seventeenth centuries gigantic sausages were carried through the streets by dozens of men, the exaggeration and innuendo

---

garish-coloured sweetmeats made of eggs, sugar and almonds, formed into a variety of suggestive shapes using currants where necessary to make 'angels' breasts', 'ladies' thighs', 'dream longings' and *tochino de cielo*: 'bacon of heaven'.

both typical carnival images: 'a low mind has a continual feast', as the saying goes. In Britain, carnival has never really been celebrated in quite the same spirit as elsewhere in the world; plays, masques, football, bear-baiting and cock-fighting have been more usual, and other violent activities such as the rumbustious behaviour at Shrovetide when apprentices went on the rampage to storm brothels and theatres (both of which were closed for Lent), sometimes nearly destroying them. Accounts of Shrovetide feasting and carousing showed they sometimes cost as much as Christmas celebrations. Thomas Dekker describes such an occasion in *The Shoemaker's Holiday* (1600), when at the sound of the pancake bell everyone hurried to table and found that the food presented itself to be gobbled up, as though for the Lord of Misrule himself: '... there's cheere for the heavens, venison pasties walke up and down piping hote, like sergeants, beefe and brewesse come marching in drie fattes, fritters and pancakes comes trowling in in wheele barrowes, hennes and orenges hopping in porters baskets, colloppes and egges in scuttles, and tartes and custardes comes quavering in mault shovels.'

Along with the guzzling of food and bacchanalian carousing went hilarious, boisterous disorder, a lampooning of the Church and anything or anyone else that represented establishment. While not approved of, this behaviour was condoned, the rationale being that allowing people to misbehave for a defined period would make them more biddable in Lent.[11] Whether or not this turned out to be so, people seized the opportunity to be as abandoned as they wanted, to make a mockery of anything, to wreak

---

11 It didn't always work: in the fifteenth century some monks near the Belgian town of Stavelot were banned from celebrating carnival for being lazy and lax. They found the six weeks of Lent unbearably long, so they escaped from their monastery in mid-Lent covered in sheets and wearing carrot noses as disguises. The Carnival of the Blancs-Moussîs (Blanc-Moussî means clad in white) still takes place on the fourth Sunday in Lent. The Blancs-Moussîs scamper about putting up irreverent posters. In the afternoon there is a cortège of floats from which the Blancs-Moussîs shower the crowds with confetti while others run around flogging them with pig-bladders.

havoc and cause as much confusion as possible. At carnival, as at the Saturnalia and other pagan extravaganzas, nonsense takes over from rationality, anarchy replaces order, roles are reversed. Identities are concealed in a riot of masks and fantastic costumes; debaucheries explode in drunken dancing and a roar of noise.

Carnival burlesque is timeless and ancient. Its raucous humour, full of scatological absurdities and heavy with sexual imagery, is a huge subject, proof of its universal appeal to a human need that the Church dared not deny. Such ribaldry can be seen everywhere. Peer under the seats of a medieval choir stall and there are misericords[12] carved with bizarre scenes of pagan monsters making mischief. Outside, gargoyles pull grotesque faces and spew out rainwater. Look in the margins of illuminated manuscripts and you find people dancing and jesting, making love and music. The van Beuningen collection of medieval carnival badges in Rotterdam contains wonderful parodies of those worn by pilgrims. Instead of being souvenirs of a shrine, these crude devices take the form of male and female sexual organs engaged in comical activities – a vagina walking on stilts, for example, or penises scampering off with a vagina. In Italy, Pulchinello[13] emerges masked from an egg which may itself have legs. Thomas Rowlandson's eighteenth-century cartoons show drunk people vomiting and rolling around to reveal their bloated nakedness. Seek and you will find.

A tiny medieval convent church at Mortemart near Limoges has wooden choir stalls with beautifully carved figures at the end of each row which, viewed from the aisle, appear to be ordinary people going about their daily business while suffering the gamut of miseries normal for the time (one clearly has a painful toothache). But viewed from behind, the little figures lift their robes and bare their bottoms. However, the choir-stall ends that face the entrance are carved with the pagan Green Man spewing luscious vines from his mouth, forewarning that all will not be as it seems.

---

12 Misericords are small ledges underneath choir stalls. The seat is tilted up when the person stands and he can prop his buttocks on the ledge during the long service. The word comes from the Latin *misericordia* meaning pity. They are common in medieval churches and, because they were not really meant to be there, often reflect secular images, many grotesque.

13 *Pulchinella* – little chickens – are the forerunner of Mr Punch: urban satyrs dressed in white pyjamas and conical hat, and beak-nosed to accentuate their bird-like origin. Hatching from an egg is a carnival symbol much used by the Bruegels and Hieronymus Bosch, connecting eggs with fools, and it reminds us that eggs are soon to be forbidden even though hens are likely to be at their most prolific during Lent. Hence eggs were thrown at carnival, either whole or, in more refined society, filled with rose-water.

François Rabelais wrote his bombastic tales of Gargantua and Pantagruel in the early sixteenth century, a time of great change. The New World had just been discovered and medieval attitudes were giving way to the Renaissance and humanism, but at the same time Puritanism emerged to offer a different restraint from that of the Church of Rome. Rabelais had no time for either form of cheerless doctrine. Although religious in his way, he recognised the innate human need to be bawdy and let off steam, the need to behave badly, the need to eat and drink excessively; or if these things were not possible, the need at least to fantasise about them. As a physician and good student of Aristotle he was well aware of the divine origin of laughter; unique to man[14] and good for his health. His philosophy and writings (immediately censured by the establishment, of course) can be analysed and rendered complex; but in essence they are simple, putting into words what unsophisticated people had acted out for centuries. Everyone wants to have a good time, preferably all the time, and Rabelais touched a sympathetic chord which still reverberates today.

In a liberal society with the Church less dominant, some may wonder what there is to rebel against. But there is always something to mock, and Mardi Gras still serves as an abandonment of social correctness: if you can shock, so much the better. Recently carnival has emerged as a celebration of gay and transvestite culture. Travel where you will – to Cologne or to New Orleans, to Venice with its masks or to Rio with its samba rhythms, or to one of the many less famous carnivals – and you are met with a roar of music and dancing and a succession of larger-than-life floats – even the dogs have one in New Orleans. And if the occasion is rather more organised and commercial nowadays, nevertheless the more individual expressions of carnival, sometimes protesting, sometimes sinister, sometimes just silly, continue to lurk in back streets and in the small hours of the morning. There is still rowdiness, plenty of opportunity to achieve euphoria in one way or another, and unquestionably plenty of drunken behaviour. One thing is certain, though: very few of the participants will be fasting afterwards, so the original purpose of carnival has gone and something of the true spirit of carnival has gone with it. Perhaps we need to return to rigorous fasting to appreciate the event better. As like as not,

---

14 'Better to write about laughter than tears, For laughter is the essence of mankind,' wrote Rabelais. But, as though ridiculing his own axiom, he also wrote: 'We hold not that laughing but that drinking is the distinguishing character of man. By wine we become divine.'

everyone will simply carry on laughing, which is, after all, the best medicine. As Horace says, *'Dulce est desipere in loco'*– 'It is sweet, in the season, to be silly.'

F   **A** **S** **T**

F **E**   **S** **T**

E **A**   **T**

F **E** **A** **S** **T**

F   **A**   **T**

12

The Feast of St Hubert: hunting, and a nine-course venison feast

No-one will throw away venison for squirrel's flesh.

NIGERIAN PROVERB

'Seeing my darling is absent I can no less do than to send her some flesh, representing my name, which is hart flesh for Henry, prognosticating that thereafter, God willing, you must enjoy some of mine ... No more to you now at this time, mine own darling, but that a wish I would we were together an evening. With the hand of yours, H. R.' King Henry VIII wrote this note whilst in pursuit of Anne Boleyn, the second of his six wives. His gift of hart flesh is venison and this luxurious red meat was a potent symbol of love, but there was more to his note than that. Wordplay was the language of a cultivated person in Tudor times; Shakespeare in *Twelfth Night* has the lovelorn Duke Orsino playing on the words heart and hart and their connotations of the chaste and the chased, portraying himself as the hunted hart pursued by the hounds of his desire. Orsino extends this metaphor to Viola (disguised as a lad but secretly in love with Orsino) and unwittingly compares 'him' to Diana, goddess of hunting. So it is not difficult to imagine what Henry had in mind when he and Anne were finally 'together an evening'.

Henry's words reflect beliefs associated with deer and venison that permeate many centuries and cultures, and of which some are still held today. In some cultures deer have at various times represented fidelity, timidity, resurrection and regeneration; in others, strength, virility and uncontrollable lust. They appear as the prophetic curse of a family and as the Celtic stag-god Cernunnos, they occur in fertility rituals and in early Chinese mythology, they were the object of a cult around which much Scythian art revolved, and they still play an important part in the Shinto religion. Some regarded venison as a social dividing line: John Manwood's *Treatise of the Laws of the Forest* written in 1665 mentions that, although venison was the privilege of the nobility, 'those deer that are not sweet nor meet to be eaten by the best of people ... The flesh shall be given to the poor and the lame and the head and the skin shall be given to the poor of the next Town.' Small wonder, then, that people's feelings about deer and venison today are confused, ambivalent. Are they spiritual lords of the forest, or are they pests ransacking our gardens and spreading Lyme disease? Is venison, with its naturally low fat and healthy proportions of essential fatty acids, the modern diner's dream or is it, thanks to Walt Disney's Bambi, in some curiously sentimental way different from the flesh of other animals and so taboo? Whichever the attitude, there can be no denying that despite increasing urbanisation, the urge to hunt deer remains part of Western culture. If today you combined the manpower of the world's ten largest armies, this would still amount to fewer than the number of Americans who go off as individuals every year in pursuit of white-tailed deer.[1] Whilst the majority are armed with guns, a substantial minority – about a quarter – slip into the woods armed only with bow and arrow, the deliberately primitive nature of this hunt being its principal attraction.

Where does this urge come from? In primitive societies the importance of hunting and its strong element of chance inevitably led to superstition and ritual; therein lie the beginnings of mythology. The strength and quick senses of deer earned them respect, and their fascinating annual cycle of antler regrowth, culminating in the extravagant behaviour of males during the rutting season, came to epitomise the marvel of nature's eternal regeneration as well as male potency. The Spanish philosopher José Ortega y Gasset wrote a compelling meditation that conveys man's passionate relationship with hunting, including the Dionysiac ecstasy experienced at that moment in the chase when hunter, dog and hunted animal become one, and he explains something of the longing in man's soul for this moment.[2] It is not unusual to encounter hunters today who, for no logical reason, become profoundly upset at the thought of domesticating deer. One

1 This almost unbelievable statistic was quoted in the British Deer Society's journal, which in turn was quoting the *Wall Street Journal*. I have since quizzed a number of American hunters who can all quote figures for their own states that tend to corroborate the national picture.
2 This was brought home to me by a dinner conversation during which someone described the exhilarating experience of killing a rabbit as a young boy during the war. Sixty years later he still marvelled at the sense of power conveyed by the blood on his hands and said that this excitement far outweighed the appetising prospect of eating the rabbit, hungry though he was at the time.

senses that they cannot bear the idea of the untameable stag, essence of male virility, happily accepting docility. It is as though the hunter feels he might regain, or at least experience for a moment, something in the wild animal which civilized urban man has lost. If you remove the wildness from the stag, you deprive the man of his dreams.

Although these feelings originated in primitive society, medieval attitudes to deer, religion, hunting and chivalry refined them. A white hart (stag) appeared frequently in Arthurian legends to lure a knight to some mysterious place to face his rite of passage. Be it in loyalty, bravery or courtly love,[3] the hunter becoming the hunted was a common metaphor of the period. But hunting was good because it trained men for war and kept them from the dreaded sin of idleness.[4] The hart had attained a reputation for immense longevity (anything from a hundred to fourteen hundred years depending on whom you believed). A common legend was attributed to various European rulers, including Charlemagne, Henry III of England, Charles VI of France and even Napoleon. They were all said to have caught a stag with a collar concealed in the folds of its skin and bearing the message *'Caesaris sum, noli me tangere'*. The stag was spared and anyone harming it was punished severely, for such collared stags were regarded as a metaphor for the legitimacy and longevity of the ruling dynasty. A poem of Plutarch's was responsible for changing the stag into a hind and making her a metaphor for unattainable love. Stags were also supposed to have an ability to regenerate into a pure white hart, achieving immortality by casting off earthly riches and flushing out the serpent of evil. They were consequently used as symbols of Christ himself. It was believed that they really could eat snakes; afterwards they apparently wept out the poison in the form of little pebbles which were known as bezoar stones – highly prized treasures thought to be effective against poison.[5] A stag drinking at water was a recurrent motif throughout the medieval period, not only in connection with the serpents but also as an allusion to the Forty-Second Psalm: 'As the hart panteth after the water brooks, so panteth my soul after thee, O God.'

---

3 Courtly love is the context of the legend of *Tristram and Iseult*, which was probably influenced by the classical tale of Dido and Aeneas. Several medieval Arab poets used the same device, with a gazelle replacing the hind in their imagery.

4 *Sir Gawain and the Green Knight* was, among other things, a warning to young knights of the dangers of lounging about at home instead of joining the hunt.

5 Some thought bezoar stones must be deer gallstones, but since deer do not have gall bladders it seems this was yet another example of passing-off, as happened so frequently with saints' relics at that period.

Stag eating serpents, Initial Q from the St Alban's Psalter, *c.*1120. Belief in this myth lasted from the writings of Pliny well into the seventeenth century. In Christian allegory serpents represented sins, and the stag by eating the serpent destroys sin and so runs to quench the burning sensation with the water of Truth.

Such images appear in several legends where a nobleman or king is either converted or enthused to found a religious order after being accosted by a stag which proves to have a crucifix between its antlers. St Eustace is the earliest example but St Hubert is probably the best known, he being the patron saint of deer-hunting. He lived in the eighth century and became Bishop of Liège after his conversion; his relics supposedly cure rabies[6] and, usefully, toothache. His feast day, 3 November, is celebrated at the village of Saint-Hubert in Belgium and resembles a cheerful Bruegel painting come to life. In early November the Ardennes are likely to be looking at their most beautiful. Rolling hills covered with mixed beech, birch and pine forest have turned into a mottle of browns with sheets of yellow and slabs of dark green. Early morning mists and steam lifting from frosty grasses herald

---

6 Rabies was a serious concern to the medieval huntsman because of the crucial role played by dogs.

an eruption of chanterelles, boletus and the many other mushrooms that emerge after a sharp temperature drop. The woods have an encouragingly fragrant fungal smell and from the depths of the forest you can imagine, if not actually hear, the scuffles of wild boar and the distant roar of a rutting stag. There could not be more perfect hunting country. At Saint-Hubert a grand procession of the green-cloaked Compagnons de Saint-Hubert prepares to make its way to the basilica. They are followed by the hunters with their hounds, the hunt followers, the *sonneurs* carrying huge circular hunting horns, flag-throwers and, this being Belgium, a strong contingent from the brewers' guild.

During the high mass, hounds stand next to scarlet-coated hunters in the church, good-naturedly waving their tails and tilting their heads in recognition whenever the otherwise typical service is punctuated by the refrain of the hunting horns whose rasping chords reverberate amid the soaring columns. Like the sound of the ancient *lur*,[7] they disturb something primordial in those who listen, and it is almost possible to understand the elusive moment of Dionysian ecstasy. After mass the hounds are blessed with holy water and outside the church a throng of people hold up their pets to be sprinkled. If the hunters' quarry is flesh of the earth, bread represents the land's fruit, so piles of rolls are blessed and people bring along their own, bought as well as home-made. In the case of one hungry pilgrim patiently waiting outside the church, only the last crust remains but it is solemnly and joyously beatified all the same. Finally the hunting horses are blessed round the back of the basilica. (When I was there, a group of pilgrims had ridden for four days from France to Saint-Hubert; they sang a song about the glories of hunting and its empathy with nature, and then clattered off into the frosty sunshine.) Back in the square, tots of fiery *genever* are offered to warm the stomach, a great many bottles of specially brewed Cuvée Saint-Hubert beer are opened, and booths dispense chips with mayonnaise, spiced escargots and *matoufé* – a cross between an omelette and scrambled egg. Those with the foresight to book in advance enjoy Belgium's legendary cuisine. Increasingly merry songs are sung by the guildsmen, two women dressed in peasant costume totter unsteadily down the pavement, and the four-part conversations of the *sonneurs'* horns echo round the buildings. Everything

---

7 A *lur* is a long, curved Bronze Age trumpet. Until very recently it was used in parts of Scandinavia for calling in the cattle.

has been cheerfully sprinkled with holy water. Everyone is protected against rabies and toothache, and good hunting is secured for the next twelve months.

Today's followers of St Hubert uphold hunting traditions that have varied little from medieval times. Although the most challenging hunt used dogs in the forest, the many deer parks created in the Middle Ages afforded a more genteel version – sometimes attended by women – and more reliable entertainment. These hunts must of necessity have been fairly restrained, since the deer would simply have jumped over the park walls had they been seriously pursued for any length of time. There were around two thousand deer parks in medieval Britain, many quite small. Given the population at that time (about four million), this is a remarkable number. Hunting was enjoyed as a sport, but these parks' main function was as reliable sources of meat for the wealthy. Ordinary people did not have legal access to deer in parks, though clearly many tried their hand at poaching. Shakespeare, for example, was supposed to have been caught poaching deer in Charlecote Park in Warwickshire in 1586; the deer park still exists.

But whether hunted in wild or tame fashion, deer were so much a part of chivalrous life that even the way they were 'unmade' or cut up afterwards was highly ritualised; everyone knew their rank, in what order the carcass must be dismembered and who would receive which portion.[8] This even extended to the hounds, who had their *curée*[9] or ritual reward ceremony after the kill. This account from *Sir Gawain and the Green Knight* was written around 1385:

> And the lord of the land rides long at his sport
> Hunting yeld hinds through wood and heath.
> When the sun sank low he had slain such a number
> Of hinds and other deer, it is a marvel to recall.

In those days fat was a desirable trait, so

> Those who were assigned the assay of the fat
> Found fully two finger-widths on even the leanest.

---

8 Many versions of *Tristram and Iseult* give lengthy descriptions of Tristram's skill in the unmaking of his stag, citing it as an example of his prowess as a chivalrous hunter.

9 Despite its similarity to *curee* or *cury*, the medieval term for food preparation (see p. 17), the word *curée* derives from *cuir*, the French for leather, since the dogs ate it off the deer's hide.

There follows a lengthy description of how the carcasses were unmade which would make perfect sense to a butcher today, and afterwards the meat was divided, 'To each person his portion most proper and fit'. Here is how the dogs received their *curée*:

> They fed their hounds on the hide of a hind,
> On liver and lights and the skin of the paunches
> And bread well sopped in blood of the deer.
> They blew the kill with high horns and set the hounds a-baying,
> Then packed up their meat and went home merrily.

The dogs were held back, straining at the leash, until the *sonneurs'* horns rang out, so that they would always associate hunting horns with their reward. Many illustrations and tapestries feature dogs relishing this feast of umbles.

Red deer and wild boar (classed as 'greater game') were the food of kings and warriors[10] and an essential ingredient of the medieval table, appearing in the accounts of great feasts, though they feature more heavily at northern and eastern European feasts than in the south, or even in the British Isles which was devoted to and renowned for the quality of its beef (see chapter 8). The Emperor Charlemagne's favourite food was apparently large game which had been hunted, spit-roasted and carved by his nobles, and 'the time of grease' when these animals were fat after feasting on nuts and lush summer browse was the most glorious time to hunt them. The word venison (coming from *venari*, to hunt) meant any meat of the chase and was not originally confined to the meat of deer; in those days wild boar and even hare could have been called venison. At what point the English word venison came to be restricted to deer meat is not clear;[11] in modern English the term for hunted meat is game, whereas the equivalent German term, *wild*, has remained unchanged since the Middle Ages. Nevertheless, that venison was regarded as a noble meat is without question. Beef, being fatter, was much relished, but venison, with its sporting and seasonal cachet, was serious feast meat. John Russell wrote around 1460, 'Fatt venesoun with frumenty hit is a gay plesewre your souerayne to serve with in season to his honowre;' and 'I am sure it is a Lordes dysshe . . .

---

10 The same class differential existed in Japan: whilst most of the country was vegetarian or vegan, the samurai classes hunted and ate deer, wild boar and game birds.

11 Robert May writes in 1685 of 'the flesh of a hinder part of a hare, or any other venison'.

It is a meate for greate men,' wrote Andrew Boorde in 1542.

It is not difficult to infer how the highly ritualised chivalrous hunting behaviour embraced by medieval nobles evolved from their ancestors' primitive chase and their superstitions. Neither is it hard to understand how the act of co-operative hunting, which required planning as well as the promise of bringing home a substantial quantity of meat requiring distribution, helped to shape early social structures. At the beginning of the seventeenth century Samuel de Champlain founded a hunting and feasting club in Canada, initially to raise the morale of his garrison; but he found coincidentally that his French troops made a lasting bond with the native Canadian Micmac tribe who went out hunting with them. After a disastrous few years of scurvy and depression, de Champlain's *Ordre de Bontemps* proved invaluable:

> We spent this winter very pleasantly, and had good fare by means of the Order of Good Cheer which I established, and which everybody found ... more profitable than all sorts of medicine we might have used. This order consists of a chain which we used to place with little ceremonies about the neck of one of our people, commissioning him for that day to go hunting. The next day it was conferred upon another, and so on, in order. All vied with each other to see who could do the best, and bring back the finest game. We did not come off badly, nor did the Indians who were with us.

In a hunter-gatherer society, when hunters brought back a large quantity of fresh meat it had to be distributed and eaten quickly before it went bad. A glut was inevitable, and people gleefully consumed it – perhaps this is the origin of feasting. Hunted meat was special, of high status, nutritious, and generally provided by dominant males. Absolutely the right food for a feast, especially when roasted.

In northern countries, the darker a meat is, the more effort is required to produce it and the higher is its status. Thus, particularly, beef was preferred to lamb which in turn was more highly regarded than pork. This even extends to poultry, where peacock, swan, goose and turkey,[12] all dark meats, were preferred to chicken. Venison, being as dark a meat as swan, was also highly regarded and crops up at feasts

---

12 Turkey was a dark meat initially; it is only with comparatively recent intensive breeding that it has evolved into the pale and insipid travesty deemed more acceptable to the modern consumer.

through the ages roasted and baked and turned into elaborate pies and pasties. Venison feasts were a popular event in Tudor London, so much so that Queen Elizabeth I had the Lord Mayor ban them to avoid 'the excessive spending of venison and other vitails in the halls of this citie and which we understand to be offensive to Her Majesty'. Double standards seem to be in place here, for Elizabeth, like her father, was an inveterate stag-hunter, and the Tudors were notorious for completely denuding deer parks on their visits. Although she continued the chase well into her sixties, Elizabeth's forays were more refined affairs than Henry's. In 1591 she arrived at Cowdray Park in Sussex, 'where was a delicate bowre prepared, under which her Highness' musicians played; and a crossbow, by a nymph with a sweet song, was delivered into her hands to shoot at the deere; about some thirty were put into a paddock, of which number she killed three or four.'

In the eighteenth century, entry to some gentlemen's clubs could sometimes be gained by donating a sufficiently creditable gift. The original charter to the Royal Society allowed 'any nobleman or gentle-man complimenting this company with venison, not less than a haunch, shall . . . be deemed an honorary member'. By the nineteenth century, many deer parks were used for grazing cattle. In the few that remained, some used to castrate fallow bucks and feed them up in stalls to produce fatter venison. In the case of Richmond Park, it meant they could also provide out-of-season venison legally for the Royal Venison Warrant.[13] Alexis Soyer, remarkable chef of Reform Club and Sebastopol fame, still placed venison alongside turtle as the backbone of a feast, calling them 'the Gog and Magog' of the event. Although Soyer advocated serving roast venison 'so that the blood runs down the carving knife', another approach soon prevailed after Queen Victoria and Prince Albert popularised the Scottish Highlands as a ruggedly romantic place where one roamed the hills in uncom-fortable but sportsmanlike pursuit of the noble stag. The techniques of Albert's native Germany were adopted and became the accepted way to deal with this rich and sometimes tough royal meat. Lengthy

13 The Royal Venison Warrant dates back to the fifteenth century, possibly earlier. In return for giving up the right to hunt in the royal parks in and around London, the citizens (or rather their representatives the mayor, sheriffs, town clerk and so on) were granted the right to a certain amount of venison (which nevertheless had to be paid for) and occasionally the right to take deer themselves. The practice was interrupted during the Commonwealth period, and also from 1918 to 1920 and from 1940 to 1949. When it was restored in 1950, recipients, who now included some cabinet ministers, were given just one haunch of venison at a cost of ten shillings. In 1997 the Royal Warrant was finally discontinued.

marinating followed by long slow cooking with strong spices and sweet fruits were the last remnants of a European style dating back to the Middle Ages.

As with hunting traditions, cooking rituals were perpetuated among what was until recently a very select band of venison-eaters. So much so that it is only in the last few decades that venison has experienced a renaissance. With its lack of fat, young venison is surprisingly refreshing in warm weather if quickly cooked, and venison has always provided richly flavoured comfort food for cold winter days. These two approaches yield results which, luscious as they both are, might as well be from different meats, so dissimilar are they in eating quality.

Some years ago I was asked to present a venison banquet for an international congress of deer experts. I wanted to correct a few erroneous beliefs but more importantly to demonstrate to them, in the course of one meal, some of the historical importance of deer, and also the diversity of ways in which they have been used by people all over the world. I presented nine dishes, each one with deer produce in it. Some were culinary curiosities and there were even vegetarian options.

To start off the banquet I made a perfectly transparent venison consommé with little stags cut from thin slivers of celeriac prancing in the bowls. A tiny flake of gold leaf floating on top added visual sparkle.

The next course was a platter of venison charcuterie: slices of smoked haunch, venison salami and some dry-cured venison rather similar to Parma ham. These were served with a refreshing mixed-herb salad. Alternatives I considered were a smooth liver pâté or a rough country venison terrine; or even a slice from a monstrous raised venison pie, its crust gilded as in medieval times, with a pastry stag sitting on the top.

Then came venison steak tartare. Venison is lean and healthy enough to be ideal for steak tartare because, provided the steak has been hygienically prepared from a single uncut muscle and is served immediately, the meat is safe to eat. The tartare was served alongside a raw egg yolk and some caviar, together with horseradish sauce, aïoli and pickled capers.

The fourth course gave respite from meat, being a small pouch woven from green and white tagliatelli and stuffed with a fresh cheese made from curdled reindeer milk. This cheese had been flown over from Finland where research is being conducted into reindeer cheese for modern markets. Nomadic tribes of reindeer-herding people still

The Land of Cockaigne. Pieter Brueghel the Elder, 1567. A never-never land of dream foods asking to be eaten. The carnivalesque imagery is emphasized by the eggshell in the foreground.

Hell – Gluttony. Detail from a fresco in San Gimignano by Tadeo di Bartolo, 1396. A common theme: the link between gluttony, lust and damnation.

A Sumptuous Still-Life. Jans Davidsz de Heem, c.1648. On the face of it, a celebration of Dutch prosperity, but the suggestively shaped ham bone and seductive lobster appear to convey other messages.

Dr Wilson, Lt Bowers & Cherry-Garrard on returning from Cape Crozier, by Herbert Ponting, 1910–13 British Antarctic Expedition. Jam sandwiches and hot chocolate from a chipped enamel jug are a feast after the worst journey in the world.

Meal before the hunt, and La Curée. From Gaston Phoebus' *Book of Hunting*, French, 15thC. Trackers present deer spoor to the lord in the hopes that their trail will be chosen. After the hunt there is a feast for the hounds who are fed on the hide.

La Matança: the pig-killing. Ceramic plate, Portugal, 1998. There is usually a feast afterwards to thank the helpers for their hard work.

Three prize pigs outside a sty. English school, 19thC. Ideal cottage pigs: so fat their feet can hardly support them.

Apparato di convivo. Francesco Ratta, 1693. A splendid example of an elaborate trionfi for the banquet course: an impressive quantity of edible sugar sculptures, and the centrepiece is charged with dishes of 'banquetting stuffe'.

Large food display. Georg Flegel, 1622: The banquet course in detail: thick fruit paste glistens in its box; sweet wine accompanies spicy biscuits and sugar-coated comfits; fresh and dried fruit sit next to a pile of lacquered wooden trenchers.

Dinner in the iguanodon model. Illustrated London News, 1854. A precursor of the Acclimatisation Society's inaugural dinner, this one took place in the Crystal Palace, scene of the Great Exhibition.

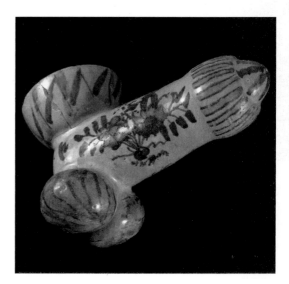

Bawdy drinking cup. Delftware, c.1690, found in the river Thames. This contrast to the elegant scene opposite exemplifies the Restoration humour deplored by Richard Warner.

landum eciā lururia
malium ꝗ̄ accuſare
aliꝗ̄ſto facilius eſt
qua virtute operi nō inſerat. Non
quidem ut illi honorem ꝛeꝛpiat
ſed ut ſeipſam recognoſcens ad
poententiā impelli poſſit iuuigat
ille libido qui eo hiſdem vicioꝛum
pncipiis oꝛitur neꝗ̄ a reprehecē

aut ab emendatione ſeparent· eiꝰ
mentie errore conuenꝛe· tranſlateur
Er ceſte partie Valerius commence
ſon vyᵉ liure qui eſt de Bie z de
faiꝯ dignes de memoire de la cite
de romme z des eſtrangiers· ou il
apꝛes ce que Valerius eū vny liure
precedent a determine des vertuz z
operatiōe vertueuſes· en ce vyᵉ

A feast in the bath. Master of Anthony of Burgundy. 15thC miniature illustrating a
translation of Valerius Maximus's work; so popular that over sixty manuscripts still
survive. See p170.

inhabit a vast area of land stretching across the far north of Europe and Russia; their methods have changed little for thousands of years and their ancestors are perhaps the earliest known managers of animals for the provision of food and drink. Reindeer cheeses were not traditionally made for sale, but preserved in the snow or on elevated caches for later use. The soft cheese that I produced was spiked with crunchy strips of carrot, lightly cooked with spices in a mild honey vinegar. The woven pouch was steamed and served with a vegetable purée.

The main course consisted of meltingly tender venison loin, briefly roasted and served medium rare alongside a chunk of ossobuco[14] that had been slowly simmered in wine and vegetables until the meat and sinews had dissolved together. The juices from the roasting and the stewing were combined, strained and reduced to make a rich dark sauce which married the flavours of two styles of cooking venison. A refreshing vegetable cake accompanied this, made from layers of mashed potato, leek purée and spinach.

The dessert course contained some curiosities popular at medieval banquets, starting with hartshorn and hindberry jelly. Hindberry is an old north-country name for raspberries, presumably because hinds (female red deer) love nibbling them as they pass through the dappled woods. Hartshorn is an ingredient commonly seen in old recipe books. It is simply shavings of hard antler boiled for a long time until they produce a form of gelatine. I found that ground-up antler made only a very light jelly, so I added venison knuckle-bones to make it firmer. Clarifying the liquid was a lengthy process, but once it had been diluted with white wine and flavoured with sugar, lemon, mild spices and the raspberry juice, the result was light and delicious. With this came a real mincemeat tart, that is to say pastry cases were filled with a rich forcemeat of minced raisins, currants, prunes, almonds and fresh apples mixed with grated venison suet and ground venison meat. The tart also contained mixed spices, candied citrus fruits and some brandy to plump the fruit and act as preservative. To complement its richness I made an ice cream from reindeer milk, simply flavoured with vanilla pod.

Reindeer milk is extremely rich and syrupy in texture, and highly nutritious. It has a wonderful flavour slightly reminiscent of fresh cobnuts. The simple cheese course therefore consisted of some softly

---

14 Ossobuco is generally made with veal shins, but obviously I used venison for my banquet..

pressed fresh reindeer cheese served with a savoury hazelnut biscuit.

To finish, there was a tisane made of powdered velvet antler (a Chinese tonic for at least two thousand years) mixed with Hungarian herbal tea. This was served with a choice of two liqueurs, one called Stag's Breath, a Scottish whisky-based liqueur, and the other called Royal Velvet, a fiery ginger liqueur from New Zealand containing extract of velvet antler and finely powdered gold leaf which sparkles invitingly. And so, with the gold leaf bringing it full circle, the banquet ended. My hope was that, after experiencing these diverse flavours and armed with a little more knowledge of venison's wide-ranging importance to so many cultures, some of these delegates – who were largely of a practical bent – might be encouraged to delve further into the background of their specialist subject. And maybe they would appreciate that their own efforts were just the latest chapter in the long partnership of man and deer.

13

Ephemera at the feast:
perfume and flowers

In emerald tufts, blue and purple, blue and white
Like sapphire, pearl and rich embroidery.
SHAKESPEARE, *The Merry Wives of Windsor*

To elevate a good meal into a feast there must be an extra dimension; and although this chapter does not describe any particular feast, it would be remiss to leave the subject of ambience untouched. Many feasts exalt themselves by visual impact. Sometimes, as we have seen, this is achieved by covering walls and floors with rich tapestries; in contrast, flowers and perfumes represent less durable treasure. However, as with music, their role is to lift the spirit, to enhance the performance, to make the guest feel special. Like a bower bird's nest, extravagantly decorated with flowers and shiny objects to attract a mate, beautiful surroundings impress as well as delight the guest. Although the biological function of flowers is simply to attract attention, nevertheless their colour, scent, ephemeral quality and association with secret languages[1] have led them to appear at banquets in most cultures.

Many festivals involve processions for which the streets are dredged with flowers and fragrant herbs. In some cases this was originally to mask street smells and protect against the plague, but flowers can be purely decorative. In 1830 Hans Christian Andersen described arriving at a festival in Italy: 'The whole long gently ascending street was covered over with flowers, the ground was blue; over these lay in long green stripes, green (leaves) alternating with rose-colour, then a dark red colour to form a border to the whole carpet. The middle of this

---

1 In the nineteenth century numerous books were written about the language of flowers. Unfortunately different books frequently ascribe different attributes to the same flower: for example foxglove could either mean 'I am ambitious only for you' or 'Insincerity'; a dahlia could mean either 'Forever thine' or 'Instability' – which must have been confusing, if not heartbreaking at times.

represented suns and stars formed by a mass of yellow, round, and star-like flowers. The whole was a living flower carpet, a mosaic floor. Not a breath of air stirred, the flowers lay immovable as if they were heavy, firmly set precious stones.'

Flowers welcome us to the feast. Just as visitors in the Pacific islands are presented with a *lei* and guests in Thailand with orchids, so wreaths and garlands were a feature of banquets from Roman through to medieval Europe and beyond. The *Mesnagier de Paris*, written around 1393 and one of the earliest books on entertaining, reminds the reader that when preparing for a banquet, branches, greenery, violets and chaplets (garlands) must be bought in good time from the flower-sellers at Porte-de-Paris. In 1560 Queen Elizabeth I made an ephemeral banqueting house in Greenwich Park to welcome the French ambassador's entourage. It sounds interestingly like a bower bird's nest, being made of fir poles, 'decked with birch branches and all manner of flowers both of the field and of the garden; as roses, july flowers, lavender, marygolds and all manner of strewing herbs and rushes'. Elizabeth had a very sweet tooth, and so in this fragrant bower was presented her 'banquetting stuffe': sweet spicy wines and the daintiest of sweetmeats whose beauty would have equalled the bower itself. If Elizabeth's rustic bower was a charming seasonal gesture, out-of-season flowers might characterise the feast-table as a status symbol. At the wedding of one of Louis XIV's illegitimate daughters in 1680, *Le Mercure galant* (the French equivalent of the *Illustrated London News*) comments on the great tables fifty-four feet long which were decorated all the way down the centre 'in a wholly original manner, which had something elegant, magnificent, and supernatural about it, considering the season. There were nineteen open-work baskets, as many gilded as silver, which dominated all the length of the table. They were filled with anemones, hyacinths, Spanish jasmine, tulips and orange leaves, and with little garlands of flowers crowning them above. There was nothing more natural, and seeing these baskets it was difficult to remember that it was the sixteenth of January.'

Tablecloths at Georgian banquets were heavily swagged with fresh flowers. In contrast the table top was decorated with exquisitely fashioned artificial flowers, sometimes made from cut paper, sometimes from porcelain, sometimes from sugar paste, their beauty reflected in the fashionable new hand-painted porcelain plates. At Victorian banquets the plant life was sometimes so exuberant that it could be difficult to see across the table. Heated glasshouses produced exotic blooms, grapes and pineapples (some of which even contrived to be growing out of the centre of the table) to celebrate the achievements of a successful colonising nation. By 1913, just before the First World War put an end to large-scale extravagances in Europe, society hostess Mrs Lucie Heaton Armstrong welcomed with some relief the demise of these grandiose displays. In her book *Etiquette and Entertaining* she wrote: 'The cumbersome épergne is never seen at the modern table ... An appearance of carelessness is prized above all ... the favourite fancy of the moment is to get long branches of roses, roots and all, and lay them all along the table. The roses are wired to the stem, and the roots are carefully cleaned, and then partly veiled in asparagus fern, but the idea that the rose tree has been carelessly plucked up by the roots and laid on the table is voted extremely charming in this artificial age.'

Flowers were also used to colour festive food: pickled, crystallised and powdered, they were widely employed in medieval and Renaissance times. Custards and creams, tarts and jellies gleamed with rich colours; in his *Historie of Plants* Gerard describes the rich red obtained from bugloss: 'The roots of these are used to colour sirrups, waters, gellies, & such like infections as Turnsole is ... The Gentlewomen of France do paint their faces with these roots, as it is said.' Violets produced blue and crushed herbs gave green. Saffron, most expensive of all, supplied a deep rich perfumed gold, though, as Gerard also noted, pot marigolds were widely used as a cheaper substitute: 'The yellow leaves of the floures are dried and kept throughout the Dutchland against Winter, to put into broths, in Physicall potions, and for divers other purposes, in such quantity, that in some Grocers or Spice-Sellers houses are to be found barrels filled with them, and retailed by the penny more or lesse, insomuch that no broths are well made without dried Marigolds.' Marigolds were also a popular ingredient in salads along with seasonal flowers like primroses and cowslips, violets and lavender, bugloss and borage, all of which must have been especially appreciated after a long winter without fresh salad leaves.

Other than for decoration and cooking, plants have one more important role which has largely disappeared from the Western feast: perfume. Some food and wine enthusiasts frown on the idea of perfume because it masks the 'true' flavours and bouquets of food and wine. This notion first appears in nineteenth-century Britain when people were at pains to dissociate themselves from louche eighteenth-century habits and from the unwashed mass of perfumed foreigners. The *Epicure's Yearbook* for 1869 reports a 'Banquet de Degustation' given by the Le Havre International Club and echoes the predictable reaction to one member's contribution: 'The scent vaporised by Rimmel unpleasantly disturbed the tasters; anything more barbarous than a scented dinner-table it is impossible to discover. How to taste a truffle, or catch the flavour of a wine, in an atmosphere charged with hair-dresser's scents!' Now that current hygiene practices eliminate natural smells from almost every part of life it is easy to forget the pleasing impact of perfumes and scented oils when used on skin and hair, clothing and floors; but the role of perfume in entertaining has a long and noble history, probably starting when people first squatted on a sunny carpet of fragrant herbs. The *hetaerae*, courtesans who were often hired for ancient Greek banquets, applied the heady scent of violets to their breath as well as their bodies. The Roman emperors loved roses: Lucius Verus stuffed his banquet couches with rose and lily petals; Nero's dining room was lined with movable leaves of ivory that wafted sweet perfumes around the room and rained down petals onto his guests; Elagabalus once almost smothered his guests with rose

Greek hetaerae dancing for Dionysos, Black Attic vase painting *c.*430 BC

petals as they waited for their feast.[2] Throughout medieval Europe costly aromatic spices – ambergris, musk, rose- and orange-flower water[3] – were included in celebratory dishes, and the water for hand-washing was often scented with herbs. No banquet during the Italian Renaissance was complete without its phials of perfume on the table, ready to sprinkle over napkins and cloths.

Such practices arrived in Europe as a result of the crusades. The Middle East and Asia still have a place for perfume in entertaining and cooking: delicate rose-petal conserve in Persia, the drops of rose-water added to a cup of strong coffee in Turkey, almond sweetmeats moistened with rose- or orange-flower water, guests' feet and hair anointed with balms and essences. Jesus received this gesture of hospitality in Bethany: '. . . as he sat at meat, there came a woman having an alabaster box of ointment of spikenard very precious; and she brake the box and poured it on his head.' Not much had changed by the seventeenth century, when Sir John Chardin described a wedding in Persia: 'They threw a Bottle of Rose-water upon the Body which held about half a Pint, and another larger Bottle of Water colour'd with Saffron, so that the Vest was stain'd with it: Then they rubbed the Arms and Body over with a liquid Perfume of Labdamum and Ambergrease, and they put upon his neck, a large string of Jessamin . . . This manner of caressing and doing of Honour, is universal among the Women, who have the wherewithal to provide this Profuseness.' Perhaps the current revival of aromatherapy will lead to some Westerners appreciating once more the pleasures offered by perfume at the feast.

---

2 A less frivolous significance of roses at the ancient banqueting table was confidentiality; if a rose was suspended above the table it was acknowledged that private conversations made *sub rosa* during the meal would remain confidential.

3 The symbolic significance was different for Christians and Muslims. Roses were sacred to Muslims as they were believed to have sprung from the Prophet's sweat, whereas to Christians they symbolised incorruptibility (the Virgin Mary is known as the Rosa Mystica) and orange flowers signified virginity, hence their popularity at weddings.

14

The Feast of St Antony: pigs – the peasants' feast

The race of pigs is expressly given by nature to set forth a banquet.

MARCUS TERENTIUS VARRO

In most feasts the prestigious meats to serve were beef, swans, peacocks and venison, in some societies sheep and camel. Pork, although of course it appeared at banquets, was not rated at high table because it was considered too ordinary.[1] Even today chefs know that for every ten dishes of beef, they will only sell one of pork – most people do not consider it a special treat. The ceremonial boar's head which appeared at university college feasts may appear to contradict this statement, but wild boar was classed as game, indeed its meat was included in the original generic term venison, meaning the meat of venery (the hunt). Wild boar were respected as a fearless and dangerous quarry by hunters throughout Europe and Asia; domestic swine were regarded as an entirely different class of beast. These early pigs were herded through the wooded countryside by peasants exercising their feudal rights to pannage (grazing on acorns).[2] Scrawny, long-legged and hairy, they resemble wild boar to our undiscerning eyes – indeed in 1658 Edward Topsell used the same engraving for both animals in his *History of Four-footed Beasts.*

As time went on and the feudal system broke down, even manual labourers were able to keep their own animals, in the towns as well as in the country. Those who took it upon themselves to advise the poorer classes – writers such as Gervase Markham and John Worlidge in the seventeenth century and William Cobbett in the nineteenth – extolled

---

1 The one exception is sucking pig. In Chinese cooking, too, this was and is the case: although pork is one of the most widely eaten meats in China, it is rarely used for a banquet.

2 In Saxon times lands for pasturage as well as the swine themselves were sometimes bequeathed in wills: 'I give food for seventy swine in that woody allotment which the countrymen call Wolferdinlegh.'

Of the Swine, Edward Topsell, 1658. In his *History of Four-footed Beasts*, Topsell's illustration for wild boar is identical to that of the swine.

the virtues of the cottage pig as an economical way to provide food for a family. The pig's omnivorous diet and its ability to create nourishing meat and valuable fat from the most unsavoury waste material inspired misgivings about the undiscriminating greed[3] of the beast; this perhaps explains why it was less highly esteemed at the noble feast-table, but deemed a more suitable highlight for the festivities of lowlier classes. Describing the pig in her *Book of Household Management* in 1868, Mrs Beeton (an industrious scavenger of other people's writings herself) declares

> ... he is everywhere known for his gluttony, laziness, and indifference to the character and quality of his food. And though he occasionally shows an epicure's relish for a succulent plant or luscious carrot, which he will discuss with all his salivary organs keenly excited, he will, the next moment, turn with equal gusto to some carrion offal that might excite the forbearance of the unscrupulous cormorant. It is this coarse and repulsive mode of feeding that has, in every country and language, obtained for him the opprobrium of being 'an unclean animal'.

In some places pig-keeping was neither traditional nor common: large parts of Scotland, for example, and some areas of southern France. This dates back to times when the population was very poor and the land unproductive. Crop failures were common, and because pigs are omnivorous they were in direct competition for food that people needed for themselves. They couldn't afford a cow to yield whey, and grain or potatoes were too valuable to give to pigs; in some parts of France they could not even spare chestnuts, these being part of the

---

3 In Buddhist thought, too, the pig symbolises greed.

human diet, as is demonstrated in old regional recipes. Consequently, until the standard of living rose only the better-off were able to keep a pig. Sheep, goats or geese, which live on grass and furthermore might also produce wool, milk or fat, were favoured. In south-west and central France, the goose was the substitute for those whose budget would not stretch to a pig. The bird could be finished, if not hugely fattened, on grass alone, and from there it was only a short step to making *foie gras* when times became easier. Even though people in those regions can now afford to feed pigs, you still encounter fewer pork products at markets and cafés than in other parts of the country.

In Scotland, where even today pork is not especially popular,[4] the exceptions demonstrate the point. Both Ayrshire in the south-west of the country and the Isles of Orkney in the far north have fertile soil and productive climates mellowed by the Gulf Stream. Both are dairy-cattle areas with a strong cheese-making tradition that means plenty of whey for pigs. These were the only two areas of the country that also produced traditional bacon and pork recipes. In Orkney (whose name means pig-island, from *ork*, pig, and *en eye*, an island) little kitchen gardens called planticrues were made by piling soil inside stone walls that protected their plants from the wind. They were turned into temporary pigsties at the end of the winter, when the pigs were shut in to clean up all the remaining roots and vegetable waste and manure the plot at the same time. 'Pork and kail and knockit corn'[5] was the delicious result.

It has been suggested that anxiety about pigs competing for scarce food resources may help to explain the Jewish and Muslim prohibition of pork, though the whole story is clearly more complex than this. Mrs Beeton touched on a second reason, and the obvious risk of contracting diseases or parasites from eating pork in a hot climate is another. Thus a significant number of people do not associate pork with a feast; nevertheless across the world the pig has given many others the chance to enjoy a glut of meat and fat which is all the more appreciated for its infrequency. A case in point is China's custom of killing a pig for the

4 Mutton pies rather than pork pies; haggis rather than faggots, and sweet Angus beef rather than pork crackling, are the Scot's preference.

5 It is a wonderful peasant dish when made with good fat pork. Knockit corn is pearl barley, i.e. with its husks knocked off. The k in knockit is sounded, perhaps because it is onomatopoeic. Kail, as well as meaning curly kale, is also a generic Scots word for any brassica leaf, and the Scots word for a kitchen garden or planticrue is a kailyard.

New Year celebrations, one of the few times when poor people might eat meat.

So whilst the aristocracy feasted on gilded peacocks, turtle soup, chivalrous game and fatted barons of beef, the peasantry deployed their ingenuity in concocting more homely delights from the carcasses of monstrously fat pigs;[6] naïve paintings of these bulging creatures testify to their owners' aspirations and achievements. Many families' most important times of feasting came in the days after the killing of their pig. The most sensible time for this momentous event was in the autumn when kitchen scraps, garden waste and other economical ingredients of the swill bucket were coming to an end, the pig was at its fattest and cool weather prevented the meat from deteriorating. Pig-killings went on all through the winter, providing not only the rare treat of fresh pork and all the delicious parts that had to be consumed at once, but a gamut of preserved products since pork takes readily to being salted and preserved. And if this modest type of feast was spurned by the nobility, it was no less eagerly anticipated by the lower orders.

Throughout Europe, the killing of a pig and the hard work of preserving it is marked by special days: in Switzerland the traditional pig-killing spawned a sausage feast known as *die Metzgete* which some-times coincided with Martinmas on 11 November. That 11 November is also the Feast of Bacchus only increases the merriment. Many people associate Martinmas with goose, but November is an obvious time to kill any domestic animal: 'His Martinmas will come, as it does to every hog' was the old adage.[7] Many Swiss country restaurants still serve '*La Martin*', a menu '*tout cochon*' – unashamedly vast quantities of sausage and trotters, roast pork and sauerkraut, brawn and black pudding. Long cold winters also encourage home distilling and, as food writer Sue Style writes:

one of the best Swiss spin-offs from the distilling process are the sausage feasts called *Treberwurstfrass*[8] that happen on the shores of Lake Biel from November to February. The wine growers are a bit short of work in the freezing winter months before they can start pruning, so some of them get distilling instead. The said feast consists of steaming the

---

6 See p. 65 for Varro's description of an over-fat pig.

7 In the seventh century Bede called November 'Blod-monath', referring to the slaughter and salting of meat.

8 *Treberwurstfrass* translates as a 'grape-husk sausage gobbling', which is a pretty good description.

most wonderful, huge, horseshoe-shaped smoked pork sausages in the upper part of the burnished copper still, just under the domed lid. After an hour or two, the sausages emerge reeking of marc and practically walk out of the pan unaided. You sit at huge trestle tables in the caveau of the vigneron and eat them with lashings of potato salad, and of course wine and marc from the property. Wonderful stuff.

In Hungary pigs are killed for the feast of St Elizabeth on 19 November and fiery paprika-reddened salamis and *gyulai* are hung up to dry afterwards. In Italy pigs are transformed into sublime *salame, pancetta, mortadella, coppa* and *prosciutto* and their stuffed trotters into *zampone* to be served with lentils at New Year's Day celebrations; from Germany come *Speck, Frankfürter* and more varieties of *Wurst* than you would think possible; in Belgium there are *bloedpens*, pâtés and *cochonnailles*, and in Scandinavia *leverkorf* and *leverpostej, polse* and salami. In Britain it was formerly traditional to kill a pig to provide fresh roast pork for Christmas, so the feast of St Thomas on 21 December was often chosen as it heralded the start of a two-week holiday: 'If you have a pig now, kill it, if you don't have one, steal one; St Thomas will forgive you' went the saying, and everyone enjoyed pig's fry and chitterlings, faggots and fat, puddings and pies, Bath chaps and bacon, great hams studded with cloves, and crisp crackling on their Christmas roast. In Spain a pig-killing is called *la matanza*, and is a major event in the family calendar which produces fragrant *jamón serrano* and *jamón de Jabugo*, and spicy *chorizos, embutidos, salchichas* and *morcillas*, the last rendering a delicious orange fat for spreading onto toasted bread. Eating pork assumed a positive religious significance after Christians wrested Spain from the Moors after eight centuries of occupation. Both Muslims and Jews were persecuted by the Spanish Inquisition, so conspicuous consumption of pork could deflect the dangerous charge of heresy.

The patron saint of herdsmen and pigs is St Antony of Egypt whose feast day is 17 January. In France, this is the one time when pigs are not killed, partly in recognition of their important role in truffle-hunting. Instead, the village of Richerenches holds a *messe des truffes*. Everyone attending the mass must bring a truffle which is auctioned off afterwards for charity. Once Saint-Antoine is over and the truffle pigs are back at work in the forests, ordinary pigs are turned into pâtés and *jambonnettes, hure* and *galantines, saucissons, cervelas, andouillettes*[9] and

---

9 'Tasty little bags of mystery', André Simon called them.

boudins, *oreilles*, *museaux* and *pieds de porc*, all testifying to the inventiveness of country people who would not waste any part of their
precious pig; every last piece is relished or put to use: trotters, cheeks,
bristles, ears, fat, meat, snouts, hide – nothing is wasted except the
squeal. And then the products are celebrated. Festivals and eating
competitions for black puddings and sausages are still serious business in northern France, overseen by the appropriate *confréries* or
brotherhoods who, dressed in ceremonial costume, lead processions
of cheerful spectators to join in the eating and drinking as competitors
manfully gulp down another sublime slice of *boudin noir*. '*Il fera venir
l'eau à la bouche de tous les touristes gloutons*' (It will make every visiting
gourmand's mouth water) states one tourist leaflet, encouragingly.

In Andorra, Saint-Antoine used to be marked by a pig auction in aid
of charity. A wealthy farmer would donate a pig or two and the less
well-off would donate a piece of pig, perhaps some trotters, ears or
cheeks or even just a *coca*: a large flap of pastry shaped like a pig's ear,
sprinkled with sugar and nuts. A more recent custom is the free lunch
of Escudella. Margaret Shaida, a fellow member of the Guild of Food
Writers, wrote this account:

> It was St Anthony's today. I had forgotten until I drove down into town
> this morning and saw a row of five great steaming cauldrons set up
> along the side of the road to serve our local parish. They were tended
> by men wearing scarlet hats and white aprons over their winter coats.
> Every year, on 17th January, the parishes of Andorra organise the
> preparation of the annual Escudella, a Catalan stew, to serve every
> passer-by with a free meal. In earlier days, you had to bring your own
> bowl and spoon, but nowadays, commemorative bowls are sold nearby.
> And you can come back for more, as many times as you like. If you go
> down to the main square in the town centre, you can sit at a table to
> eat it, and if you are smart, you will pick a table where a jug of wine has
> been placed, also free.

Coming so soon after the Christmas and Epiphany celebrations it
seems likely that the Escudella is a convenient way to use up all the
leftovers and have some collective fun at the same time.

A pig-killing is of necessity a communal event because of the considerable labour required for cleaning and scraping the carcass,
preparing the intestines for sausage skins, collecting the blood for

black puddings, rendering the fat, chopping the meat, salting the bacon and so on, not to mention the initial skilled business of the slaughter. The owners had to put in a lot of advance preparation by boiling up the large quantities of water necessary for cleaning and for scalding the carcass to help remove the bristles. They also had to produce a good quantity of food for the neighbours who came to help. Sharing tasks was part of rural life; an acknowledgement that everyone joined forces at times of need for the common benefit. After a killing, English children used to be sent scampering round to neighbours with 'pig cheer': dishes of hot pig's fry or perhaps more prestigious gifts of pork chops, a raised pie, a pot of haslet given to those who had obliged with their labour or had contributed scraps to the feed trough. Throughout the rest of the year the best pieces were served up with pride at special celebrations. A christening chine was just such an example: after being taken out of the brine tub, the pork chine was deeply scored and fresh green parsley was crammed down into the slashes, so that when the joint was sliced a festive sight of glowing red meat, clear white fat and bright green parsley added to the occasion. Pork, being a cheaper meat than many others, is also a great standby for the community feasts held in village squares throughout Europe.

The institution of the communal pig lasted well into the twentieth century. I recently listened to the legendary footballer Bobby Charlton reminiscing about his childhood during the Second World War, and about occasions when his street shared a pig: '... and every time one was killed it was a major celebration; everyone came in from all over and had a little share of it.' He also remembered his impatience at having to wait until his family's share had been salted down before they were allowed to eat any. In most of Europe keeping pigs in towns died out when sanitary inspectors banned the practice after the Second World War, though the cottage pig still flourishes in the countryside. Subsequent European Community regulation outlawed pig-killing even on the smallholding, but long-held customs are not eradicated so easily.

In 1997 one of my daughters spent a year in a tiny village in the Gironde; as well as ducks and hens, her host family kept a pig at the bottom of their garden. A few weeks into the New Year came the day for the pig to be killed. A buzz of anticipation on the school bus demonstrated that, even though some pupils were embarrassed by such rustic activities, it still formed a vibrant part of their life. Everyone in the village was, if not actually related, then co-operative and most of the pupils would either take part or knew someone who would. The *tueur des cochons* was part of a large local family and was one of the few remaining butchers with 'special extra skills'; the fact that he could not only do the job but was prepared to flout EC rules added to the excitement. Dogs, children, friends, grandparents and other relations all came to work or to eat or to bark or add to the merriment. But then everything went still:

When the moment arrived I felt a bit nervous because all the girls kept insisting the pig would escape. The *tueur* went in to fetch it on its noose and when he caught it was the only time I heard it scream – very loudly. Once caught it seemed quite calm. There was a moment of quiet tension as he led the pig out to a low bench. Four or five of the men held it down; they were laughing and showing off a bit, maybe they were nervous too. I was fascinated by how quickly and cleanly the *tueur* cut the artery and by how quietly, almost resignedly the pig died; I could hear it breathing steadily till the end. I was amazed how much blood there was. It steamed in the cold air and it all had to be collected for the *boudin noir* and stirred in great cauldrons. Then there was a lot of activity, scraping the skin with boiling water to take off the bristles, blowing out the intestines to make sausages the next day, a hideous big pot with weird bits of rubbery pig bubbling away; I wasn't so keen on watching that. After the day's work was finished everything was quiet and clean and tidy. The only difference was the two pink halves of pig and its liver hanging up steaming in the garage beside Guy's gleaming motorbike.

In the afternoon came the best part of the proceedings: a convivial meal that sprawled generously on into the darkness for everyone who had worked so hard. As people came in stamping their feet and sniffing from the cold wind and steaming boilers, they relaxed in the welcome of the house. Even the dogs settled down quietly under the table, casting longing glances at the most understanding children. Some things, like the *boudin noir*, came from other recent pig-killings in the knowledge that a generous length of today's *boudin* would soon be served up in a neighbouring house, for not long afterwards Stella and her family helped some other people with their pig. There was a huge platter of dark red ham, very salty and cut thick; it had been curing in the garage since the last pig. Crunchy pickled gherkins from Martine's garden offered a sharp contrast to her well-larded terrine. In appreciation of all the hard work there were several jars of Martine's home-made *foie gras* – a coveted treat only brought out on very special occasions. A *charlotte de pêche* had been made from bottled peaches fragrant from last summer's sun, and there was fresh goat's cheese and another made from sheep's milk that dribbled ripely over the edge of its plate to be scooped up and washed down with jugs of wine from the local co-operative. The party atmosphere continued throughout the meal,

a sort of harvest supper in thanksgiving for the pig and reward for everyone's efforts, but once the feasting was finished life quickly returned to normal for there was a lot of hard work to be done next day chopping fat, sterilising the glass jars for storing the meat and terrines, making sausages, puddings and terrines and feeding the other animals. The impression I was left with is of the event being a completely natural part of life there: you work hard, you feast hard and work hard again, and that is the way I accepted it.

15

A beastly feast

Man will not abide in honour: seeing he may be compared unto the beasts that perish; this is the way of them.

PSALM 49

The siege of Paris which took place during the Franco-Prussian War of 1870 is remembered by historians as sowing the seeds of the First World War. And the subsequent civil uprising and disastrous repression of the Paris Commune[1] in 1871 provided essential lessons for the Russian Bolshevik revolution of 1917. But the images of the siege which caught popular imagination seem to be the inequality between the lot of rich and poor in society, and in particular their inventive ways of coping with the lack of food.

On the eve of war, Paris in Louis-Napoleon's Second Empire was Europe's most glittering city, its centre of power: 'It is in Paris that the beating heart of Europe is felt,' wrote Victor Hugo. Haussmann's spectacular new urban layout swept away the chaotic old town and replaced it with wide boulevards and elegant buildings. Masked and fancy-dress balls achieved a frivolity and brilliance not seen since the days of Louis XV, and every corner of fashionable Paris was devoted to the pursuit of Love; a veritable 'El Dorado of pimps and parasites, panders and wantons', as the correspondent Henry Labouchere wrote later. Society restaurants were in their heyday, and one of Paris' most famous, the Restaurant Voisin, had recently employed an eager young trainee called César Ritz.

Once it was clear that a siege was imminent, swift preparations were made. Carts were piled high with vegetables from the market gardens round Paris, granaries were packed with grain, and game in the surrounding forests was captured or shooed away so that it could not be used to feed Bismarck's army. M. Duvernois, the Minister of

---

1 Over 20,000 Parisians were killed in the space of a week when the socialist Communards who had taken control of Paris were ruthlessly crushed by forces sent in by the French government at Versailles. The guillotine used against the nobility during the 1793 terror accounted for only a tenth of that number.

Commerce, arranged for some 250,000 sheep and 40,000 oxen[2] to be folded in the Bois de Boulogne and in the smaller squares of Paris. But this apparently vast storehouse of food was inadequate, owing partly to some simple accounting errors, and as the autumn wore on the authorities began to realise that trouble lay ahead. Horsemeat had already been introduced by Parisian butchers in 1866 as an alternative meat for the poor, but the French taste for horsemeat stems from its role in the siege. In October of 1870, as an example to the rest of respectable Paris, the Central Commission for Health and Hygiene treated itself to a well-publicised horse banquet at which horsemeat was made into a progression of dishes starting with consommé followed by a concoction boiled with cabbage. The rump was served *à la mode*, the side braised, the fillet roasted, and various equine versions of charcuterie were also served. The fashion caught on, with mule and donkey being compared to veal and even Englishmen extolling the virtues of horseflesh: 'How people continue to eat pigs I can't imagine,' wrote journalist Tommy Bowles enthusiastically, after his first taste of it.

By mid-November the supply of fresh meat was drying up and the population turned its hungry gaze towards less usual creatures. In September Henry Labouchere, the 'besieged Resident' for the *Daily News*, had written to his paper, 'I presume if the siege lasts long enough, dogs, rats and cats will be terrified.' Two months later his words, jocular at the time, came true as dogs, cats and even rats were rounded up by the 'Feline and Canine Butchers' and their gastronomic merits compared. Naturally this made perfect copy for the newspaper correspondents who reported their findings in the knowledge that their British readers would shake their heads in thrilled disgust. According to the American contingent, horsemeat from light greys apparently tasted better than that from blacks; rats were said to taste like birds and cats like grey squirrel. A Frenchman pronounced dog to be 'fine, fresh, rosy' and well covered with white fat. By mid-December even Labouchere confessed to having had a slice of spaniel, which made him feel like a cannibal. In the run-up to Christmas, cats cost six francs a pound, though were often passed off as rabbit (which cost forty francs). Rats fetched half a franc per pound, leading to the popular sport of rat-hunting and to various reported menus featuring salmis of rat, rat pie,

---

2 Unfortunately he forgot to include dairy cows amongst the cattle, which was to prove disastrous for some children.

Viande canine et féline, engraving by Vierge in *Le Monde Illustré*, February 1871.
Rats, as well as cat and dog meat on sale during the Siege of Paris during the
winter of 1870–71.

and cat flanked by rats (or mice 'like sausages', depending on which
version you read).

As the winter became bleaker and colder it was the turn of the Jardin
des Plantes, whose collection of exotic animals became the object of
a new interest. Apart from the big cats[3] and the monkeys (and the
hippopotamus which was too big), all the inmates were dispatched and
sold to the now all-powerful butchers. Castor and Pollux, the two
young elephants, were shot and the joints proudly displayed alongside
camel humps and kidneys, bear, wolf and various anonymous body
parts at the Boucherie Anglaise. For those with money, therefore, there
was no serious shortage of nutrition; it was the poor that, as always,
suffered the worst deprivations. *Plus ça change*: much the same thing
had happened in 1596 while Paris was devastated by famine. The contemporary diarist Pierre de l'Estoile wrote, 'Meanwhile processions of
the poor took place in Paris, in such numbers as were never seen; they
cried for hunger while in their mansions the rich gorged themselves

3 After the looting which followed the American invasion of Baghdad in 2003, the carnivores were the
only animals to remain alive in Baghdad Zoo.

with banquets and luxuries, an abominable affront to God, whatever excuse is given.'

During the winter of 1870, all the best restaurants and cafés offered exotic animals on their menus. Antelope and reindeer met with universal approval and, despite the fact that since October they had been instructed to serve only one meat dish to each client, Labouchere noted: 'in the expensive cafes of the Boulevards, feasts worthy of Lucullus were served.' The Restaurant Voisin, renowned for its wealthy clientele, served up a Christmas feast typifying the menus of the day. It would appear that accounts became somewhat muddled in the excitement of the reportage of that whole period, since some dishes turn up on other menus, but the beastly feast prepared by head chef Choron apparently included:

> *Tête d'âne farcie*
> *Consommé d'éléphant*
> *Le chameau rôti à l'anglaise*
> *Le civet de kangourou*
> *Côtes d'ours rôties, sauce poivrade*
> *Cuissot de loup, sauce chevreuil*
> *Le chat flanqué de rats*
> *La terrine d'antilope aux truffes*

These creations were washed down with Mouton-Rothschild 1846, Romanée-Conti 1858, Château Palmer 1864 and an 1827 port. This was Voisin's last great feast, as both food and fuel shortages forced it out of business soon afterwards. Its bright young trainee would move on to further his career as maître d'hôtel at the Hotel Splendide, where he learnt how to satisfy the tastes of rich Americans before eventually founding his own eponymous establishment.

16

The Renaissance: evolution of European banquets

... a perpetual feast of nectared sweets
JOHN MILTON

Chapter 3 described the food at feasts during the Middle Ages and how it changed very little for hundreds of years. There was, of course, evolution and this speeded up somewhere around six hundred years ago. Generally speaking, dining fashions flowed northwards through Europe, so it is easy to become confused when changes happened in different countries at different times. For example, although in 1491 Lorenzo de' Medici owned a whole set of silver forks, it was nearly two hundred years before the British aristocracy used dinner forks routinely; until then they were regarded as unnecessary foreign conceits.

So what were these changes? Whether or not anyone in fifteenth- and sixteenth-century Italy realised they were involved in a European 'Renaissance', nevertheless there emerged a fascination with science and a renewed interest in studying classical purity, all of which con- tributed to a humanistic climate in which religious dogmas could be questioned and even reformed. Printing presses meant that books speeded up the flow of ideas throughout Europe. Multi-talented artists strove, using perspective and mathematics, to represent their subjects more naturally; away went the stylised medieval icon. The discovery of America to the west and the colonising of spice islands to the east brought other changes, not least to food and feasting, with chocolate, potatoes, turkeys, tomatoes and chillies all poised to make their con- tribution. And with new ingredients came a new attitude to food embodied in the *De Honesta Voluptate et Valetudine* of 1474. Its author, Bartolomeo Sacchi (known as Platina), was a humanist philosopher and papal librarian; his book marked a turning point in the literature of eating since his thesis is that, instead of renouncing the enjoyment of food as a conduit to the sin of gluttony, we may glory in it in the right circumstances.[1]

By and large, the first courses of a feast remained little changed from medieval times. The mixture of sweet ingredients with spicy and savoury ones remained popular and roasted peacocks served in their plumage continued to spout fire as a party piece, but changes in table layout were afoot. The long thin bench-style trestle (the *banchetta* from which the word banquet comes) gave way to wider tables that could accommodate an increasing number of dishes all laid out at once in symmetry; many later books contain diagrams to explain how the dishes should be arranged and the components of the courses removed and replaced. The extra size was also needed for elaborate table decorations made of silver, sugar, majolica or even glazed bread dough woven into pretty baskets filled with flowers. Rituals like the carving of meat became increasingly elaborate, and gentleman carvers – *trinciante* who practised the showy art of 'carving in the air' – held a position in Italian court circles rivalling that of the *scalco*, or steward. The medieval passion for including live animals as part of the spectacle died hard: Cherubino Ghirardacci describes the 1487 wedding banquet[2] for Annibale Bentivoglio in Bologna, which included a sugar castle full of live birds (followed by roasted game birds), a paste castle full of live rabbits which scampered among the guests (followed by rabbit *pastelli*), and another 'artful castle' enclosing a large pig which grunted and snorted among the battlements (followed by roast sucking pig). The gilding of food reached shimmering proportions, especially at weddings, where gold had connotations of longevity. Wood, metal and eventually china plates replaced the bread trencher; glassware, particularly in Italy, made its sparkling appearance on the table; forks as well as knives started to be used, and intricately folded napkins decorated the table throughout the meal. Two seventeenth-century books (Antonio Latini's *Lo Scalco Moderna* and Mattia Giegher's *Tratto*) show the art at its pinnacle: an array of napery folded into ships, castles, whales, peacocks, crabs, griffins, dogs and startling abstract patterns. Such complicated constructions usually needed a stitch or two to secure them; simpler

---

1 All the recipes (written in a quite different and practical style) have been subsequently recognised as the work of the chef Maestro Martino of Como, who wrote the *Liber de arte coquinaria*. Platina absorbed almost half of the book into *De Honesta* with little more acknowledgement than to write: 'O immortal gods, which cook could compete with my friend Martino of Como, to a great extent the origin of that which is written here?'

2 Weddings do tend to be conservative in their practices, particularly at table.

versions perfumed with rose-water were used by the guests. In 1570 Bartolomeo Scappi, chef to Pope Pius V,[3] describes concealing song-birds in the napkins for his dessert course so that a burst of twittering and a flutter of little wings charmed the guests as the birds made their escape. These creations were so popular that some artisans earned a living by going from house to house folding napkins. By the seven-teenth century, the fashion had filtered through to middle-class England where Samuel Pepys notes, with his customary attention to cost, that the man who created his napkins for the following day's dinner, 'in figures of all sorts, which is mighty pretty ... gets much money by it'.

By now chefs and chroniclers were, like Scappi, writing down their banquet menus so that we have more details of what was served. Europe diversified into cuisines still identifiable today. In Italy, while table decorations and service became more elaborate, the food itself became simpler, lighter, and less heavily spiced than medieval 'messes'. Vegetables were prominent in tempting side dishes like orach[4] tossed in oil and herbs, or spiced fungi with leeks, or braised bulb fennel drizzled with bitter orange juice. Meat featured less than in countries further north, though salamis and the renowned Bologna sausage were ubiquitous and poultry was popular – partridges and other small birds crop up regularly, served perhaps with sugared olives and grapes, or lemons. An interest in antiquity was responsible for a revival in the use of truffles and caviar, and of exotic parts of creatures such as cockscombs, fish livers, brains, pigs' ears, udders and other delicacies enjoyed by classical Roman diners. French cooking became more complex, with dozens of ingredients in each dish, larded meats, and an enthusiasm for sauces. Britain, Germany and other northern countries remained enamoured of their red meat, plain and lots of it. However, accounts start to praise the quality or rarity of food at feasts rather than only its quantity; out-of-season fruit and vegetables were highly desirable, fresh peas or asparagus in January the height of luxury.

But the biggest impact on feasts and banquets throughout Europe during this period was made by sugar. Imported from the Middle East, sugar was very expensive in medieval times so was initially used as a

---

3 Pius V was famous for his extreme abstemiousness, yet Scappi dedicated his sumptuous *Opera* to him; so either the pope's idea of frugality was on a different level to ours, or he simply liked to entertain his guests.

4 A primitive form of spinach, also known as arroche.

medicine rather than a food; its ability to preserve both fruit and meat as well as flavour them intrigued people. Naturally, as it became more affordable, sugar was used more and more extravagantly at table. Sotelties originally made of pastry were now made of sugar paste. At one fifteenth-century wedding in Rome a life-sized sugarwork composition of a turreted castle with Hercules fighting a lion, a wild boar and a bull was broken up after the banquet and thrown down to spectators waiting eagerly in the courtyard.[5] Another account, of a wedding in Pesaro in 1475, mentions that the entire table service was made out of sugar: plates, cutlery, and even wineglasses that remained waterproof for the duration of the feast, as well as imitation fruit, nuts and berries for decoration. The ladies were given sugar trinkets in the form of rings, strings of beads or rosaries to take home. When King Henri III of France visited Venice in 1574, Nicolo delle Cavalliera made 1,286 items out of sugar, including the napkins and tablecloth. Many sixteenth- and seventeenth-century cookery books describe how to make sugar plate. Gum tragacanth (gelatine would serve the purpose today) was dissolved in rose-water and lemon juice, then pounded together with egg white and fine sugar to produce a smooth malleable paste which was rolled into sheets. These were fashioned into plates, wineglasses and decorations. The dried paste is not crystal clear, being more like translucent porcelain, but its lack of transparency is more than compensated for by its sweetness: Thomas Dawson's *The Good Huswifes Jewell* of 1597 finishes with 'At the end of the Banket they may eat all, and breake the Platters, Dishes, Glasses, Cuppes, and all other things, for this paste is very delicate and saverous.'

Everybody loved sugar. Not only was it sweet, it provided endless scope for showing off. The medieval voidee, or final course, became so elaborate that it evolved into an event in its own right. Whereas the words banquet and feast used to mean the same thing, now a feast meant the meat and fish courses and a banquet meant just the sweetmeats. Indeed, a banquet was frequently offered at any time of the day, without the rest of the meal. Charming and expensive, it was the perfect entertainment; so we read that in 1535 the Dukes of Richmond and Norfolk were received by the Mayor of Coventry with a banquet in the street.

In England a particular type of architectural folly emerged as people

---

5 Such huge sugarwork constructions had been made in Egypt since the eleventh century.

built little banqueting houses where guests could retire from the dinner table and stroll about nibbling their final course in informal surroundings. Sometimes banqueting houses were built in artificial grottoes, but more often they were built in elevated places (in the extreme case of Longleat, on the rooftop) so as to profit from the view over the gardens; to the Renaissance mind, the whole purpose of a garden was to exalt the senses and stimulate the intellect. Since guests were rarely hungry by this stage of the meal, the banquet was there simply to please the eye and to titillate jaded taste buds.

The 'banquetting stuffe' served in these settings consisted of spiced wine and cordials served with dried fruits and any number of sweet desserts: aromatic seeds and nuts were coated in coloured sugar to make crisp comfits of all shapes and sizes; creams, jellies, leaches (rather like Turkish delight) and marmalades were smooth and sticky; marchpane (marzipan) was coloured, rolled, cut and fashioned into any shape that took the confectioner's fancy; ice creams and syllabubs were served in tiny glass or porcelain cups to be eaten while guests strolled around admiring the view; delicate wafers, jumbles and spiced biscuits were made in colourful patterns. There were dry suckets (crystallised fruit) and wet suckets (fruit preserved in sticky syrup); the latter were eaten with a spoon or dessert fork, or even, like the syllabubs, sipped from a little dish while one wandered about. The word sucket comes from succade, referring not to the way these items should be eaten but to the method of preserving them in sugar. Invariably some splendid edible centrepiece would show off the chef's skill and the generosity of the host. It might be a classical statue, or a large sculpture worked into animals and flowers. Sometimes the decorations were a little risqué, reflecting the understood but unspoken aphrodisiac qualities of some banquetting stuffe. A gingerbread bull or ram (both emblems of lust, and fiery ginger was supposed to 'provoke Venus'), or perhaps a motto broken off a sugar plate, could be passed to someone else who would understand its meaning. Looking back at this period from the 'enlightened' eighteenth century, the Reverend Richard Warner writes with distaste in *Antiquitates Culinariae* of 'an extraordinary species of ornament, in use among the English and French, for a considerable time; representations of the *membra virilia, pudendaque muliebria*, which were formed of *pastry,* or *sugar,* and placed before the guests at entertainments, doubtless for the purpose of causing jokes and conversation among them.'

It is in the nature of extravagances that they tend to become more and more exuberant until further refinement seems impossible, at which stage either a political revolution or a complete change in fashion occurs; this is what happened with the feast and the banqueting course. Throughout the sixteenth and into the seventeenth century, kings, queens, archdukes, popes and the aristocracy staged a succession of lavish festivals designed to display their wealth and power. By the seventeenth century the banqueting course had turned into a vast architectural affair often referred to as a collation.[6] Huge tables were covered with elaborate swirls of candied and fresh fruits, interspersed with dishes of colourful sweetmeats stacked up into tall columns or pyramids. Their forms echoed the towering centrepieces portraying classical allegorical scenes; these were often edible too. Some accounts of Italian outdoor events boasted entire paths and flowerbeds made of cured sausages and sweetmeats. The French *croquembouche*, a caramelised pyramid of profiteroles sometimes served at weddings nowadays, is a relic of this architectural style of presentation. Inevitably these huge stacks sometimes toppled over. One eighteen-foot-high creation proved too large to fit into the room; the indignant chef could not understand why his employers didn't simply raise the ceiling.

It was no accident that the Bologna wedding mentioned earlier featured three kinds of castle. As a symbol of power, the castle was a universal theme of banquet architecture. Entertainments, centred round a triumphal procession or a mock battle, were the excuse for a dramatic combination of spectacle and allegory, everything symbolising the glory and wisdom of the host or his illustrious guest. Largesse was extended to bystanders too: handfuls of comfits or coins were tossed to the crowds; onlookers not grand enough to take part at a feast nevertheless stood at the fringes ready to descend on the food and demolish it after the principal guests had departed for their banqueting course. John Evelyn's diary for 1685 records a banquet given in London by the king for Signors Zenno and Justerini, the Venetian ambassadors. It consisted of:

---

6 A collation, meaning a light meal (though these affairs were often substantial), could contain meat and game dishes as well as the much-vaunted sweetmeats. A cold collation usually meant savoury food (Pepys mentions a 'collacion of gammon and anchovies'). The use of the term as a repast taken between meals is supposed to have come from the light meal taken in a monastery whilst the *Collationes* of St John Cassian was being read out.

12 vast Chargers pild up so high, as those who sat one against another could hardly see one another; of these Sweetemeates which doub(t)lesse were some days piling up in that exquisite manner, the Ambassador touched not, but leaving them to the Spectators who came in Curiosity to see the dinner, & were exceedingly pleas'd to see in what moment of a time, all that curious work was demolish'd, & the comfitures &c voided & table cleared: Thus his Majestie entertain'd them 3 dayes, which, (for the table onely) cost him 600 pounde as the Cleark of the Greene-Cloth Sir W. Boreman, assur'd me.

Every major post-Renaissance feast worthy of the name had to have some sort of mechanical device bearing a political message – of congratulation, of threat, of gratitude or of self-aggrandisement. It is hard to believe that people did not become a little weary of the succession of conch shells, Titans, Herculeses, Dianas, Junos and satyrs, but chroniclers continued to express astonishment at their splendour, inventiveness and magical qualities; they were, after all, paid to do so and in many cases had organised the displays as well. And the devices were indeed extraordinary. The festivities given by the queen dowager, Mary of Hungary, at Binche in Belgium in 1549 for the future Philip II of Spain became a benchmark against which other celebrations were rated. Amongst revels that went on for several days was a banquet in which a huge canopied table reaching up to the ceiling lowered each of its three courses in layers. Later on, wild men (knights in disguise) appeared to carry off the ladies and hold them prisoner in a magic castle, to be rescued by the other guests. If this seems a little ridiculous today, nevertheless one cannot but admire the skills that went into staging such events. The messages they conveyed were of importance to the host and were often a palatable way of making a point that his guests might not necessarily want to take.

The Binche festival and another staged by Catherine de' Medici at Bayonne spawned paintings and tapestries of their 'magnificences'; these are often quoted. However, a less widely known but particularly good example took place in the Great Hall at Stirling Castle in 1594. It was minutely recorded by William Fowler, the pageant master, who published his *True Reportarie* in 1603. The event was the christening of Henry, son of King James VI of Scotland, later James I of England as well. James was building on an example set at his own christening twenty-eight years earlier by his mother Mary, Queen of Scots, who had imported the new style of allegorical entertainment from France in order to glorify the Stewart line. Mary had the delicate task of reconciling her Catholicism with the Protestantism not only of Scotland but of England as well, and was emulating on a modest scale Catherine de' Medici, who a year earlier had staged a series of 'magnificences' at Bayonne in which she had also tried to placate both Protestants and Catholics. Mary's event very nearly ended in disaster because the English ambassador and his retinue, being unused to the continental courts' fashion of allegorical messages, mistook the tail-flicking of some 'counterfeit devils' (intended to represent the soon-to-be-vanquished forces of Evil) for obscene gestures against their party and a skirmish broke out.

James, no doubt aware of this, took particular care that his messages should not be misconstrued. In any case, such allegorical festivals were by now understood by all his guests who, as well as his Scottish noblemen, included ambassadors from France, Denmark, the Low Countries of Holland and Zeeland, and of course England. The state of relations between Scotland and England was interesting, to say the least. Elizabeth of England was unmarried and James of Scotland was by that time the nearest claimant to her throne. Relations were cordial, if occasionally strained because Elizabeth had beheaded James' mother. Be that as it may, Elizabeth was now godmother to young Prince Henry. James hoped to rule over both countries, so the whole event was created to compliment the English ambassador's party and to demonstrate that the prince was a suitable future monarch.

Preparations had started months beforehand, beginning with the demolition of the old Chapel Royal because it was too small for the occasion James had in mind. This took longer than expected, so it was fortunate that the English ambassador fell ill and that the Earl of Essex had to be sent to deputise for him, which conveniently delayed the event. The other ambassadors were entertained at the king's expense, with 'Magniffique[7] Banqueting, Revelling, and daily Hunting, with great Honour'. Before the feast came a series of tournaments in which James was disguised as a knight of Malta. Although the Scottish Presbyterians thought he looked popish, he was actually paying a compliment to Elizabeth by staging a version of a popular English event: the Accession Day

---

7 This French version of 'magnificent' is the consequence of the close ties between Scotland and France. Many remnants of the Auld Alliance can be found in Scots words today.

tournaments that her devoted subjects celebrated annually. Henry's baptism followed the next day, after which 'the Cannons of the Castle Roared, that therewith the Earth trembled, and other smaller shot, made their Harmony after their kind' and there was 'great quantity of diverse species of Gold and Money cast over among the People'.

In the Great Hall there was a 'delicate banquet . . . ordered with great abundance' for the party. Once again King James wished to make a point by seating his guests in the English fashion, which was to alternate lords and ladies at table, rather than the Scots fashion of segregating them. After the courses of meat and side dishes came the first of the mechanical devices. This 'triumph' was announced by the sound of oboes and took the form of a Moor pulling a huge chariot twelve feet long and seven feet broad. The pageant master's original idea was to use a lion[8] (the emblem of Scottish kings for four hundred years) to draw the chariot, but 'because his presence might have brought some Fear to the nearest, or that the sight of the Lights and Torches might have commoved his Tameness, it was thought Meet that the Moore should supplie that Room'. The mechanics were concealed so that 'it appeared to be drawn only by the strength of the Moor which was very richly attired, his Traces being massie Chains of pure Gold . . . Apon this Chariot, was finely & Artificially Deviced, a sumptuous covered Table, decked with all sorts of exquisite delicats and dainties of Patisses, Fruitages and Confections.' Round this table were six 'Gallant Dames': Fecundity, Faith, Concord, Liberality, Perseverance and Ceres, their leader, who carried a sickle in her right hand; and 'upon the outermost part of her Thigh was written this Sentence *Fundent uberes omnia campi*, which is to say, the plenteous Fields shall affoord all things.' This sentiment is exactly contemporary with Shakespeare's use of innuendo. The Moor duly hauled his chariot with its precious cargo to the king's table where the goddesses delivered their confections to the servers to distribute.

After the chariot had retired there entered

a most Sumptuous Artificial and well proportioned Ship, the length of her Keel was 18 Foot long, and her Breadth 8 Foot long . . . her Motion was so Artificially devised within herself that none could perceive what brought her in . . . The Bulk of this Ship was curiously Painted . . . Her Masts were Red, her Tackling and Cordage was Silk of the same Colour,

---

8 King James had recently been given a lion by the King of Norway. For hundreds of years live animals had been transported surprisingly long distances, apparently successfully, and were popular royal gifts.

with Golden Pullies. Her Ordinance was 36 pieces of Brass, bravely mounted, and her Anchors Silver Guilt, And all her Sails were of double White Taffety ... Her Tops were all Armed with Taffeteies of His Majesties Colours, Gold and Jewels, and all her Flags and Streamers suitable to the seamen ... The Sea under her, was lively Counterfit, with all Colours; on her Forestern was placed Neptune having in his hand his Trident, and on his Hand a Crown, his Apparel was all of Indian cloth of silver and Silk, which bear this Inscription *junxi atque reduxi* which in sense importeth That as he joined them, so he reduced their Majesties.

This was a reference to James' voyage over the North Sea to Norway some years earlier to fetch his queen to Scotland, resulting ultimately in this baptism. The ship was so enormous that part of the entrance to the hall had to be widened to let it in and out. This permanently weakened its structure, as Historic Scotland found to its cost some four hundred years later.

Ships, like castles, were popular motifs in these allegories. The ship represented the state, sailing solidly through difficult seas and arriving safely with its bounteous cargo. This one's mariners were gorgeously attired and her pilot wore cloth of gold. 'And now at this her Blessed Delivery, [he] did bring such things as the Sea affoords, to Decore withal this Festival time, which immediately were delivered to the Seuers, furth of the Galleries of the Ship, out of Christalin Glass, very curiously painted with Gold and Azure, all sorts of Fishes, as Herrings, Whiteings, Floks, Oysters, and Buckies, Lampets, Partans, Lobstars, Crabs, Spout-Fish, Clamms, with other infinite things made of Sugar and most lively represented in their own shape.' This 'magnificence' disappeared mysteriously in clouds of smoke generated by the real cannons on board. Then, as if there had not been enough sweetmeats during this 'Merry and Joyful Repast', some guests went off to another hall where 'for the Collation, a most Rare, Sumptuous and Prince like Desert was prepared', which they enjoyed until about three in the morning. In and amongst the tournaments, the hunting and the costly food, King James' entertainment conveyed the unmistakable message that his son was a fitting heir to the throne of England. In the event the much-loved Prince Henry died in 1612, and his younger brother became Charles I of England.

During the next hundred and fifty years, countless events of this kind took place throughout Europe. The mechanical 'triumphs' bedecked with sweetmeats gradually gave way to concerts, theatre, outdoor masques and the beginnings of ballet. 'Sumptuous and Prince like' collations developed into vast geometric constructions typified by those on display at the baroque festivals of seventeenth-century Versailles and illustrated in contemporary engravings. In both France and Britain, however, they dwindled with the decline of absolutism. By the time of the French Revolution, extravagant displays were ready to give way to the more restrained style of the Age of Reason. Across the Channel too, despite the restoration of the monarchy in 1660 and probably owing to continuing Puritan influence, entertainments seem to have become more modest.

The last British entertainment in the Renaissance style was the coronation banquet of King George IV in 1821, for which he insisted on a pastiche of James II's. Before the king's arrival at Westminster Hall, flower girls entered the hall, strewing petals over the floor. The Regency had been a period of flamboyance in male dress, and this was given full rein as the participants dressed up in Tudor costume. Sir Walter Scott wrote, 'I must not omit that the foreigners, who are apt to consider us as a nation ... without the usual ceremonies of dress and distinction, were utterly astonished and delighted to see the revivial of feudal dresses and feudal grandeur ... in a degree of splendour which, they averred, they had never seen paralleled in Europe.' Everyone glittered: Prince Esterhazy's diamonds, which 'glimmered like a galaxy', were worth £80,000, and the Marquis of Londonderry, one of two knights of the Garter, 'added very considerably to the splendour of the occasion by his graceful and elegant appearance ... his hat was encircled with a band of diamonds, which had a most brilliant effect ... Of the splendour of the whole spectacle it is impossible for me to give you the slightest idea,' wrote Lord Denbigh to his mother.

The table took two hours to lay with 336 silver plates, each one having two silver spoons placed near it. There was also a sideboard displaying solid gold plate.[9]

This sparkling show was enhanced by nearly two thousand candles. However,

Such a vast display of artificial light would be calculated to add considerably to the splendour of such a scene, if it took place after sun-set;

9 Such customs die hard. At the coronation of Queen Elizabeth in 1952, many of the same pieces were displayed on a long bench behind her.

but in the broad glare of the unclouded sun, which beamed through every window, any number of lights could not be found a desirable acquisition. On the contrary, they detracted considerably from its splendour ... To those gentlemen whose seats happened to be placed immediately under the chandeliers, the great increase in temperature – and that was very considerable – was not the only inconvenience; for occasionally large pieces of melted wax fell, without distinction of persons, upon all within reach. The very great heat was no where more visible than in the havoc which it made upon the curls of many of the ladies, several of whose heads had lost all trace of the friseur's skill long before the ceremony of the day was concluded.

The seated guests were fed on venison, beef, goose, lobster, turbot, salmon, pies and hams along with turtle soup, pineapples and innumerable side dishes – the new king was a noted trencherman.

The coronation feast of King James II, 1685. This is the event on which George IV based his own coronation banquet in 1821, and an almost identical engraving was made of it.

They were watched by a similar number of hungry spectators in the galleries; one man took pity on his wife and threw her a cold capon wrapped in his handkerchief.

Once His Majesty and his attendants rose, the spectators transferred their interest from the food to the tableware, and there was a rout in the hall when

> the gathering crowds of spoliators, by a simultaneous rush, in a moment surrounded the royal table. For a few seconds delicacy, or a disinclination to be the first to commence the scene of plunder, suspended the projected attack; but at last a rude hand having been thrust through the first ranks, and a golden fork having been seized, this operated as a signal to all, and was followed by a general snatch ... The Lord Great Chamberlain managed to rescue the large plate so plunder was confined to small items and inexpensive plates and items ... The scene which was now presented scarce admits of parallel in modern times.

George IV's ambitious Renaissance-style coronation was the last of its kind. Although eulogised by official recorders, in actual fact by the 1820s such flamboyance was considered to be in very bad taste; future coronations were celebrated with private dinners.

17

Thanksgivings: celebrating relief

Some hae meat and canna eat
Some hae meat that want it
We hae meat and we can eat
And sae the Lord be thankit
ROBERT BURNS, 'THE SELKIRK GRACE'

Gratitude has spawned many feasts and is a component of others: the return of a prodigal son, the end of a war, passing an examination, the birth of a baby, a departed life, the completion of a difficult task, a harvest successfully gathered in – all these are occasions for thanksgiving. Although some are celebrated annually, others remain sporadic or impulsive. In Afghanistan, for example, there is a charming custom of showing gratitude by giving away food. *Nazer*, as it is called, is a religious act that can be prompted by anything from a completed pilgrimage to recovery from an illness.[1] The offering may be something basic like newly baked bread or it could be more elaborate: *halwa* – mildly sweet and delicately flavoured with cardamom, almonds, pistachios and rose-water – is a popular choice. Fresh, warm portions are scooped onto a piece of *nan* bread and taken out on a tray into the street to be offered to passers-by and poor people alike, a spontaneous sharing of food and happiness with strangers.

The two most important instances of thanksgiving feasts are those connected with emigration, of which more later, and those connected with harvesting crops. As long as harvests are the most important part of rural life, the knowledge that the year's crop is secure represents a genuine celebration of relief from potential or – if the previous year's stores have already run out – actual hunger. Even in rich countries where a good harvest no longer spells the difference between life and death, and farm workers no longer experience the hunger that comes from the hard physical labour of scything corn and binding sheaves,

---

1 According to Helen Saberi, *nazer* has not been diminished by recent wars, rather the reverse.

English harvest home, Illustrated London News, 1843. At harvest suppers farm labourers were given lots to eat and drink as a reward for relentless hard work.

the elation when the last bale of straw has been stacked seems irrepressible; the atmosphere of the harvest suppers in George Eliot's *Adam Bede* or Thomas Hardy's *Far from the Madding Crowd* has not utterly faded away.

Although most of us are removed from intimacy with food-growing, many will be familiar with the sense of security that comes from seeing jars of jam settled on the shelf or a freezer crammed to bursting point with produce. The urge to gather and hoard is very basic – who can pass a hedgerow studded with plump blackberries and resist picking them? And ever more people find another kind of harvest compelling beyond all nutritional logic: fungi. The truffle-hunters of Italy and Périgord may be renowned, but many others swarm into the forests to collect boletus, chanterelles, wood blewits, field mushrooms, puffballs, lawyers' wigs and more. In the far north of Europe, the Saami even gather fungi for their reindeer. There is something about the smell, particularly of ceps and truffles, that is exhilarating, beguiling, provocative; apparently the aroma is related to animal pheromones. This may explain why every year so many people are seduced into eating their harvest before being quite sure that what they have gathered is safe.[2] Except for truffle-hunting, the passion for seeking out fungi is most deep-rooted in eastern Europe and Russia, where

2 For this reason all pharmacists in France and Switzerland are qualified to recognise fungi, and anyone can take theirs in for free identification.

it is by no means restricted to country people.[3] The annual journey from town to forest to gather woodland treasure is nothing less than a pilgrimage in honour of pagan tree gods, and consuming their fungal manifestations nothing less than a communion. After a fragrant orgy of these near-mystic growths, the rest of the harvest is dried and laid up as treasure to be given away or used for special occasions.

Thanksgiving has a straightforward connection with harvests, but a more complex one with emigration: exile is not always a chosen state. Most emigrants take their food and feasting customs with them as a tangible link with their original home, often with the result that they keep alive and sometimes exaggerate usages that may have declined or disappeared in their country of origin. This is the case with the world-wide diaspora of Chinese, and also with that of the Jews, who for thousands of years had no home country at all. Like the Chinese, Jews cling to their culinary traditions and nurture them, their rituals reflecting ancient shared memories. The excitement generated by the mere mention of home cooking is a graphic demonstration of how domestic food traditions are inseparable from Jewish cultural identity. That cooking and the closely knit family epitomise Jewishness is largely because their dietary laws used to make it impossible to mingle freely with indigenous communities; so although Jews everywhere adapt their cuisine to local conditions, it always remains identifiably Jewish. As Claudia Roden points out, this is the 'cooking of a nation within a nation, a culture within a culture' – the exact opposite of French home cooking, which is based firmly in its *terroir*, its native soil.

Important festivals in most cultures involve food symbolism, and the meal at the Jewish feast of the Passover – the *seder* – is no exception. Its rituals are part of what binds Jews together, for Passover is a festival of thanksgiving for deliverance out of bondage in Egypt. First comes a ritual purification of the whole house[4] and total separation of permitted and forbidden items in the kitchen. Only when everything is not only actually but also ritually clean can the special Passover utensils be brought out and preparations for cooking begin. Six foods on the

---

3 Emigrants to Britain cannot understand our suspicion of toadstools, though no doubt they welcome the lack of competition since patches back home are fiercely concealed and protected. I have been quizzed for tips on where to find the best patches in the woods round Auchtermuchty and I must confess my answers are usually rather vague.

4 Most cultures have a ritual cleaning before a feast at some point in the calendar; New Year is a common time.

seder plate symbolise the Hebrews' life in Egypt and their exodus: a green vegetable dipped in salt water represents new growth and the slaves' tears; bitter herbs represent the bitterness of slavery; *haroset*, a paste, represents by its colour the mortar the Hebrews used to build Pharaoh's treasure cities; a roasted egg symbolises the burnt offering of an animal in the Temple; a lamb's leg bone replaces the lamb sacrificed the evening before the exodus; and matzos[5] represent the bread which had no time to rise as the Israelites fled.

Even if emigration is undertaken voluntarily, the struggle to re-establish family life in an unknown country can be daunting; so it comes as no surprise when thanksgiving celebrations are held to mark these momentous survivals.[6] The word Thanksgiving, however, has only one meaning for an American: feast 'n' football – a family gathering at which huge amounts of food are consumed, followed by a bleary-eyed look at the football. With no presents or decorations to worry about, this is simply a blow-out meal. Nowadays the celebration is largely a secular event; perhaps just as the Pilgrim Fathers fled from religious authoritarianism, so their descendants felt that too much religion can be divisive and gradually phased it out.

The Pilgrims held a feast in 1621 to celebrate surviving their first year in America – an achievement made all the more remarkable by their ineptitude at fishing and their fussy eating habits. One hundred Pilgrims had set sail on the *Mayflower* from England the previous autumn in order to be able to worship freely in a new world; the intention of these middle-class merchants was to make a comfortable living off the plentiful fish stocks they had heard about. Unfortunately they chose the worst possible time of year to set sail, and arrived in December with little in the way of fishing equipment and even less knowledge of how to use it. Neither were they adept at farming or hunting, and nearly half the group died in starvation that winter. The fifty-eight who survived until autumn did so only by stumbling upon hoards of corn, beans and pemmican (dried meat pounded with cranberries) stored by the Native American Wampanoag. After a period of

5 Unleavened Passover bread made from specially purified wheat.

6 One such is an Italian feast still held by the family of Angelo Lorenzato to commemorate their arrival in Brazil from Italy in 1888 to work on the coffee plantations. Every so often the expanding family joins together in Ribeirão Preto for a huge family lunch followed by music and dancing. The most recent was in January 2000 when 2,350 relatives from Canada, the United States and Italy joined their Brazilian kinsmen. An open-air mass was held by the eight priests in the family. How times change; not so long before there would have been many more priests in a group of that size.

hostility these generous people made a truce with the beleaguered Pilgrims and showed them how to grow corn and fertilise it with fish; taught them how to hunt deer and wild turkeys; and explained how to harvest the abundant shellfish on the coasts. But clams, steamers and mussels were regarded with distaste by the newcomers, who spurned them as unfamiliar and only grudgingly ate lobsters as a last resort; so it was indeed something of a miracle that more than half of them survived. Determination and faith are a potent combination, and we can imagine how jubilant the Pilgrims must have felt after their first harvest. This account of the 1621 feast[7] is attributed to Edward Winslow who sailed on the *Mayflower*:

> . . . our harvest being gotten in, our Governour sent foure men on fowling, that so we might after a more speciall manner re[j]oyce together, after we had gathered the fruit of our labours; they foure in one day k[i]lled as much fowle, as with a little helpe beside, served the Company almost a weeke, at which time amongst other Recreations, we exercised our Armes, many of the Indians coming amongst us, and amongst the rest their greatest King Massasoyt, with some nintie men, whom for three dayes we entertained and feasted, and they went out and killed five Deere, which they brought to the Plantation and bestowed on our Governour, and upon the Captaine, and others. And although it be not alwayes so plentifull, as it was at this time with us, yet by the goodnesse of God, we are so farre from want, that we often wish you partakers of our plentie.

Although Winslow's account is not specific, the likelihood is that the fowl included wild turkey; and it is their domesticated descendants, served with cranberries and followed by pumpkin pie, that now form the backbone of this all-American feast. Thanksgiving meals are above all celebrations of family, of comfort foods that must conjure up the essence of your own home – as an American colleague, Marc Millon, so endearingly described to the Guild of Food Writers:

---

7 This event is often referred to as 'The First Thanksgiving', but such a claim is incorrect. The English colonists who had settled in Jamestown in 1607 had already celebrated several days of thanksgiving before the arrival of the Pilgrims in Massachusetts. Others claim even earlier 'First Thanksgivings'.

Understand: this is not gourmet food; . . . it's family food. It's about the tastes that you remember from childhood and pass on to your own children. Indeed, I think it is sometimes hard for British friends to understand what Thanksgiving is all about: a secular holiday that centers around a basic and universal primeval urge to gorge – yes, eating in outrageous and uncouth quantity is part of the experience – born from a time of hardship; a celebration of survival, of simply being alive; of eating until quite literally you can eat no more because who knows what tomorrow might bring? Who knows indeed.

And so we enjoy foods that the rest of the year we never consider eating, each of us with our own family traditions and recipes: stuffing (nothing varies more from household to household; nothing is more important than this essential centerpiece to the meal; certainly stuffing, in this household, is far more important than the turkey itself); strange foods like candied yams, bathed in lashings of butter and brown sugar; mashed potatoes and cranberry sauce and apple sauce; gravy, lots of it, thickened with flour and stock from the giblets; carrots in dill, butter and vinegar; creamed onions. But not a sprout in sight. And of course pumpkin pie and pecan pie (sickeningly sweet but also an essential), and in our house, lemon meringue pie too.

Perhaps it's because I'm an expat, yet at this time of year, and at this time only, we crave – indeed need – the tastes of foods which we absorbed, like milk from our mothers, in our earliest days and years and as we grew up, and so have become a very part of our being, of who and what we are.

A simple feast which means everything; there is no more to add.

Gallus Indicus – The Turkey, from John Johnstone's *History of Birds, c.*1650.

18

A Victorian banquet: dinner for the Acclimatisation Society of Great Britain

When it is considered how few amongst the immense variety of animated beings have been hitherto applied to the uses of Man...it is impossible not to hope for many new, brilliant and useful results in the same field, by the application of the wealth, ingenuity, and varied resources of a civilized people.

PROSPECTUS FOR THE ZOOLOGICAL SOCIETY OF LONDON

The menu reproduced at the end of this chapter epitomises the Victorians' fascination with associations like the Acclimatisation Society, which transported curios from far-flung parts of the empire with a view to increasing the useful gastronomic range of the home country. At this, their first annual celebration dinner, the society's members sampled 'many natural products which do not often find their way to our tables, and some of which might be advantageously introduced into this country.' Many parts of the world subsequently regretted such zeal for introducing foreign species – red deer, possums and gorse in New Zealand, rabbits in Australia and rhododendrons on the west coast of Scotland have proved environmentally disastrous. But in the 1860s these introductions seemed progressive. The Great Exhibition of 1851 had proudly displayed technological discoveries from all over the world and there was an explosion of achievements in science and technology, including Charles Darwin's evolutionary theory, William Smith's geological maps, David Livingstone's explorations, and innumerable expeditions in search of flora and fauna.[1] Fashionable chefs like Alexis Soyer were fascinated by technology.

---

1 It was largely due to the co-operation of overseas exhibitors at the Great Exhibition that the remarkable array of dishes was dried, canned, bottled, pickled and bred from imported stock for the society's commemoration dinner.

Places and people were commonly celebrated in the menus of the day, a habit that lingered on until the Second World War. Reading through these menus leaves us frustrated by the impossible names of the items listed: *'Crème de la Grande Bretagne à l'Albert'*; *'Riz de veau à la Palestine'*; *'Vol au vent à la Talleyrand'*. They sound so pompous and are so uninformative that they do nothing to stimulate the gastric juices. However, when we discover what the dishes consisted of – for instance that the *'Côtelettes de bécassines à la Souvaroff'* made for Edward VII's coronation banquet in 1902 was actually made from halved boned snipe stuffed with foie gras and a delicate fluffy forcemeat, then shaped into small cutlets which were crisped in butter and served in a silky reduction sauce – it is possible to imagine flavours and textures, and to appreciate that the dish was indeed a highlight 'extremely rich in flavour, and each piece melted in the mouths of the guests'.

Elaborate neoclassical, partly edible table decorations, which had gone out of fashion during the eighteenth century, reappeared on the Victorian table with a vengeance. Like the menus, their names give little indication of what they looked and tasted like unless they happen to have been both illustrated and described, as was the case with *'L'Extravagance culinaire à l'Alderman'*, created in 1850 by Alexis Soyer for a banquet given by the mayors of Great Britain and Ireland for the Lord Mayor of London. The event took place in York and served to raise funds for Prince Albert's Great Exhibition the following year. There was a lavish menu for 248 guests with a more sumptuous version for the royal table. 'The opportunity of producing some gastronomic phenomenon for the royal table ... was irresistible, accordingly, the following *choice morsels* were carefully selected from all the birds mentioned in the general bill of fare, to form a dish of delicacies worthy of His Royal Highness and the noble guests around him.' The 'phenomenon' consisted of five turtle heads, parts of their fins and their green fat (the most highly prized part of a turtle). These were adorned with 6 whole plovers, 6 dozen larks, stuffed, some ortolans from Belgium, and the two small *noix* – sometimes called the oysters – from each side of the backs of 24 capons, 18 turkeys, 18 pullets, 16 fowls, 10 grouse, 20 pheasants, 45 partridges, 100 snipes, 40 woodcock and 3 dozen pigeons. Some of the *noix* can be seen impaled on silver skewers rammed down the turtles' throats; the rest are arranged on the ornate silver dish along with coxcombs, truffles, mushrooms, crawfish, olives, American asparagus, paste crust (which forms the central structure), green mangoes, and 'a new sauce'. Soyer was well versed in the classics and knew of the Romans' legendary dishes made from hundreds of obscure parts of birds; this construction looks as though it was inspired by the 'Shield of Minerva'.[2] He does not say what Prince Albert thought of it, but does comment that the ingredients cost one hundred guineas.

Extravagance Culinaire. Soyer's Hundred Guinea Dish as described in his *Pantropheon* of 1853.

The Acclimatisation Society's first annual dinner took place on 12 July 1862 in Willis's Rooms[3] in St James's. The room was decorated with stuffed animals, birds and gigantic horns; a case containing the birds that make edible nests was produced during the soup course, 'and afforded an interesting corollary to the culinary lesson which the Society was illustrating with plates'. The menu, published in *The Epicure's Yearbook* of 1868, is unusual for its time because we can understand quite easily what the dishes were, presumably because it was necessary to identify each country's produce. The arbitrary mixture of English and French in the menu is typical of its time. It looks a formidable meal and would have required considerable planning in order

2 According to Suetonius, Emperor Vitellius' dish 'The Shield of Minerva, Guardian of the City' was so called because of its colossal size (Vitellius was a noted glutton). It consisted of a gallimaufry of costly rarities – including pike liver, peacock and pheasant brains, roe of lampreys and flamingo tongues – that had to be gathered from all over the Roman Empire.
3 Willis's Rooms were built in 1765 in King Street, St James's, as an offshoot of Almack's club. Willis's started life as a ten-guinea subscription club for dining and gaming but latterly rooms were let for balls and public dinners such as this one.

Tables laid à la française, detail from the engraving of the coronation of James II in 1685 showing the dishes arranged to cover the whole table; peoples' individual plates were tiny.

to cook and serve it. Since there were so many different dishes to taste, the dinner may have been served in the old way – *à la française* – a style of table service that had been used with little modification for hundreds of years, but which by 1868 was being replaced a new style: dining *à la russe*.

The Epicure's Yearbook describes these two basic styles, the French one representing the last adjustments to the old medieval method. The writer has clearly not become accustomed to the new style: 'Dinners served in the French style are parted into three categories or services. The first service comprehends the soup, hors d'oeuvres, relevés, and entrées; the second comprises the rôts, vegetables, and sweet dishes; the third is the dessert. All the dishes appear on the table. This style is to the gourmand the best.' However, it put more responsibility on the host, who had to do the carving himself, since the carvers of medieval times had long since gone. Each course consisted of masses of carefully arranged dishes which completely covered the table and were after a while removed, that is, replaced by those of the next course. The advantage for the diner was that he could choose for himself which dishes he wanted and how much of each. There were also drawbacks:

conversation was interrupted as people asked for dishes to be passed around, hot dishes would cool down, and inevitably food was dropped onto the tablecloth. And although the anonymous nineteenth-century Epicure favoured the French style, it had not pleased everyone. In 1588 Michel de Montaigne wrote, ' I hardly ever chuse my dish at table, but fall to of the next of hand, and unwillingly change my dish. A confusion of meats, and a clutter of dishes displeases me as much as any thing whatever. I am easily satisfied with few dishes, and am an enemy to the opinion of Favorinus, that in a feast they must snatch from you the meat you like, and set another plate of another sort before you, and that it's a pitiful supper, if you do not sate your guests with the rumps of several fowls, and that the beccafico [a songbird much prized as a delicacy in Italy] only deserves to be all eaten.'

By 1913, when dining *à la française* had become a memory, Mrs Lucie Heaton Armstrong wrote rather disparagingly of it in *Etiquette and Entertaining*: 'It must have been terrible to go out to dinner in the days when the host carved and it was the fashion to press people to eat. Politeness in our grandfather's day demanded that no-one should accept anything without first offering it to his neighbour and the progress of dinner must have been greatly hindered by these strange little passages of arms . . . it is really much nicer to dine à la Russe when the waiting is perfect and the food appears at your elbow . . .' The 1868 Epicure describes the 'new' way of dining: 'Dinners served à la Russe, means a table tastefully adorned with flowers and fruits, and the triumphs of the confectioner's art; indeed all the cold dishes. The hot dishes are served, carved apart, to the guests. This regime is served when a banquet of ceremony is to be served.' The kitchens took care of the job of carving and the tablecloths would not be sullied. The dishes were divided up into a logical sequence of courses which we have more or less kept to ever since. To begin with, the great number of courses gave the diner less chance to opt out of any dish, since each was presented as part of a relentless stream; so service *à la russe* meant that more food was eaten. Fortunately the Victorian appetite seems to have been prodigious; people, or at any rate men, really did consume vast quantities of food and managed to devour these large banquets with surprising speed. Perhaps this is why the writer favoured what he perceived as being the more leisurely and less formal old style. It is not entirely clear from looking at the Acclimatisation Society's menu which style was adopted. The fact that it is not broken down into three

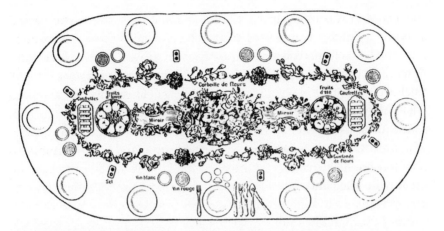

Table laid à la russe, from Urbain Dubois' *La Cuisine et la table moderne*, 1900 edition. The individual's place setting (only one has been drawn in) has become very elaborate, giving plenty of opportunities for social gaffes, and most of the table's surface is now occupied with decorations rather than dishes of food.

services but divided into courses of specific types of dish, and also the fact that the courses are not quite in order, argue against service *à la française*. And after all, the writer did suggest that banquets of ceremony were now served *à la russe*. On the other hand the large number of items for tasting in each course, and the use of terms such as *relevés des rôts*, suggest service *à la française*. There is also mention of cards placed against dishes (the kangaroo's was swapped with the wild boar's by mistake). In any case gentlemen's clubs tended to be conservative and may have preferred the old-fashioned style; the subject matter meant there was more discussion and less ceremony than at a formal banquet. The process of change was a gradual evolution, but the fact that the list is headed by the word Menu tips the scales towards *à la russe*, since menus came into prominence with this style of service.

Whichever way the dinner was served, there was nevertheless much deliberation over the dishes. The gelatinous quality of the bird's nest soup was pronounced excellent. Some found the tripang (sea slug) unpalatable while others ate it with delight – the flavour was reckoned to be 'something between a bit of calf's head and the contents of the glue-pot', a consistency repeated in the soup made of deer sinews. The kangaroo steamer had been too highly salted (probably on purpose, because the tin can provided was not over-tight and the kangaroo was 'a little "gone off", but not bad for all that'). A dried kangaroo ham was also over-salt, but owing to the muddle over the name cards, everyone thought it was wild boar. The Syrian pig was 'practically approved by being eaten up' and the pepper pot (a mixed stew flavoured with cassava) was so greatly enjoyed that Frank Buckland, supervising in the kitchens, 'was obliged to tap [the waiters'] fingers with the spoon, to keep them and their plates out of the way'. And so it continued. The eclectic array of fowl, fruits, fish, meat, biscuits and seaweed was washed down with palatable wines and some Algerian liqueurs, of which 'Oued Allah' and 'Nectar de Garibaldi' were the favourites. The Acclimatisation Society was short-lived, going into voluntary liquidation around 1868, but not before several similar societies had started up across the world.

MENU[4]

Potages

Bird's-nest soup (China); tripang, or bêche de mer (Japan); semoule (Algeria); nerfs de daim (Cochin-China); purée de pois; mock turtle; à la reine; crécy au riz; consommé au princesse; à la bisque aux écrevisses.

Poissons

Tranches de saumon racollées; saumon de Perth; rougets; whitebait; truite à la Tartare; turbot à la sauce.

Entrées

Kangaroo steamer (Tasmania); pepper pot (West Indies); Kromiskys à la Russe; supreme de volaille à l'eclarte aux haricots verts; ris de veau à la chicorée; coteletts d'agneau aux petits pois; poulette en karic à la Siamoise; ris de veau à l'oseille de Dominique.

Relevés

Chinese lamb; kangaroo ham (Australia); wild boar ham (Spain); ox tongue (New South Wales); petits poulets à la Macedoine; selle de mouton; jambon de Yorck [*sic*]; vol-au-vent au ragout à la Japonaise; quartier d'agneau.

Rôts

Syrian pig; Canadian goose; the Hon. Grantley Berkley's pintail ducks; Guan (Central America); Curassow (Central America); Honduras Turkey; dusky ducks; couple of leporines (France); brent geese (Holland) ; oisons au jus; canetons.

---

4 It looks as though either the writer or the typesetter became overwhelmed with this lengthy and exotic menu since the spelling is rather erratic.

Légumes

Chinese yam; potatoes; peas; cauliflower; &c.

Entremets

Sweet patates (Algeria); sea weed jelly (Queensland); petites pois à l'Anglais; gateau Condé aux pistaches; petites bouches à la creme; suédoise aux fraises; asperges en branches; gelée d'ananas; bavaroise à la vanille; petites cupes de groseille; gelée de millefruits.

Hors d'oeuvres

Lobster salad; Digby herring salad; Botargo (Ionian islands); &c.

Relevés des rôts

Soufflé glacé; babas à la Polonaise.

Glaces

Fraise; ananas; orange.

Dessert

Cerises; fraises; dried bananas (Ile de Réunion); preserved pine apple (Ile de Réunion); bibas (Ile de Réunion); preserved cassareep; Guava jelly; rosella jelly (Queensland); Australian biscuits; meat biscuits (Australia).

Vins et liqueurs

Port, sherry, claret, champagne, moselle, erbach; Australian wines (presented by Sir Edmond Barry): hermitage, chablis, ceres Burgundy, red Burgundy, white Longfield wine, hock, sauterne, white Victoria, ancorat, red Victoria, sweet-water.

Wine from New South Wales (presented by Sir Daniel Cooper).

Camden wine, New South Wales (presented by L. Mackinnon, Esq.); pine apple wine (Queensland); plum wine (Queensland); vin de pommes d'acajou (Guadeloup); liqueur amer Oued Allah, nectar de Garibaldi (Algeria); creme de citron (Ionian Islands); crème d'orange (Ionian Islands); rosoleon (Ionian Islands); mentha (Ionian Islands); vino de vino pastra (Ionian Islands); muscat (Ionian Islands); rum (Martinique).

Tea, coffee, &c.

Ayapana tea (Réunion); Cassia orientalis coffee (Réunion).

19

Cha-Kaiseki: a vegan feast at the Japanese tea ceremony

Chrysanthemum
silence – monk
sips his morning tea.
MATSUO BASHO

Within many cultures a feast would not be a feast without flesh, but in the Buddhist tradition this is not the case. If ever there was a feast that encapsulates a country's traditions and culture, then *cha-kaiseki*, the formal meal served in conjunction with the full Japanese tea ceremony, is the perfect example. Its origins lie in vegan temple food which embodied simplicity and humility, a retreat from materialism,[1] so the ingredients were seasonal and inexpensive and portions small, though adequate. This is a spiritual feast, one in which the host and guests, by temporarily withdrawing from everyday life, can achieve together a period of harmony and tranquillity in which the aesthetic and the spiritual can be appreciated. Because the deliciousness of the food is appreciated in a *cha-kaiseki*, it is not the same kind of spiritual feast as, say, the Christian sacrament; nevertheless, if the concept of a simple, tranquil meal seems at odds with that of a feast, then for some it will remain a puzzle. Others will understand the saying '*Chazen icchi*' (Tea and Zen are one) and will appreciate the complexity of the event, seeing it as one of many apparent contradictions presented by Zen philosophy.

It would probably help to explain the background to some of the main words in this context. First there is *cha*, which is tea. The ritual of drinking tea was imported from China where, as early as the third

---

1 Even today, when the meal is often less basic, being vegetarian rather than vegan (some may even include meat as well as the usual fish), it remains simpler than many Japanese banquets. A *cha-kaiseki* will never be as elaborate as the formal *kaiseki* banquets served at exclusive *ryotai* restaurants in Kyoto and Tokyo because such lavishness would not be in keeping with tea-ceremony principles.

Chazen itchi: Tea and Zen are one, and *Ichigo-ichie: One life, one meeting*, calligraphies by Emi Kazuko 2003. Soji, a pupil of Rikyu, made the word *Ichigo-ichie* to encapsulate one of the most important teachings of the tea ceremony: to treat your guests as if it was to be your only encounter with them.

millennium BC, it was regarded as a source of immortality. By AD 450 it was a recognized medicine, and in the eighth century Buddhist monks brought ritual tea-drinking to Japan. Next there is *dō*, meaning a way of studying something in such intimate depth that it becomes a personal path of spiritual learning in the Zen tradition. The way of tea, therefore, is *chadō*, whose measured rituals are an expression of Zen Buddhism embodying the spiritual art of hospitality. *Shodō*, the art of calligraphy, and self-defence arts like *aikidō* are other examples of *dō*.

The lengthy ceremonial offering of tea by someone trained in the Way of Tea is known as *chanoyu*, which means simply hot water for tea. Once tea was grown widely in Japan it became a refined form of entertainment for the nobility, who enjoyed tea parties and tea competitions, as well as serving its original ritual role in monasteries. The appreciation of art forms, especially ceramics, assimilated from Song-dynasty China introduced the aesthetic component, and disciplined samurai classes contributed rules governing the presentation of tea. Over a period of four hundred years the two approaches to tea – the religious and that of intellectual entertainment – merged and were refined until the *chanoyu* of today was formalised by Sen-no Rikyu, a sixteenth-century tea master. His philosophy and teachings became so highly regarded that eventually he was considered too powerful by Shogun Hideyoshi and was forced to commit suicide. However, Rikyu's three grandsons each established schools to teach *chanoyu*, and these continue little changed today.

When the ceremony of *chanoyu* is performed after a formal meal, the whole sequence is called a *chaji*. The formal meal, *kaiseki*, which nowadays means a Japanese banquet, translates as embraced stone and refers to the heated stone that Zen monks hugged in their robes to keep warm during their long meditations. *Cha-kaiseki* is therefore the banquet element of the full *chaji* ceremony, though it is only one of several ancillaries to the main event which is the sharing of a bowl of tea.

Rikyu's guiding principles for *chanoyu* encompass harmony, respect, purity and tranquillity; these four elements are present throughout the occasion. He taught his adherents to be in harmony with the seasons through their choice of food and flowers or through heating or cooling the tea house; how to prepare the event with minute attention; to know intuitively how much of everything to use so that none is wasted; to avoid ostentation; to respect companions. All the actions of a *chaji* are in essence the everyday activities of housework and preparing a meal. Carried out with the forethought and consideration of a tea host, though, they assume meanings on other levels which are appreciated by the guest well versed in the philosophy. Whenever hospitality is offered it is important that both host and guest behave appropriately; in the tea ceremony it is as crucial for the guest to know what to expect and how to behave as it is for the host to stage the event correctly. It is a truly interactive occasion, and for this reason one of the most difficult feasts at which to be a guest if one has little understanding of the sequence of events.

For guests, a formal *chaji* starts on entry to the tea garden. This is the point at which they leave the outside world behind, observing a silence as they go and meeting their host who brings a basin of water to rinse their mouths and wash their hands. The really diligent host may even have got up before dawn to draw the purest of spring water for the event. The garden will have been scrupulously prepared and will have an air of calm beauty, though not necessarily perfection in the Western sense. There is a story about an apprentice who swept and tidied his garden, arranging every stone scrupulously until there was not anything out of place. But still his master insisted it was not perfect, and the puzzled student was at his wits' end. Suddenly a puff of wind tossed a few leaves onto his neat arrangement. 'Now the garden is perfect,' said the teacher.

A tea house is a small hut made of untreated wood and built without using nails, in the pure Japanese shrine-building tradition. Entry to the house is remarkable for the fact that the opening is so small that the guests, entering in the correct order, must climb in on their knees: worldly dignity is left behind at the entrance. Throughout the *kaiseki* and the *chanoyu*, the host will converse mainly with the guest of honour; the other guests say little. It is said that the tea ceremony teaches you your place in society; knowing your place remains an essential part of Japanese culture. The distress caused by a meeting between two groups of people who have not been briefed as to each other's status demonstrates clearly that Japanese people need to know where they stand – or rather, kneel. A full *chaji* can take four or five hours, and kneeling for this long can prove trying to those not used to it. One Japanese man even commented that he was apprehensive about his father's dying, not so much for the loss of his father but because he dreaded having to kneel for the long hours of his funeral ceremony.

Furnishings are sparse and rustic in style: the floor is covered with *tatami* mats made of rush-covered straw, the window is covered with translucent paper that sheds a soft light but affords no view, the walls are a soft green or beige. At first glance the space seems almost dowdy to the uninitiated Western eye, but its beauty becomes apparent with time. A scroll with calligraphy makes a perfect decoration: like the tea ceremony, the brushwork must be perfect at the first attempt and its message will prompt conversation. Small pieces of aromatic wood – juniper, perhaps, or sandalwood – are laid on the side of the brazier to produce 'the scent of Buddha's paradise'. Flowers are perfectly positioned, and chosen to reflect the season. Rather than a profusion of blooms, the tea host is more likely to have chosen a few twigs whose buds are so far off opening that only a chink of colour – a moment of potential – is displayed.

Although *kaiseki* means banquet, a *cha-kaiseki* dinner is meant to be a frugal but nevertheless satisfying meal consisting of three dishes and soup. Rice and pickles, both essential Japanese staples, appear throughout the meal. The style of temple cooking served by the Buddhist monks who developed the tea ceremony is called *shojin-ryori* and it is strictly vegan. At its best, it is the most beautiful and delicious of all Japanese cooking, quite unlike any other cuisine. The seasons are always reflected in the choice of ingredients and rarely are any repeated (except rice, of course) elsewhere in the meal. The meal described here is an autumnal *shojin-ryori*-style menu.

Rice will appear in four guises during the meal. At first it is very moist, only just cooked. A small portion is served to each guest by the host, and the way it is placed in the bowl will reveal which school of *chanoyu* the host follows. The Omote-senke school, for example, serves the rice in the centre of the bowl while Ura-senke followers serve it in a wedge shape placed towards the guests, and so on.[2]

Rice for the second serving is still fairly moist and steamy. It is served in a *hanki*[3] – a lacquered rice-tub – for the guests to help themselves to two or three bite-size amounts. By the third serving all the steam has been absorbed, the rice is drier and the guests may now help themselves freely. By the end of the meal, rice cooked in a traditional iron rice-pot will have stuck to the bottom and become brown and crispy.[4] This relished treat is crisped a bit more then cooked with hot water and lightly salted to make a refreshing palate-cleanser. Rice is so revered in Japan that it has acquired an almost spiritual status; for this reason it is treated with respect, and should never be wasted. 'For every grain cooked, one must be eaten,' said the fifteenth-century Zen master Dogen. Indeed, the best advice for a novice at a *cha-kaiseki* dinner is never to waste so much as a grain of rice; but if there should be any left, arrange it in a neat pile in the centre of your rice bowl.

These four stages of cooked rice set the pace of the meal: the moment it is ready, our autumnal meal begins. The first rice is carefully distributed and a *miso*[5] soup is served alongside in a simple black lacquer bowl on the guests' trays. The colour of the soup reflects the season. For example, in spring the *miso* is made with rice so will be a pale and milky colour; later on it might be made with barley and be pale red;

---

2 The first rice is also called *ichimonji* – character 1 – because in its just-cooked state it resembles a single brush stroke forming the number 1. Calling it *ichimonji* symbolises the importance of rice to Japanese food. The Japanese symbol for 1 is a horizontal stroke like a long hyphen and so when, for example, the Ura-senke school places the first tiny serving in its wedge shape, all the grains are laid like so many horizontal brushstrokes. Ura-senke is based in Kyoto and is the most elaborately ritualised of the three schools.

3 The *hanki* was originally a wooden rice box with a cloth placed under the lid; the wood and cloth absorbed moisture from the rice.

4 These scrapings are greatly enjoyed, as they are also in Persia, where the last rice scrapings are called *tahdeeg*. Since few people in Japan still use the traditional iron rice-pot, the rice grains are now usually toasted, then cooked till very soft, and lightly salted to make a thin, watery gruel which is served in a *yuoke*, or water pot. A really simple temple meal might just have plain hot water poured into each guest's rice bowl to mop up the remaining rice.

5 Miso is a widely used Japanese seasoning made from fermented grains or soya beans. Depending on what it is made from – sometimes it is a mixture – it can range from a sandy colour to almost black. It is sold as a crumbly paste which is added to soups and stocks for flavour and makes a refreshing hot drink.

autumn soup is deep brown, reflecting the stronger taste of soya beans. In this peat-brown broth nestles an autumn composition made from a perfect *maitake* mushroom, a few pine kernels, a small shape made from *fu* (a gluten product made with millet starch rather than the usual wheat starch), and some little pieces of white daikon roots. All the flavours and textures complement each other perfectly; the colours are brown, beige and white.

Next comes some sake to sip while eating the first of the dishes. *Mukozuke* means far dish because it is placed on the far side of the tray from the rice and soup bowls, and it includes something cured, or pickled in light vinegar.[6] Temple cooking does not of course employ fish; instead we have a neatly cut piece of *kabu* (turnip) which has been simmered in vegetable stock delicately flavoured with soy sauce and *yuzu* (a Japanese citrus fruit) rind. For a little garnish there is a colourful heap of vegetables which have been salted and pickled so that they are softened yet still crunchy, and a steamed chrysanthemum flower reminds us of autumn. The second rice and smooth sake which accompany *mukozuke* complement the salty pickle flavours. In contrast to the lacquer soup-bowl, the *mukozuke* has been served on a rustic ceramic dish painted with casual brush stokes.

Nimono-wan is the simmered dish, the highlight of a kaiseki. The covered bowls (*wan*) for this course are the most splendid of the meal: gorgeous decorated lacquer. *Nimono* is essentially a clear broth containing a stunning composition of other items that have been meticulously planned for flavour and colour. Our *nimono* bouillon contains a piece of fried tofu which is made from sesame rather than the usual soya, so has a different, almost elusive, flavour. There is also a *matzutake* mushroom which grows wild under the red pine trees. To add the green element there is a small heap of simmered *mizuna* leaves (*mizuna* is rather like rocket – green and peppery) and some tiny diced particles of fragrant yellow *yuzu* zest. The clear broth is made from *dashi*: a stock normally flavoured with kelp and dried bonito-fish flakes; in vegan cooking vegetable stock, or the water in which dried shiitake have been soaked, is used instead. When these stocks are made, some of the flavourings are steeped for so short a time that it seems impossible they can impart much flavour, but they do: the result is a complex

---

6 When it is not vegan, *mukozuke* is usually shellfish or fish, sometimes delicately flavoured by wrapping it in *konbu* (kelp) and then pressed. *Wasabi*, a fiery green horseradish paste, is likely to crop up in this intensely flavoured dish .

yet elusive flavour, always wonderfully balanced. Such exquisitely tiny morsels in this light clear soup do not indicate a substantial main dish. However, the *hanki* with its heap of perfectly cooked rice is to hand, and the perfectly balanced collection of flavours and colours in this simmered dish, so thoughtfully compiled, leaves us with a sense of well-being verging on euphoria.

The grilled dish is called *yakimono*, and is served with little or no garnish. Fish or sometimes duck is the favourite at a normal *kaiseki*, while tofu is common for the vegan version. However, to avoid repetition of ingredients, we are given grilled aubergine garnished with a few shreds of fragrant *shiso* leaves served on top of elegant long pine needles[7] in a plain square dish.

At this point the traditional 'one soup and three dishes' that constitute the basic *cha-kaiseki* are completed, but the host may well add a few extra dishes before finishing the meal. If so, there is likely to be *azuke-bachi*, meaning 'leaving the serving dish', because this is when the host retires to eat his own meal alone. *Azuke-bachi* is a small but exquisite assemblage, one for each person, left on a dish to be passed round by the guests, whose conversation is a little less formal at this point. Our vegan example is some lily bulb pounded into a ball (lily bulb has a nutty flavour) with a diamond-shaped piece of fried fresh *fu* (made of wheat gluten this time) and a stem of *mitsuba*, a salad leaf rather like coriander. The dressing is made of ground sesame seed and *mirin* (sweet rice wine) to complement the other flavours.

To start preparing for the tea ceremony, the next dish is called *hashi-arai*, or chopstick-wash. This is such a mild bouillon that it is virtually clear water with just a little dried kelp briefly steeped in it. There are one or two shreds of fresh ginger to cleanse the mouth, and a tiny piece of *umeboshi*, dried and salted Japanese apricot,[8] as a digestive; in the spring there would probably have been cherry-blossom petals instead. *Hashi-arai* is plain and refreshing; just enough for one or two sips is served.

The host now pours sake for the main guest, who returns the gesture; this is repeated with the other guests. With the sake comes *hassun*, which the host shares with his guests. *Hassun* means eight-sun – an old Japanese measurement similar to an inch – and is the name for

---

7 Pine trees represent longevity and so are auspicious.

8 Sometimes translated as plum, *ume* is one the oldest fruits grown in Japan. Inedible when fresh, it is either salted and dried (*umeboshi*), or made into sweets and jams.

an eight-inch-square serving dish, on which two kinds of food are served. *Hassun* is another savoury course which, in conventional cooking, would contain one item of animal protein from the sea and a vegetable to represent the land. A vegan *hassun*, since both items are vegetable, contrasts mountain and field, so we have a grilled mountain chestnut with a small aromatic clump of steamed *shungiku* leaves. *Shungiku* is a vegetable chrysanthemum.

To finish the meal, pickles[9] are served with the burnt-rice broth. A small, bite-sized amount of rice should still be left in the bowl, into which the broth is poured. After the broth has been drunk, a piece of pickle is used to scoop up the last remaining grains of rice so that the bowls are left clean and empty.

After the meal, moist and rather glutinous rice sweetmeats called *omogashi* are served and the guests adjourn to the waiting room to talk in a more relaxed way among themselves while their host prepares for the tea ceremony. At various stages in the *chaji* the guests will show their appreciation of the artefacts chosen by the host: an incense case, the scrolls, the flowers, the utensils for the tea ceremony and, most important of all, the tea bowl itself, which represents communication and intimacy since it has touched everyone's lips. Most objects are rustic and characterised by the absence of obvious value, since ostentation is alien to *chadō*. Each piece has been selected with great care, but, unlike a Western arrangement, none will match. However, this apparently haphazard collection of colour, form, age, texture, material and subject matter somehow works artistically and has a specially poignant beauty when it reflects the inner harmony of the host. Part of the ethos of *chadō* is respect, which means respecting even the most insignificant object. No matter how old or plain, or how humble a role it plays, it is handled reverently. The history of a utensil is of great value, and should one be broken, it may well be repaired and used again with increased reverence – not unlike the Kwakiutl coppers on p. 42 whose value is counted in different terms to our own. In the British Museum is a simple rustic tea bowl which clearly suffered a breakage, but whose owner did not try to disguise the damage. Instead, the gaps and cracks have been lovingly filled with brilliant gold lustre,

---

9 These pickles are known as *konomono*, or fragrant things, and in this case comprise yellow *takuan* which has been pickled with rice bran, some burdock root pickled in salty *miso*, slightly bitter pink *myoga* (a curious vegetable which is at its best in autumn), and the attractively shaped white *renkon* root. Japanese pickles have a lovely crunchy texture; the rice-bran tubs are used for years, improving all the time.

turning an imperfection into something startling and beautiful, not least because of the care that was taken to do it. All these things will be understood by the guest familiar with the Way of Tea.

The tea ceremony itself is, like any ritual or task carried out by a competent craftsman, a seamless flow of movements which are in themselves beautiful to watch. The utensils are purified with water ladled from the iron tea-kettle and carefully wiped dry. So that it makes no smoke, the burning charcoal will have been washed and dried beforehand, and exactly the right amount is used. The sound of the simmering water indicates when it is ready for use: at the right moment the noise is like the wind in the pine trees, a distant roar overlaid with a light seething hiss. I was once involved in making an iron tea-kettle, and the cleaning process involved boiling up clean water many times over to get rid of the residue from the casting. Suddenly, the cleared water started to make an extraordinary rustling roar: the kettle was working, an exciting moment. However, water for Japanese green tea should never boil, only simmer, for boiling water makes it bitter; so cold water is ladled into the kettle to reduce the temperature.

Tea for *chanoyu* is a fine, pale green powder called *matcha* which has been grown under protective shades so that the perfect leaf can be harvested before being steamed, dried and ground. The first bowl of tea, very thick and extremely strong, is called *koicha*. It is whisked to a batter-like consistency with a small bamboo *chasen* and the bowl is handed, with a bow, to the guest of honour who returns the bow, takes the tea bowl and rotates it before taking a few sips. He then wipes the bowl deep down inside the rim and passes it to the next guest who also turns the bowl before sipping. This custom is said to date back to the samurai who would share a bowl of sake with guests to assert their mutual ties. When everyone has had his turn, the bowl is handed back to the host. The various utensils such as the tea container, the scoop and the hot-water pot, are appreciated by the guests while the host makes more tea (*usucha*), this time frothy, and thin enough for each person to drink a whole bowl. *Higashi*, beautifully formed dry sweets,[10] are served with this thin tea. The tea ceremony is now finished and after the host has thanked and spoken to each guest, he retires, leaving the guests to talk for a while before returning to the outside world.

---

10 Higashi, often stamped into the shape of flowers or leaves, are quite different from the dense and sometimes sticky *omogashi* sweetmeats served after the meal.

Thick green tea is extremely strong, with a pleasant bitterness nicely counteracted by the soft, sticky sweets served beforehand. The smell is invigorating and fresh, redolent of spinach purée, 'the essence of chloroform' as wine writer Andrew Jefford described it. To those not used to *koicha*, its effect can be quite a shock – it is stronger than espresso coffee – but the perfect bowl of tea, the climax of the *chaji*, leaves the guest with a sense of elation encapsulating all the elements of *chadō*: harmony, respect, purity, tranquillity. On the face of it, the contrast between a slowly measured ceremony and a shot of green tea appears to belie tranquillity. An abstract concept is difficult to translate, but one Japanese lady likened tranquillity in the context of *chadō* to a bead of dew at the tip of a leaf. Complete in itself and in repose, the droplet is nevertheless not static because it encapsulates latent energy.

20

A feast in the bath: how not to behave

I know that more things were lost in the depths of those waters than mere earrings.

PETRA CARTER

The picture at the end of the second colour section is of a feast in the bath. This remarkable scene was painted for Antoine de Bourgogne about 1470, around the same time as the more famous *Très Riches Heures du Duc de Berry*. It is the finer of two paintings of the same scene that I have seen, both of them in fifteenth-century French books. The features are so similar that, as was common at that period, one artist has clearly copied the other. Bizarre though it appears, pictures of people eating in the bath are not unusual in books of this period. Many show scenes from everyday life, and communal bathing, like communal sleeping, was the norm; nakedness was not necessarily shameful, although some public bathhouses or 'stews' were frowned upon as steamy and vice-ridden. Other examples in art are more unusual, like an illustration of a couple bathing in a draped wooden tub hanging in front of a banqueting table. This could have illustrated a romance being enacted as an entremets or soteltie but it could equally have been a representation of the *pensiles balneae* mentioned by Pliny. These were small bathtubs suspended in such a way that the bathers could divert themselves by literally rocking the boat.

So what is going on in this beautifully detailed scene? It displays all the characteristics of a late medieval banquet: there is a handsome canopied top table (matched by the draped four-poster bed in the next room); vivid blue and gold tapestries brighten the walls; a minstrel plays sweet music on his lute and a little dog scampers about. A crisp white embroidered surnap lies neatly over a central board carrying dainty pointed knives, fine rolls of manchet bread, and polished pewter plates with sweetmeats on them. Some of the men drink from mazers (maplewood drinking bowls), and a pitcher of hippocras (sweet spiced wine) stands ready at either end of the table. There are ripe greengages and suggestively luscious cherries to eat, and the lady at the front holds up a jellied tart. In short, this would be a typical banquet of its time were it not for the lack of clothing, the unconventional seating, the explicit goings-on in the adjoining chamber and the expressions of the king and his bishop peeping through the door.

The Old French text underneath is a 1407 translation of Valerius Maximus, a popular Roman Stoic writer who lived in the first century AD and was a collector of wise sayings and lightweight moral stories about the great and famous of his day. The addition of a few prurient details ensured popular appeal in the Middle Ages. The fact that the chosen text was written by a pagan scholar reflects a typical combination of Renaissance interest in antiquity and Christian moralising. The excerpt, from *On High Living and Lust*, runs: 'High living is a pleasant vice, which it is easier to condemn than to avoid. We shall insert it in our work, not indeed so that it should receive any honour, but so that recognising itself it should be impelled to penitence. Lust may be joined to it because it arises from the same principles of vices, nor may they in being condemned or amended be separated from one another, having been connected by a twin error of the mind.' Valerius Maximus continues with stories of wealthy people who built ornate bathhouses and dissolved ground-up pearls into their drinks, amongst other extravagant vices. So the painting is a charming portrayal of the kind of high living that the devout fifteenth-century Christian should avoid at all costs. Why these deplorable vices should then be described and illustrated in quite such exquisite detail will be easily understood by any populist publisher. Since the text does not specifically describe this scene anywhere, the miniature also reveals that its creator had a colourful imagination typical of his period.

21

Rites of passage: universal symbols

Weddings, christenings, duels, funerals, swindlings, diplomatic affairs – anything is a pretext for a good dinner.

JEAN ANOUILH

By now it will be apparent that many feasts are public demonstrations of superiority, power, even aggression. But rites of passage (except weddings sometimes, of which more later) tend to be private family celebrations, benign affairs demonstrating pride at achievements and hope for the future. But the most important event in life – birth – is traditionally the one least fêted on any grand scale. This is partly because the timing of births is unpredictable (to stage a feast usually requires preparation) and partly because until very recently infant mortality was so high that to celebrate a birth prematurely with a lavish feast was tempting fate. All too often a small funeral followed. Instead, foods connected with birth tend to be offered in small quantities either for good luck or for nutrition. The red-coloured eggs given away by proud Chinese parents after a birth are one example (red represents luck and joy); another is salt, which in eastern Europe is considered important both nutritionally and as a symbol of good fortune, and is given to the mother and placed on the newborn baby's tongue. Sweetness is another common element in these foods since it not only gives some quick energy to the mother after her labour but is also a token of the sweetness of life. The forms in which the sweetness appeared often represented fertility as well, and were thus also on display in wedding foods. So we see 'groaning cakes' bursting with dried fruit and seeds, sugar comfits,[1] rum butter (buried in the garden and then resurrected to be shared between mother, midwife and baby),

---

1 An Englishwoman, giving birth in a gleaming sterile state-of-the-art maternity hospital in Holland, was surprised to be offered 'for tradition' a *beschuit met muisjes* (biscuit with 'mice'): a buttered rusk liberally heaped with tiny coloured grains of sugar-coated aniseed which spilled off the rusk and bounced exuberantly all over the pristine floor of the recovery room. This custom is common all over Holland and the 'mice', a traditional cure for colic as well as a fertility symbol, are identical to medieval comfits or modern Italian confetti, which are more usually associated with weddings.

Feast given by the Duc D'Albe to celebrate the birth of the Prince of Asturies. G. Sestin, 1707. Only four of the 38 seated guests are male, which is unusual, but it is, after all, to celebrate a birth.

sweet wines and almonds. In the days when births of important people had to be witnessed (to make sure nobody swapped the baby or that the midwife didn't secrete the placenta to give to a witch), a mother's sweetmeats were often enjoyed instead by her trusted witnesses (known as gossips; the word comes from godsib, meaning a relation standing in for God; the meaning of spreading idle talk came later) who cheerfully feasted on the luxuries while the mother lay exhausted.

But none of these (bar perhaps the gossips' junketings) really constitutes feasting. This is reserved for later rites of passage, of which there are many. Sikhs mark the first shaving of a baby son's head with a full day of feasting; Orthodox Jews celebrate the first hair-clipping. There are feasts for baptisms and for circumcisions (some of the Ottoman sultans went to enormous lengths to celebrate the circumcision of an heir – in 1582, for example, two years of preparation went into a feast for Sultan Murad III's son; it went on for fifty-two days and included entire edible gardens created out of marzipan flowers). Anniversaries and birthdays are also honoured. Children's birthday parties are of course embryo feasts, events at which children learn about special food and behaviour for festive occasions. With both savoury and sweet things laid out on the table and the lack of cutlery (not to mention the amount of food dropped or thrown as a consequence), the proceedings resemble a Tudor banquet right down to the soteltie of the birthday cake, sparkling with candles and decorated to illustrate some current enthusiasm in the child's life. In China one's sixtieth birthday is the most auspicious because it represents five[2] rotations of the twelve-year cycle (rat, snake, dragon, monkey, rabbit, tiger, sheep, etc.) and it is the occasion for a special feast at which the elderly person will probably be offered the Eight Delicacies – in Chinese the word eight sounds like the word for good luck. Colours and textures are important aspects of these delicacies. In the past these included exotic titbits like gorilla's lips, tiger's placenta, dog's liver or fat from a wolf. Nowadays it is more likely to be chicken, pork, prawn or squid; a vegetarian version might include mushrooms, fungi, lily roots and

---

2 Five is a special number in China. Deh-ta Hsiung writes: 'All nature is made up in combinations of five elements or powers of nature: metal, wood, water, fire and earth. The earliest Chinese book on medicine, written over two thousand years ago, proposed that the body needed five flavours to live, five grains for nourishment, five fruits for support, five animals for benefit, and five vegetables for energy. This ideal is perpetuated not just in the famous Chinese five-spice powder, but also in the traditional flavours fundamental to Chinese cooking: sweet, sour, bitter, hot and salty.'

bean curd. The list of celebrations goes on, with bar and bat mitzvahs which can last all weekend, or a *cresima* (confirmation) that will constitute one of an Italian's most important rites of passage. There are school and university graduations after which children join the adult world, and in some African countries there are ordeals to be undergone before young men can be initiated into adult society, with a feast afterwards as compensation. In northern Thailand even the menopause justifies a hearty spread of meat and poultry to mark the virtual gender change from woman to honorary man.

Apart from the last, all these rites of passage are in preparation for the greatest one: the marriage ceremony. Throughout all cultures and ages, no family occasions have been as exuberantly celebrated as weddings. The abiding themes of hospitality and fertility are entertaining adjuncts to the main purpose of the ceremony, which is to sanctify the production and nurturing of descendants since – biologically speaking – genes are the most enduring thing we have on earth. The prospect of a couple's new beginning generates an infectious feeling of hope, and the festivities are usually enlivened by the unpredictable spirit of Carnival amongst the younger guests.

When marriages are unions of power and wealth, the feasts must be seen to be lavish and consequently weddings have provided some of

To make an extraordinary Pie, or a Bride Pye of several Compounds, being several distinct Pies on one bottom. From Robert May *The Accomplisht Cook*, 1671. See p. 181 for details of how to fill them with birds and frogs.

the most extravagant feasting occasions.[3] In the Middle Ages, they were often combined with coronations to create an even greater impact. The thirteenth-century writer Matthew Paris describes the joint coronation and wedding of Eleanor of Provence and Henry III in January 1236:

> to this nuptial entertainment, there came such a multitude of the nobility of both sexes – such hosts of religious persons – such crowds of people and such a variety of clowns and buffoons, that London could scarcely contain them in her capacious bosom ... why need I describe the profusion of dishes which furnished the table – the abundance of venison – the variety of fish – the diversity of wine – the gaiety of jugglers – the readiness of the attendants – whatever the world could produce for glory or delight was there conspicuous.[4]

To honour the marriage of Edward I of England (who also married an Eleanor), the King of Scots released five hundred horses; anyone who caught one could keep it – a splendid display of munificence which no doubt conveyed more than one message. For wealthy dynasties such a union was the culmination of protracted negotiations to safeguard property, money and social prospects. The rest of us express the occasion more modestly as a time of happiness shared with family, friends and sometimes the wider community; a time of giving and of receiving. Money is the universal present: pinned on the bride's dress at a Jewish wedding; pressed into a peasant's hand in rural France; thrown by bridegrooms to children scrambling outside the church. Dowries took many forms, from food to jewels to whole countries. What was given used to be of great interest to the community, and in Britain the custom of displaying wedding presents a few days before the ceremony lingered on into the late twentieth century. A more pragmatic approach used to be taken in Hungary in situations where it was obvious that costly gifts would not be forthcoming. A professional reader was hired to announce the list of wedding presents, and, as George Lang described,

> Judging by the list one would have thought this was a royal wedding, such were the astounding jewels and other riches. But what really happened was that for a modest fee the reader embroidered a little and

3 I have just read about a recent double Indian wedding which cost the two families £7 million.
4 This was ascribed to Matthew Paris by Robert Huish writing in 1821, but is now thought to be by Roger de Wendover, whose *Flowers of History* included Paris's *History of England*.

Plan of a tea house in its garden. Japanese school, late 19thC.

A wedding fête at Bermondsey. Joris Hoefnagel, c.1570. The decorated bridal cup is filled with sprigs of rosemary, and heading the procession are bearers of bride cakes so massive they need a sling to support them.

Peasant wedding feast. Pieter Brueghel the Elder, 1568. The bride sits demurely beneath a symbolic circlet; a small child and the corner of a cot are a reminder of the purpose of marriage.

Macaronenberg. German, 19thC. Perfect wedding symbolism: circles of almond paste stacked up ready to be pierced with a knife.

Soup and stews of beef and veal being prepared for a wedding feast. France, 1953. Frank Scherschel. Preparations for a post-war country wedding suggest a generous feast in the offing.

'Gathered': Lawson Park 2000. Jenny Brownrigg. The surreal atmosphere of our banquet high above Lake Coniston is captured in this photograph taken as dusk was falling.

The Inauguration of Robert Burns as Poet Laureate of The Lodge Canongate Kilwinning. William Stewart Watson, 1787. Photograph by Antonia Reeve. Although it is probably a coincidence, it does appear that Robert Burns has a plaid-covered halo.

Cannibal scene. Theodore de Bry, 1592. The text this gruesome picture illustrates makes it plain that cannibalism is not common but is part of a lengthy ritual involving captured enemies.

Fijian ceremonial 'i saga'.
Ceremonial wooden forks
are used to convey the
flesh of a captured enemy
to the mouth of the priest
or chief.

Quirky and colourful, Mexican Days of the Dead
skeletons are made into sweets or *papier mâché*
figures that satirise human activities.

New Year at Auchtermuchty
A Millennium feast to welcome the year 2000

MENU

Numerical vegetable consommé
Home-made bread and rolls
(Fino sherry, Tio Pepe)

* * *

Whitebait 'soteltie'
Whitebait with watercress salsa, caviar and
spicy salad leaves
(Jurançon sec, Clos Guirouilh 1995)

* * *

Two Swan 'sotelties'
Swan raised pie
Saltire potatoes
Colourful vegetables and reduction sauce
(Château Sociando-Mallet, Haut Médoc 1993)

* * *

Cheeses
Celestial Oatcakes
(Pécharmant, Bergerac 1992)

* * *

Deux Millefenilles of passion fruit
(Jurançon Moelleux, Clos Guirouilh 1994)

* * *

Banqueting course
— Bleeding stag 'soteltie' —
(Port, Taylor's 1975, Hungarian Tokai)

Swansong at Hogmanay: Millennium feast December 1999. Clockwise: the author with the reconstructed swan; the sword is removed from the stag; the wine pulses out like blood; one of deux millefeuilles; the large swan pie; the joke pie; silver platter of whitebait that appeared after the accident.

The morning after a birthday feast, Auchtermuchty; September 2003. Tatyana Jakovskaia, Sharmanka.

when it came to imagination no expense was spared. Thus the present of a rolling pin was transformed into a signed Louis XIV ebony masterpiece, the simplest object became an heirloom. Since everything sounded better graced with a French name even the reader himself was called, elegantly, M. Chamaisse.

Wealthy families who already had more than they could possibly need gladly accepted more. An account of the marriage of Lionel,[5] Duke of Clarence (Edward III's third son) with Violante Visconti, daughter of the Duke of Milan, in 1368 describes the wedding feast's thirty courses, each of innumerable dishes – one featured peacocks served with green vegetables and beans –

> ... and betwixt every course, as many presents of wondrous price intermixed which John Gelafius, chiefe of the choise youth, bringing to the tabel, did offer to Lionel. There were in onely one course seventy good horses, adorned with silkes and silver furniture, and in the others, silver vessels, falcons, hounds, armour for horses, costly coats of mayle, breast plates glittering of massie steel, helmets and corslets decked with costly crests, apparrell distinct with costly jewels, souldiers girdles, and lastly certain gemmes by curious art, set in gold; and of purple, and cloth of gold for men's apparrell in great abundance.

But to the feast, via another universal custom: the wedding procession. Whether it is a walk down the aisle of a church or through streets or fields, a column of cars honking their horns as can be heard throughout the summer in France, the 'hamefaring' of a Shetland wedding or a modern Chinese taxi motorcade scooping up the bride, they all symbolise the couple's journey to a new life, and this starts with the best meal the family can afford. Wedding feasts vary from country to country and within societies but invariably contain the same elements: abundance, luxury and fertility. People commonly spend rather more than they can afford on the occasion; excess is important, as it represents riches for the couple. To run out is bad luck and, worse, could be misconstrued as meanness; so sugared sweets are distributed

---

5 The teenage Geoffrey Chaucer was taken on as a page in Lionel's household and in 1359 went off to France as one of his yeomen. He was captured at the siege of Reims but, fortunately for countless English scholars, was ransomed and some thirty years later wrote *The Canterbury Tales*. Chaucer, therefore, would have known about, and more than likely took part in, this fabulous wedding.

to guests to take home, fountains overflow with wine and no one is barred from drinking it. Whilst paintings of state weddings feature the grandeur of the setting, the splendour of the jewels and sometimes the food too, those of lowlier weddings emphasise the excitement over the food. Even though it is less elegant, nevertheless it is being prepared in profusion and served up and handed round and vigorously danced off; sometimes there is an expectant look in the eye, sometimes one of misty stupor from overindulgence. If a grand hall was not affordable then trestles were set up in a barn or under a bower of flowers, and planks were placed over them. If there were no planks then doors were taken off their hinges. The boards were then piled with provisions until they creaked with the plenty; always there would be more than enough for everyone.

As well as being plentiful the food at wedding feasts must be special; what constitutes luxury depends upon local specialities as well as the family's circumstances: foaming spicy chocolate and turkeys for the Aztec, an enormous piece of meat to roast for the Zulu, reindeer cream and marrowbones for the Saami, smoked salmon for some, cakes and spiced bread enriched with fruit and eggs for others. Since sweetness is an important symbol of the couple's future relationship, everywhere there are rich cakes and confectionery made with fruit and nuts, honey and sugar; in India or Persia these might be wrapped in silver and gold leaf. Anything, in short, which is not everyday food.[6]

Most cultures have their deities of fertility and fruitfulness: Demeter, Lakshmi, Yue Lao, Ceres, Dionysus – one or other of them will be lurking somewhere at a wedding distributing his or her riches with abandon, so just as important as abundance and luxury is the inclusion of tokens of fertility. Fruits with masses of seeds or which come in generous clusters, such as pomegranates, strawberries, dates or grapes, are obvious choices. With their huge shoals and thousands of eggs, fish appear in many ways: they represent plenty at both Jewish and Chinese weddings (the Chinese words for fish and for surplus sound exactly the same, apart from the intonation);[7] salmon is a popular wedding-

6 Tony Green argues that late twentieth-century British weddings are the opposite. So careful is the bride's family not to appear to threaten the groom's by being aggressively showy that they produce food which is conspicuous by its ordinariness. Lavishness is expended on other parts of the ceremony instead.

7 The reason for serving a whole fish is the fact that, even if every other dish on the table is finished, the head, tail and backbone of the fish will remain on its dish to symbolise food to spare for the next occasion.

breakfast choice in Britain and a brilliantly decorated carp forms part of a Hindu dowry. Caviar, aspired to more often than produced nowadays, is appropriate wedding fare since the word comes from the Persian *khayeh* meaning both eggs and testicles – eggs and also milk dishes have obvious connections with childbearing. I went to a wedding in Ayrshire where we were served chicken formed into the shape of an egg out of which tumbled spiced raisins, symbolic food indeed. In medieval times women ate quinces in the hope that this would make their children clever. A popular fifteenth-century wedding dish was *viande royale*, a quince paste decorated with ginger, sugar, and a cross of gold and silver leaf. Almonds have long been thought to promote fertility (they are very nutritious) and appear coated in coloured sugar, or perhaps pounded with chicken to make a delicate *blanc manger*, or ground into marzipan to decorate the cake. Seeds and grains are the most visual reminders of fertility and are wedding staples in the form of seed-covered breads in eastern Europe, Indian dishes of pulses, a golden Iranian saffron-rice pilau or the enriched rice custard popular at Spanish weddings.

And who can forget the hissing sound of seeds or rice[8] thrown over the bride and groom? Or flower petals or paper confetti? The history of confetti goes back to the tiny sweets called comfits which first appeared in Europe around 1100 in Venice. They were brought back from the Middle East by traders, and their use spread throughout Europe when sugar became cheap enough to use as a luxury food instead of being purely medicinal. Like many foods with exotic and expensive ingredients in those times, comfits were originally regarded as a palatable form of digestive. They were made from 'souls' of aromatic seeds like aniseed, fennel or caraway which were laboriously coated in pastel-coloured layers of sugar in a wide copper pan over a carefully controlled fire, producing masses of tiny little sweets whose shapes and size were determined by the soul. The process took many hours and therefore they were expensive treats. Comfits were hugely popular in the late medieval and Renaissance periods and were always present at banquets and collations. Queen Elizabeth

---

8 Rice is also used decoratively at Hindu weddings and other rites of passage to make *alpana*: intricate patterns applied to the furniture, across patios, up wooden columns or over floors. The rice is ground to a fine powder which is held between thumb and index finger and drizzled out to produce startling white patterns. Sometimes the rice is dyed into vibrant colours. These patterns are never documented but are passed down from generation to generation.

I of England was very partial to them, to the detriment of her teeth. During Carnevale in Venice, noble families would throw comfits – *confetti* – down from their balconies to the thronging crowds below, and at weddings throughout Europe the well-to-do would throw handfuls of comfits at weddings that would be eagerly gathered up by bystanders. In France, those who could not afford sugar started making artificial comfits out of coloured plaster. Eventually, after someone was blinded in Marseille by one of these pellets, Napoleon III banned them. By this time many people threw flower petals instead of comfits so, spotting an opportunity and combining the two, an enterprising Englishman started making paper 'confetti' and soon had a thriving export business. He even commissioned Toulouse-Lautrec to make an advertising poster. Sugared almonds, though larger, are a direct descendant of comfits and are still commonly given wrapped in tiny bundles as favours to wedding guests. Fellow food writer Carla Capalbo wrote the following about confetti:

> The Italians are completely dotty about these wedding confetti, and there is at least one shop in every town, no matter how small, that is dedicated to them ... they produce the most elaborately decorated bundles with flowers, china trinkets, lace, ribbons and good luck charms attached. Many cost a fortune, but it would be unthinkable to have an Italian wedding (or baptism or first communion) without them ... confetti represent yet another status symbol in a country that is obsessed by them, so people go to incredible lengths and expense to outdo their neighbours.

The other wedding food to which a great deal of effort has usually been devoted is the cake. Depending on custom it might be sweet cake or enriched bread, and it has usually been symbolic of reproduction: a cone of profiteroles, tiers of cakes or a ring shape. A wafer was a common emblem, its pieces being distributed after it had been broken over the head of the bride. The Romans' was made from ground wheat bound with grape must, the Brahmins' out of ground lentils, British ones from shortbread or thin currant biscuit. Enriched breads are a feature of eastern European weddings. Hungarian *palók* (meaning joy-cake) is made from dough shaped into a large pretzel with space to hold a bottle of honeyed brandy. Polish wedding bread is circular with a hole cut into it to form a small cup covered by a lid and filled with salt for good luck. In the Ukraine *korovai* bread evokes pre-Christian traditions; the groom's *korovai* is intricately decorated with berries and ribbons, the bride's has two stalks supporting two flying lovebirds, a third is decorated with greenery and used with wine and salt during the blessing ceremony, and the fourth is cut up and given to the guests.

The evolution of the tiered rich fruit cake of many western weddings began in pre-Christian times when a cake made of seeds was buried by the ploughman in the first furrow of the season as a fertility offering. By the sixteenth century these had evolved into substantial roundels of dough which were stuffed with fruits and nuts.[9] Such bride cakes could weigh up to ten kilos (25 lb) and since they were often paraded in the wedding procession, the bearers had to use a sling to support their weight. The cracking of the crust (which was not eaten as it was too hard from its lengthy baking) to reveal the rich contents is symbolic in the same way as opening the chicken stuffed with raisins or breaking wafers over the bride's head. Sometimes smaller versions of these cakes were piled up on top of each other, or perhaps a bridal pie was served instead, its very hard crusts supporting a variety of contents. Marchpanes were much featured at sixteenth-century weddings: elaborate table decorations made of iced almond paste, they were thought to promote fertility. They might include a sprig of rosemary, a herb often used at weddings owing to its associations with the heart (it was used as a tonic) as well as its connotations of fidelity and remembrance.

By 1671 Robert May was giving directions for making a five-layered 'Bride Pye' in *The Accomplisht Cook*; his diagram is reminiscent of a gâteau Pithiviers. As chef to several large households he had clearly overseen a number of weddings and, having carefully described his fillings (designed to ensure that the different layers will support each other – the book is wonderfully practical), he offers the following suggestion: 'You may bake the middle one full of flour, it being bak't and cold, take out the flour in the bottom, & put in live birds, or a snake, which will seem strange to the beholders, which cut up the pie at the Table. This is only for a Wedding to pass away the time.'

---

9 Scottish black bun served at New Year is a remnant of this kind of rich fruit cake encased in pastry.

At the same period in Hungary, a joke cake with rubbish (nails, cut-up clothing and so on) baked into it was served up to the best man at breakfast the following morning before the start of another day's feasting. Similarly, in 1674 Hannah Woolley describes decorations made of sugar plate fashioned to look like 'Snakes and ... any venomous Creature you can think of'. Other decorations were more explicit: a hen with a brood of chicks or a 'wif lying in childe-bed' made it quite plain what was expected. In case there should be any doubt, sometimes written messages spelled it out as well. By the end of the eighteenth century, marzipan covered the cake and was itself covered in icing. This is the sort of thing Lord Byron would have been thinking of when he wrote anxiously to Annabella Milbanke in 1814 about his marriage: '"The Cake" dearest – I am in such an agitation about it – if it should be spoiled or mouldy – or – don't let them put too many eggs and butter in it – or it will certainly circulate an indigestion amongst all our acquaintance.'

By the end of the century, white and pastel shades were the accepted colours. The modern tiered white wedding cake swagged with flowers and ribbons is a simulation of the bride in her white dress, and the couple who jointly cut through the crisp white covering to reveal the fruit inside sustain the allegory as do the guests who must all eat a little piece of cake. Wedding symbolism is so obvious and universal that it is impossible to escape it. The egg-shaped chicken stuffed with fruit was one example – the bride was unaware of its relevance and was more preoccupied with other aspects of her wedding; she simply chose that dish because she thought people would like it. A Danish couple provided another illustration: they wanted something different from the customary Danish wedding cake, which is a sweet sponge cake covered with jam and cream. Instead they decided on a *Kransekage*, simply because 'it tastes good and goes down incredibly well with champagne'. *Kransekage* is made from enriched marzipan baked into concentric rings which are stacked up into a tall cone with sweet white icing dribbling down from the top. Unwittingly they had chosen the most traditional ingredients possible and with it a symbolic shape as old as time. When the almond cone combining male and female shapes was pierced by the jointly held knife, it evoked the wedding ring being slipped onto the finger, the breaking of a circular wafer, the passing of a sliver of wedding cake through the ring and the handing of it to the bridesmaids,[10] and the circular garland suspended over the head of a seventeenth-century Flemish bride at her wedding *kermesse* (carnival). A circle, a piercing, a breaking: universal symbols. A perfect wedding cake.

---

10 In *The Pickwick Papers*, Dickens describes this custom at a wedding feast.

22

A pollen feast for Ruskin: banqueting in the high forests

The first great fact, which we have to consider respecting vegetation, is that on the whole . . . it is green in life and golden in death . . . or in the pause of perfect state which precedes it . . . it is well . . . to look upon (this) first autumnal glow as the honour of fulfilled function.

JOHN RUSKIN

At the end of a blustery, wet September day the clouds parted and an unexpectedly calm golden-green evening revealed an outdoor banquet held high up in Grizedale Forest overlooking Lake Coniston. The occasion was the culmination of artist Rob Kesseler's work on flowers, pollen and their interaction with the Wordsworths and John Ruskin, the nineteenth-century artist, writer and philanthropist who had lived at Brantwood House a thousand feet below on the edge of the lake.

As a ceramic artist, Kesseler was well versed in the historical use of flowers as decoration; he decided to study the flowers in Grizedale and take pollen samples from each one down to Kew Gardens, where they were magnified with the aid of an electron microscope. These ghostly images were screen-printed in gold lustre and the flower's colour onto a range of ceramics that also incorporated snippets of Ruskin's handwritten observations on nature and ultimately formed part of an exhibition. The autumnal feast in the forest brought together all the people involved in the project – 'the honour of fulfilled function' – and I was asked to create a menu using as far as possible foods from the surroundings, perhaps even some of the flowers Rob had studied.

As we drove up through the forest, fleeting snapshots of the Lakeland hills were sharply defined by the evening sun until we reached a clearing so high above the lake that we looked straight over to the Old Man of Coniston (immortalised in Arthur Ransome's stories as Kanchenjunga). On the steep slope in front of a low slate house had been built a level platform which contained the banquet, its tables set in a V shape so that everyone faced the stunning view. Reflecting the green and gold colours of the trees and also Ruskin's observations of natural forms at close quarters, exquisite little table pieces had been made from moss studded with small ceps, chanterelles and other fungi that had been gathered by Grizedale's artistic director, a keen mycologist. Kesseler's plates shimmered and glittered in the slanting sunlight.

Most of the guests had never met; some were clearly surprised and enchanted that they had been included in this special event. Each guest had his own table setting adorned with its particular flower-pollen images: thus the representative from Wedgwood who had provided the ceramic blanks had foxglove; one of Grizedale's artists-in-residence whose birthday it happened to be had rosebay willowherb; the director of the Wordsworth Trust had the daffodil, naturally; a local beekeeper had honeysuckle; a herbalist friend had violet; the palynologist from Kew Gardens had bog asphodel; Rob Kesseler had ribwort plantain; a writer on Dorothy Wordsworth had red campion; the current Slade Professor at Oxford, a Ruskin scholar, had Scots pine; my plates had gold and yellow Welsh poppy; the Grizedale director had sheepsbit scabious, and the head gardener at Brantwood had daisy. An interesting mixture of people and plants.

Throughout the banquet the sun provided a spectacular display. Sinking into deep orangey reds and pinks, it spotlit different parts of the hills and cast deep shadows which softened as the afterglow enveloped the scenery and contrasted with the sky. A discreet team of helpers somehow managed to prepare my menu alfresco, and as though from nowhere our dishes emerged at a leisurely pace. It was rather like Prospero's feast in which the spirits materialise a banquet out of the air, except that fortunately our banquet was not whisked away. We started with a host of golden breads scattered with nuts and poppy seeds dipped into a sauce made from oil and wild herbs; a platter of tiny delicacies including one of my specialities: ceviche of wood pigeon served with caramelised shallots, tiny toasts with grilled local soft cheese, marinated trout, wild leaves such as wood sorrel and wild garlic, and beetroot. Before the next course we enjoyed a reading from Wordsworth's *Prelude* ('Fair seed-time had my soul, and I grew up/Fostered alike by beauty and by fear'). Our next dish contained a creamy wild mushroom soup full of exciting dusky forest flavours.

After this, a reading from Dorothy Wordsworth's Grasmere journals of 1801 in which she speculates whether the seeds of the daffodils that inspired her brother's famous poem had perhaps been swept over the lake. The next dish belonged to the lake far below: Coniston char is a variety of Arctic char, highly prized and uncommon, whose taste and firm texture is not unlike trout; it had been grilled over an open fire and served with a clear sauce containing rowan berries for astringency. Next came a roasted saddle of sika venison from the forest, served with plump damsons baked in honey, a carrot purée with wild garlic leaves chopped into it, half a roasted pear filled with onion marmalade, and creamy dauphinoise potatoes. The sauce was made of wild brambles and venison stock, not too sweet.

By now it had become quite dark; the first stars emerged and candles were brought to table by the invisible spirits. In the flickering light we listened to an aptly chosen reading in which Ruskin addresses his privileged Slade students and reminds them of the moral and social obligations of an artist. Writing from his home in Camberwell in April 1870, he describes his garden: 'The air was perfectly calm, the sunlight pure, and falling on the grass through thickets of the standard peach ... and of plum and pear trees, in their first showers of fresh silver, looking more like much-broken and far-tossed spray of fountains than trees; and just at the end of my hawthorn walk, one happy nightingale was singing as much as he could in every moment.' Ruskin is aware of the ominous city noises, and knows that he can only appreciate his serenity because he had

been long able to spend a large sum annually in self-indulgence, and in keeping my fellow creatures out of my way.

Of those who were causing all that murmur, like the sea, round me, and of the myriads imprisoned by the English Minotaur of lust for wealth, and condemned to live, if it is to be called life, in the labyrinth of black walls and loathsome passages between them, which now fills the valley of the Thames, and is called London, not one could hear, that day, any happy bird sing, or look upon any quiet space of the pure grass that is good for seed.

... And now, gentlemen, I beg you once and for all to understand that unless you are minded to bring yourselves, and all whom you can help, out of this curse of darkness that has fallen on our hearts and thoughts, you need not try to do any art-work, – it is the vainest of

affectations to try to put beauty into shadows, while all the real things
that cast them are in deformity and pain.

Some fireworks cracked and rumbled on cue in the far distance, sat-
ellites traced their measured way across the sky – the nearest we would
come to man-made things in our peaceful arbour. It was not difficult
to appreciate our privileged surroundings and the magical quality of
the occasion. Our final course descended from the darkness: a fruit
compote with apples and damsons, blackberries and cherries.

Conversations ebbed and flowed; ideas swirled around and cross-
pollinated, skipped from table to table, eddied up into the air to mingle
with the dancing gnats . . . The gardens at Brantwood are to be laid out
as in Dante's *Divine Comedy* – should the car park be hell? . . . Art in the
context of a forest environment . . . What would Ruskin have made of
performance art in Grizedale forest? . . . The correct way to dispose of
a cherry-stone at table should you be at New College, Oxford . . .
The 1790 *Flora Danica* inspiring an 1,800-piece table service of Royal
Copenhagen Porcelain, every piece hand-painted . . . An inspiration to
Rob Kesseler . . . Ruskin cut up his volume and gave the sheets to his
students . . . Has the climate changed from when the Wordsworths'
daffodils grew? . . . The dates of their flowering are different now . . .
According to Osgood MacKenzie, another nineteenth-century gardener, strawberries ripened a full month earlier at the beginning of the
nineteenth century compared to the end . . . Ruskin's consternation
about pollution and its effect on nature . . . Keats' descriptions of stormy
weather which was caused by the fallout from a volcano erupting some
three years previously . . . The weather (ah, always the weather) in the
Lake District is supposedly unique, 'an island outside Britain' like
Prospero's island.

With the vague feeling that we had perhaps become the subjects of
a sorcerer's happy spell, our banquet drew towards its close. Strangely,
although few of the participants had particularly studied the elements
of a feast, nevertheless the event contained all the right components:
delectable food, stimulating conversation, impressive tableware, a spectacular setting and entertainment. At the end came tiny sweetmeats,
some made of honey and pine sap, others little aniseed pastilles flavoured with orange and violet, just like the comfits so popular at
sixteenth-century banquets. And, echoing memorable past feasts, we
were given gifts: a tiny jar of honey from the beekeeper, a delicious

Brantwood apple from the gardener, an art book from the artist-in-residence, a little torch to light our way back through the forest, and, as at the best banquets, we were allowed to keep our individual printed table napkins. One by one we dispersed into the warm night. The theatrical quality of the night's experience was enhanced by the steady curtain of rain that fell the next morning, obliterating all views with swirling mist as I trudged round Ruskin's garden gathering autumn leaves.

23

Burns Supper: feasts of fraternity, and men behaving badly

Great lords have their pleasures, the people have fun.
MONTESQUIEU

Depending on your viewpoint, Burns Night represents a robust appreciation of the honest values of ordinary people, Scottish kitsch at its worst, Freemasonry, or the racier elements of the gentleman's club. Robert Burns' poetry has universal appeal, both because of its egalitarian attitude and also because his writing expresses aspects of male behaviour that may not be condoned but are certainly both enjoyed and emulated. In any case, Burns Night is widely, joyously and noisily celebrated in more countries than any other poet could dream of. Russians are particularly enthusiastic; a combination of proposing toasts with much heartfelt socialist poetry and emotional singing is clearly irresistible.

Although Robert Burns was an inveterate womaniser, he also had pronounced social and political views. Sanctimonious establishment figures who gained satisfaction from oppressing the common man's natural exuberance were astutely satirised in Burns' verses. Conscious of the plight of working people, his own family included, Burns nevertheless had the romantic's admiration for a vagabond's perceived freedom. 'A fig for those by law protected! Liberty's a glorious feast!' goes the refrain in *The Jolly Beggar*. A supporter of America's fight for liberty as well as for the fundamental aims of the French Revolution, his egalitarian beliefs were spelt out in his song 'A man's a man for a' that', and he would no doubt have been gratified to know that his vision was eventually enshrined in both countries' constitutions.

The idea that all men are equal is at the core of modern Freemasonry, a movement originating in seventeenth-century Scotland.[1] The

---

1 This statement usually arouses incredulity but Professor David Stevenson's two books, *The Origins of Freemasonry* and *The First Freemasons* cite evidence which is difficult to refute.

Freemasons modelled their organisation on medieval masons who, because they had to move from one town to another to work on building sites, could not form closed town guilds like other trades. Instead, temporary lodges used for accommodation during the construction of a building (which could last for decades) became their 'closed shop'. Secret signs and passwords were simply a way of making sure that an uninitiated mason did not enter the lodge. By the sixteenth century, however, these lodges had either declined or disappeared entirely and there appears to be no overlap between them and the new style of Freemason lodges. The Freemasons' revival of the original masonic preoccupation with mathematics, architecture and ancient Egyptian wisdom suited the Renaissance mind perfectly, and the adoption of secret signs and passwords meant that they, too, could travel around and still be accepted as bona fide Freemasons. Protestantism was surprisingly tolerant of these emergent secret rituals, apparently regarding them as a safe outlet for people whose yearnings for ceremonial in church worship had been thwarted. Freemasonry's claim to stand for morality without religion removed it from being an open threat to the Church, even though there was some concern at its secrecy.

Equality being its fundamental tenet, it is no surprise that Robert Burns embraced this brotherhood enthusiastically. By the end of his short life he was a member of no fewer than five Masonic lodges and there is little doubt that, had it not been for the considerable help given to him throughout his career by fellow Masons who guaranteed publication of his first book of poems and eased him into elite Edinburgh circles, Burns would have remained unknown. But one could argue that, despite their admiration for 'the Heaven-taught ploughman', these Freemasons had an unbalanced view of equality. One of their guiding principles was to help the less fortunate to better themselves and so take their place in society – but there are no records of an Edinburgh lawyer being helped into the honest profession of manual farmworker.

From his initiation into the local chapter of Tarbolton in Ayrshire in 1781 at the age of twenty-two, Burns rose through several degrees in the hierarchy and in 1787 was installed as Poet Laureate of Scottish Craft Freemasonry, a unique ceremony. In the painting by William Stewart Watson we see him surrounded by the accoutrements of Freemasonry and it gives the curious impression that Burns has been sanctified. As he stands there in front of the Grand Master to receive his laurel wreath, in a martyr's pose with hand on heart and eyes uplifted, he appears to have a plaid-covered halo. I mention this only because it illustrates what some people find disturbing about a closed society that conducts secret rituals; concealment breeds suspicion, and imaginations become overheated. Early Christians attracted similar disapproval from the wider community, who regarded their mysteries – only accessible to those initiated by baptism – with misgiving. Stories about eating the body and blood of Christ sounded to Roman ears alarmingly close to the cannibalistic abominations they imagined to be part of Dionysiac worship.

As anyone who has been initiated into a club will confirm, most of these ceremonies are harmless, if messy, events designed to make initiates appear foolish or subordinate; any secrecy has no more sinister function than to enhance the fun. Clubs of this type were (and still are) usually single-sexed; getting away from the constraints of a spouse was just as important as the club's supposed activity. Since most single-sex clubs are male, what they really amount to is a few hours away from the 'sullen sulky dame' who will complain about a 'blethering blustering drunken blellum' afterwards. For drinking and bawdiness are part of many an all-male gathering – they certainly were in Burns' time and are alluded to frequently in his work. The activities of such societies, including the Freemasons, were typical of their time. With brotherly love and liberty being fashionable sentiments for an Age of Reason, the eighteenth century saw an explosion of rumbustious male clubs throughout Britain. Most celebrated their masculinity with convivial drinking and initiation ceremonies and frequently with disreputable behaviour. Many adopted curious regalia (the Wig Club in Edinburgh, for instance, included a wig supposedly made from the pubic hair of Charles II's mistresses) and many ceremonies centred on phallic symbols such as pokers, which were addressed in place of God at an investiture. Were these young men reacting against the literary and cultural associations of the period, or aping Masonic ritual? Most likely both, but their conduct was probably no worse than young men in other eras intent on behaving badly. In London, gangs of young aristocrats (the Mohocks and the Hectors, for example) vandalised the city, and members of the She-Romps Club, having fortified themselves with liquor, would rampage around the streets and drag girls into alleyways where they were forced to walk upon their hands. Even nominally respectable societies like the Dilettanti were, according to Horace Walpole, no more than an excuse for getting drunk. White's and Boodle's were just two of dozens of London gambling clubs where fortunes were won and lost.

One of the most scandalous was the Hell-Fire Club, though its members preferred to be known as the Brotherhood of St Francis of Wycombe. It was founded by Sir Francis Dashwood, who also founded the Dilettanti Society. The club members (who included the Earl of Sandwich, John Wilkes and possibly even Benjamin Franklin, as a guest of Dashwood) met in the ruins of Medmenham Abbey on the Thames. The brotherhood was regaled with seductively named French dishes[2] and plied with drink before being unleashed on the 'nuns': prostitutes who had been primed into being eager participants in the debauch. After their activities were exposed they continued their revels in the chalk caves carved into a hill just outside the grounds of Dashwood's house at West Wycombe Park. The gardens of the house itself were an extraordinary piece of landscaping which, if viewed from ground level, appeared to be a pleasant park but from the height of a tower turned out to be a huge sculpture of a naked woman with appropriately placed thickets, and mounds topped with little red flower beds which, in their heyday, sprayed out chalky water. This perhaps explains a 'divine milk punch' that Wilkes mentions drinking inside the golden ball on top of West Wycombe church ('the best Globe Tavern I was ever in'). Dashwood's gardens, but not the caves, have recently been restored by the National Trust.

Robert Burns was a man of his age too; as well as enjoying the company of Edinburgh's literati, he had bouts of inebriation that led to many amorous as well as awkward moments. Apart from carousing with the Freemasons, Burns belonged to the Tarbolton Bachelors' Club and the Crollachan Fencibles, both of whom celebrated masculinity with drinking that was phenomenal even by eighteenth-century standards. He collected and wrote many bawdy songs for the Fencibles, full of ribald references, from 'I learn'd a sang in Annandale, / Nine inch will please a lady' to wanton accounts of thinly veiled tails, notably 'Tam-o'-Shanter', a classic story that begins with comrades carousing in the pub. It develops into a voyeuristic fantasy[3]

---

2 In resolutely sticking to exotic French names for his dishes, Dashwood was distancing himself from the current English preference for plain dishes.
3 Tam was ogling a young witch whose shift (sark) was too short (cutty) to dance with any modesty.

in the kirkyard, reaches a predictable end in which Tam escapes his just deserts and comes out unscathed to win the reader's sympathy, and concludes with the cocky rejoinder to 'Remember Tam-o'-Shanter's mare'[4] who, with Tam's wife Kate, bears the brunt of his escapades.

'But to our tale,' as Burns said, or rather to the feast. Every year impressive tonnages of 'the chieftain of the puddin' race' are shipped out to overseas devotees of haggis and 'neeps',[5] to be washed down with that other essential for Burns Night: nips of whisky or *uisquabae* with which the bard and the haggis are toasted. The atmosphere at Burns Suppers varies considerably. Some are homely affairs in a village hall; others are learned academic gatherings; more robust suppers take place in the pub. Most are organised by clubs, associations, choirs, and legions of Burns societies the world over and, like the pointed jokes in a local pantomime, the speeches are especially gratifying to their target audience. A few are expensive occasions with celebrity chefs producing exotic versions of the 'hamely fare' which constitutes a Burns supper menu; it is not difficult to imagine the sort of verse Burns would have written about those. Some resent outsiders taking over the event: Hugh MacDiarmid's 'A Drunk Man Looks at the Thistle' sums up their view: 'You canna gang to a Burns supper even/Wi'oot some wizened scrunt o' a knock-knee/Chinee turns roon to say 'Him haggis – velly goot!'/and ten to wan the piper is a Cockney.' Although plenty of mixed suppers do take place now, still the majority are male-only events; 'exuberant' behaviour is much more fun without women, who were admitted rather grudgingly to Burns Suppers only in the nineteenth century. After a hundred years the female role remains a minor one. A recent attempt to arrange for a female colleague to go to a Burns Supper at short notice demonstrated that the choice for ladies can still be very limited. A man's a man for a' that, but a lassie isna, though I rather think that Burns would have allowed her in. He even wrote a poem called 'The Rights of Women', though the third right, that of 'dear, dear admiration', betrays its tone.

One dank January night I went to a Burns Supper which represented all that was best about these occasions. I was the guest of John and

---

4 The witch Cutty Sark cut off her tail.

5 Neeps is short for turnips. In Scotland, turnips have golden-orange flesh and a sweet flavour. Those with white flesh have a slightly bitter tang and are called swedes. In England, confusingly, the orange roots are called swedes and the white ones turnips. On the basis that Swedes are blond, it seems to me that the Scottish version is more logical. Unfortunately, supermarkets throughout the country have adopted the English version, so do take note if preparing a Burns Supper.

Kate MacSween whose family is now into its third generation of haggis-making. John is a member of the Kevock choir, whose supper was to be held at Dalhousie Lodge 720 in Bonnyrigg. We met at their factory outside Edinburgh, where the boilers had finally been washed out for the year, having produced 120 tonnes of haggis and neeps during the last month. The MacSweens awaited news of the final consignment's safe arrival in some distant country. Once that was resolved, we sped off to Bonnyrigg bearing two huge insulated boxes containing several enormous steaming haggises. The MacSweens have mastered the art of boiling haggis without bursting the skin; others have been less successful. John Jamieson, in his *Etymology of the Scottish Languages*, has the following solution under his entry for 'Haggies': 'A very singular superstition, in regard to this favourite dish of our country, prevails in Roxburghshire, and perhaps in other southern counties. As it is a nice piece of cookery to boil a haggis, without suffering it to burst in the pot, and run out, the only effectual antidote known is nominally to commit it to the keeping of some male who is generally supposed to bear antlers on his brow. When the cook puts it into the pot, she says; "I gie this to – such a one – to keep." ' The entrance to the masonic hall was tiled in embossed masons' symbols, but there was no time to ask about those as the haggis had to be manhandled into the tiny kitchen from which billowed steam and the promising perfume of neeps. The hall was painted light brown and was packed full of cheerful people. Long trestles were arranged in traditional fashion with a raised high table. Fragments of Freemasonry, a revolving mirrored ball and a reproduction portrait of Burns in his regalia served for decoration; other more secret items were screened off.

Burns suppers are unusual for celebrating food which is con-spicuously ordinary: haggis, neeps and mashed potato amount to no more than a humble Scots winter meal. Most celebratory dinners aim to use the most luxurious ingredients that can be afforded, but Burns made a point of praising simple peasant food for its unpretentious wholesomeness.[6] So our supper followed the traditional modest pattern: the cock-a-leekie soup had no prunes this year as some people complained about them last year; next year no doubt the prunes will be back. Bagpipes announced the ceremonial entrance of the haggis,

---

6 Two hundred years later, some of our most expensive chefs have embraced simple peasant dishes now that peasants are more likely to aspire to chicken tikka masala.

Gentlemen at dinner: the toast, 19th century engraving.

John MacSween recited 'To a Haggis' while he expertly slit open the huge glossy pudding with his dirk, and everyone toasted it with a dram of whisky. A brightly coloured Scotch trifle and Dunlop cheese with oatcakes completed the meal. It was followed by the traditional sequence of convivial toasts and responses, songs, playing of the clarsach and tale-telling.[7] The singing of 'Auld Lang Syne' is a final reminder of the origin of the Burns Supper, which is thought to have been based on Freemason Harmony Boards: fraternal meals taken after lodge meetings and finished with the linking of hands. Afterwards we spilled back out into the dark, damp air with that particular euphoria which only comes with a simple, though uplifting shared experience. It must have been fraternity.

---

7 A toast 'To the Immortal Memory of Robert Burns' is a speech which should contain as many Burns quotations as possible, neatly tailored to its audience and current events. It is an honour to be asked to deliver this toast. This is followed by a toast 'To the Lassies'; its tone will depend on whether or not there are ladies present. In any case, it is meant to point out their shortcomings from a male view. The lassies' response is normally replied to with good-humoured revenge. Unless women form part of the music and singing afterwards or have been chosen to accompany the haggis procession, this is the only part women play in the formal proceedings. The clarsach is the ancient small Celtic harp which is held on the lap. It used to be the instrument which provided the music at feasts at the Scottish courts. Since its revival in the twentieth century it is generally played by women.

24

Eating people: cannibal feasts

Different countries, different fashions, and, in like manner, different gods.

TAU CHIEF, 1840

Only certain instances of cannibalism are relevant to this book. Those occasioned by hardship or famine, by political extremists or by psychopaths occur but cannot be construed as feasting. Nevertheless, eating people in a loving or ritual way – which in some cases also included communal enjoyment – played a crucial part in maintaining some cultures' community. Sometimes it also served to control or frighten. One notion common to several cannibal rituals is that by eating someone you assimilate some of their character. This theory may not be as far-fetched as it sounds: after all, scientists have suggested that primitive life forms such as flatworms may be able to acquire skills (such as finding the way through a maze) from eating another flatworm which has learned this skill.[1]

Control through fear was a major reason behind Aztec cannibalism in Mexico. When the Spaniards invaded in the early sixteenth century, some oppressed Aztecs regarded the conquest as an opportunity to rebel against a terrifying regime whose universe was based around the sun and the moon, both created by the self-sacrifice of two gods. The all-important and life-giving sun was associated with warrior castes and Aztec kings, who believed it necessary to make human sacrifices at regular intervals in order to ensure that the sun continued to rise every day. Quetzalcoatl (the Plumed Serpent), god of the winds, the war god, and several gods of fertility, rain and crops also required

---

1 Nothing to do with biology is that simple: ways of ingesting vary greatly, and the human gut tends to digest material more thoroughly than more primitive organisms. Creatures such as flatworms can regenerate by joining together the single cells of more than one worm. It is also likely that they can ingest molecules of another worm without destroying them in the digestive process, and so theoretically the learned ability could survive to regenerate in the new flatworm. Human babies can gain immunity from their mother's milk because a baby's gut does not destroy the molecules of the necessary bacteria, but as far as we know, the adult gut does break down molecules and so human knowledge or characteristics are unlikely to be able to survive the process.

appeasement by human sacrifice – sometimes involving children – to prevent the collapse of ordered life. The Aztec warrior, therefore, devoted much of his effort to procuring prisoners from his enemies to provide sacrificial material. If there were not enough prisoners, then slaves and other disadvantaged people were used instead. As well as pictorial texts created by the Aztecs themselves to describe their rituals, there are contemporary accounts written by Spanish priests who lived in the Aztec communities and learnt their language. Victims were given a fortifying drink of chocolate mixed with the blood of previous sacrifices before being dragged up by their hair to the top of the Great Temple. There they were cut open, and their still-beating hearts plucked out[2] and offered to the god. The blood was collected and the bodies were thrown over the parapet or down the steps to the chapel for dismembering and distribution according to rank. According to some reports hundreds, even thousands, of people could be sacrificed in a day and enormous feasts were prepared with the flesh afterwards; these practices were an integral part of the rituals of war. The Aztecs had a pragmatic approach to the body, and as long as the sacrificial victims were from an inferior caste such as prisoners or slaves their carcasses were simply commodities: useful sources of religious offerings, of food for ceremonial feasting, of trophy skulls to frighten opponents, of skin and bones for making both everyday and ritual artefacts; in fact, they received very much the same treatment as animal carcasses.

Brutal though these sacrificial descriptions are, they need to be considered in the context of their time. The *conquistadores* who professed to be so shocked at Aztec customs had come from a country where torturing and burning infidels alive during the Spanish Inquisition was commonplace. Clearly it was the consumption of human flesh they found abominable rather than the cruelty beforehand, which is interesting because the Catholic Church upheld the doctrine of transubstantiation. This is the actual (rather than symbolic) transformation of communion wafers and wine into the real body and blood of Jesus ready for consumption by the devout Christian cannibal. Indeed there was understandable confusion over this issue, and others to do with meat-eating in general. On the one hand, since all meat is a gift of God, to actively reject it as food was considered heretical by

---

2 Supposedly this was a metaphor for plucking a corn cob from its husk (corn had godlike status), though in most societies the norm would be to pluck the corn from the cob as a metaphor for plucking out the human heart.

some. On the other hand there were those who believed that eating meat led inexorably to lust and savagery of the worst kind: in a word, cannibalism. The Catholic missionaries who gradually converted the Aztecs found it very difficult to stamp out covert sacrifices and cannibalism; a succession of laws in the first half of the sixteenth century indicates that the old ways persisted. Clearly, superstitions surrounding the fertility of vital crops were deeply rooted. It took great faith to reverse Quetzalcoatl's teaching and risk crop failure; after all, the reality of a human corpse is much easier to grasp than that of transubstantiated bread and wine, which, even if it has turned into Christ's flesh and blood, still looks just like bread and wine.

The Hua of New Guinea did not especially want to be cannibals but thought they had to eat *nu* – a vital essence which was the source of all fertility and growth – in order for their children, animals and crops to remain prolific. Thus a man had to eat his dead father and a woman her dead mother (never the man his mother or the woman her father) as part of a continuum that perpetuates the bodies and spirits of their ancestors. In slightly similar vein, as part of their funeral rites the Yanomami in Venezuela would grind the cremated bones of their relatives into a powder and add it to a soup made of plantain. Small amounts of the powdered relative would be reverently consumed at subsequent memorial events, and this was regarded as a loving and intimate way to keep in touch with the deceased. I remember a fascinating interview with Salvador Dalí in which he revealed that he and his wife had made a pact that whoever died first should be eaten by the survivor as the supreme act of love; he confidently pronounced that it would be the subject of a great and joyous feast. Some time after Dalí's wife died, I heard him give another interview in which he confessed that he could not bring himself to keep his vow. Different countries, different gods indeed. In finding himself unable to break such a strong taboo, Dalí turned out to be more of a conformist than he wanted the world to believe.

So strangers are eaten to placate the gods who control life through fertility, relatives are eaten to stay close to them. There is also cannibalism as a means of taking over and/or annihilating another person's spirit. This justification for eating foes was used in parts of North America and throughout much of Polynesia, most notably in Fiji.

For some Native Americans, torturing, killing and then feasting on an enemy fulfilled a curious function which was accepted by both the

Comment les sauvages rotissent leurs enemis. From André Thevet's *La Cosmographie Universelle*, 1575.

perpetrators of the act and their victims. The Huron believed that if a relative was killed in a war, one of the enemy's people had to atone for the death by taking the spiritual place of the dead relative. At the same time, they also believed that the feelings of vengeful anger expressed in their dreams could be dangerous if not acted out and neutralised during this ritual killing. Consequently the victim was often horribly tortured, although his captors were courteous and even kind to him. It was the role of the victim to 'die well' and with dignity, thereby enhancing the status of his own people as well as giving his captors the opportunity to ingest his strength and stoicism afterwards.

In the Fijian islands, cannibal feasts were held not merely to acquire the spirit of an enemy but to annihilate it – the worst possible fate for the victim and for his tribe, particularly if he was their chief. Fijian culture was founded on ancestor worship, of which human sacrifice was a fundamental part because the ancestor god was fed on human flesh through a living intermediary. As with the Aztecs, many different ceremonies demanded a human sacrifice: the dedication of a war canoe, the celebration of a victory, the creation of a temple, the installation of a new chief. Again as with the Aztecs, individuals had to be procured to serve this need. Anyone outside the tribe was fair game: prisoners, conquered people, slaves, visitors from the outside world, could all be used as a *bokola* or offering. During Fiji's ferocious wars, the killing of the enemy was merely the first step; bringing back the bodies for consumption was by far the most important part of the operation, and desperate battles were fought in order either to capture an enemy body or to regain the captured bodies of fellow tribesmen.

It was believed that the spirit of the deceased stayed in the body for four days after death, so all *bokola* had to be consumed within that period. The ceremony surrounding the feast was considerable, the captured bodies being first painted and then propped up in the long-boats to resemble the warriors they once were. Once the captors were back at their village, dancers would deride the captive dead and praise the returning heroes. The triumphant warriors also performed dances with their war clubs, and then the *bokola* were offered to the gods and dismembered with great care and according to an exactly prescribed sequence. The joints were roasted in a large pit oven; sometimes pieces were wrapped in banana leaves to form a cylindrical parcel, the euphemistically named 'long pig'. The *i sigana* – the choice parts reserved for the gods – were taken to the spirit house and fed to selected chiefs and the *bete* (priest), who ate his portion on behalf of the war god. The remainder was distributed among the rest of the clan. A chief was a potential god; if he could manage to enter the spirit world without being consumed by a neighbouring tribe, he turned into a *kalou* or ancestor spirit, a source of power who was able to direct his tribe in warfare for ever. Previous *kalou* were represented on earth by the *bete*, so both he and the chiefs had to be ritually fed. Food for the gods was taboo and could not be touched. Instead the ceremonial diners were plied with sacrificial offerings on curious forks called *i saga* which were so designed that the food never touched their bodies. Once the *bokola* had been eaten, their bones were treated similarly to those of animals[3] since their spirits had now been annihilated along with their flesh.

Unfortunately, although early explorers were more than willing to seek out cannibals and to report their discoveries in often lurid ways,

---

3 They were made into everyday tools.

most were at pains to express disgust at what they had found. Their censure became further justification for conquest, and for condemning whole societies to oblivion without an attempt to understand these undoubtedly unusual rituals. For most societies find cannibalism profoundly disturbing. Just as early advocates of vegetarianism were adamant that eating any kind of meat would lead inexorably to cannibalism, so it seems that much of the dismay surrounding BSE and its transformation to human variant CJD stems from the notion of 'forcing vegetarian animals to eat meat and become cannibals', even though many ruminants routinely eat their own placentas and sometimes, indeed, other animals.[4] The origin of the closely related disease, *kuru*, found among the Fore tribe in Papua New Guinea has been traced to their funeral rites, which involved ceremonial handling of the deceased's brain and possibly its consumption as well (the practice died out in the 1950s and there seems some doubt as to whether cannibalism actually did take place). Once again, it was the possibility of cannibalism as well as the apparent vindication of those who preached that cannibalism leads to madness and death which fascinated people so horribly. Even as a highly ritualised feast it seems that, for the majority of us, eating people is still wrong.

---

4 I and several others have observed cattle and deer occasionally eating rabbits, and a scientist noted how deer on the island of Rum used to lie in wait for Manx shearwaters returning to their burrows so they could kill them with a blow from their hooves and then eat them. Reindeer living near the coast also commonly eat fish given to them by herders.

25

A feast on horseback

Men are generally more careful of the breed of their horses and dogs
than of their children.

WILLIAM PENN, 1693

Apart from an uncorroborated account that I once read of Brahmins
who apparently bathed their sacred cows in sandalwood water, adorned
them with rose garlands and bhindi and served them an eighteeen-
course banquet, feasts in honour of animals seem to be few and far
between. A horse dinner is as near as I could get. Sometimes people
are inspired to extravagant gestures by reading ancient accounts, and I
wondered if this one could have been inspired by an occasion in
England in 1535 when, as the Coventry City Annals record, 'Also this
yeare the Dukes of Richmond & Norfolke came to Coventry & were
honourably receaued of the maior & Citizens in there liueries & had a
banquett in ye streete one horsebacke'.

The photograph and details of the modern event were sent to me
by an American friend whose father, Frank Vincent Burton, is the
gentleman to the right of the steps turning round to face the camera.
Burton's host was Cornelius K. G. Billings, one of the richest men in
America at the time. His wealth came from being president of the
People's Gas Light and Coke Company; with it he built a huge mansion
on his newly acquired Manhattan estate, complete with an exclusive
driveway cut into the side of the cliff to allow access from Riverside
Drive. Billings was also an art connoisseur, but above all he was a man
with a passion for horses, especially racehorses, and was affectionately
known as the American Horse King.

Although he had stables at three other locations, he seems to have
been most pleased with those he built at Manhattan in 1903; they cost
him $250,000. The turn of the century was an era of outlandish parties
and Billings' reputation as a host was legendary. On 28 March 1903, to
celebrate the imminent opening of his new stables, he invited thirty
members of the New York Equestrian Club to a horse dinner for which

Horseback dinner at Louis Sherry's restaurant, New York, 1903.

he hired the ballroom on the fourth floor of Louis Sherry's restaurant in Fifth Avenue. The entire dinner was held on horseback. Billings' own horses, being racers, were too skittish to be used for the event so thirty more placid steeds were hired for the occasion. One by one they were hauled up to the fourth floor in the freight elevator, where a pastoral scene had been prepared for them. The walls had painted backdrops and in the centre of the circle of horses was a clump of bushes containing, apparently, real birds which twittered away throughout the proceedings. The right-hand wall panel had a jaunty harvest moon, and stars made from festoon lamps twinkled overhead. The floor was turfed, very wisely, with shaggy grass-like material, and sets of mounting blocks were arranged in a circle with two horses between each one.

Attached to the pommel of each horse's saddle and firmly secured to the animal's flanks was a tray table with a crisp linen covering. The guests, smartly turned out for their equestrian meal, were each assigned a mount by the waiters who were dressed as grooms in scarlet coats and white breeches. A number of real grooms were available to hold the horses' heads. Billings' elevated dining companions enjoyed a fourteen-course meal. Although the menu for this occasion no longer exists, it would have been similar to, though probably more lavish than, one offered to the Corn Exchange Bank of New York for its fiftieth anniversary meal only two months previously. The bank's guests ate their way through '*Huitres; Potage Ambassadeur avec olives, radis, celeri & amandes; Aiguillettes de Bass, Rayes Dieppoise; Selle d'Agneau Richelieu; Jambon de Virginie aux Epinards; Canard Canvasback avec Hominy & Celeri Mayonnaise; Glace Fantaisie; Gateaux; Fromages; Fruits; Café.*' The wines were Laubenheimer, G. H. Mumm's Selected Brut 1892, Romanée 1881, Apollinaris and liqueurs.

Billings' guests, however, drank champagne throughout their meal, perhaps owing to the unorthodox setting and the difficulty of serving other wines. Suspended from the horses' shoulders were two saddle-bags stuffed with ice-buckets and champagne which the guests suckled through nippled rubber tubes. A fourteen-course meal would undoubtedly help to mop up two bottles of champagne apiece and save you from falling off your mount – drinking champagne through a straw makes it more effervescent and therefore more quickly intoxicating. After the meal a vaudeville show was laid on to amuse the guests while the horses were being lowered back down to ground level. They ate oats throughout.

26

Midwinter feasts:
light in the darkness

I have often thought, says Sir Roger, it happens very well that
Christmas should fall out in the Middle of Winter.

JOSEPH ADDISON

Midsummer madness is a more common phrase than midwinter madness, which is curious because there is far more unruly behaviour, more desperate overeating and drinking when nights are long and cold, and almost every culture has some ritual to mark the winter solstice. The purpose of these midwinter festivals is to banish darkness and cold (death) and reawaken life, so lights, fire, dance, noise,[1] greenery, warming food and drink are common features. These are coupled with feelings of pride and regret, and a good dose of carnival spirit to bridge that disconcerting period between the old year and the new, when Janus the two-faced Roman god looks both backwards and forwards. It is a time when ghosts are abroad and animals can have the magic power of speech. Once, on a snowy New Year's night, I witnessed a mouse, cornered, standing up on his hind legs to shriek a challenge at our cat. The cat stayed his pounce and the mouse went free.

European midwinter celebrations are a mishmash of ancient festivals, scooping up the remnants of Roman Saturnalia and Nordic Yule, and combining them with innumerable New Year revelries, bean feasts and Mithraic sun-worship rites. Many of these customs, like Santa Lucia, Sweden's feast of lights, were incorporated into the Christian festivals of Advent, Christmas and Epiphany. Almost everything to do with Christmas tradition is of pagan origin: the Christmas tree is a pagan evergreen, as is the holly that symbolises Christ's blood and

---

1 One of my most vivid childhood recollections of New Year's Eve is of pulling open our huge sash windows at midnight to listen to the ships' foghorns booming down on the Clyde – a haunting, disharmonious pagan sound.

crown of thorns; the twelve days of Christmas reflect the twelve days of Roman revelries; candles echo the Roman gifts of lamps and oil given to ward off darkness. The Saturnalia embodied the notion of equality because Saturn's mythical Golden Age was supposedly so egalitarian that there were no slaves and no need for private property. During the Roman revels, normal social structures were upturned in order to redress the balance, and servants were allowed to mingle with their masters for a glorious but brief period. Rumbustiously, they exploited this to the full by dressing up as goat-men and devils, gambling and getting drunk on wine, much in the manner of carnival. The Saturnalian master–slave reversal still exists in the British army, where a variety of traditions are still upheld. Most regiments have a Christmas dinner at which the commanding officer and other senior officers serve all the other ranks, right down to the youngest troopers and privates. And on the last working day before Christmas, the officers of one regiment do the rounds at reveille and serve the unmarried soldiers tea (laced with a drop of rum) in bed.

The notion of those in authority handing over control at the winter solstice was evidently appealing, since it continued in various guises from Roman times. In Britain, a Lord of Misrule and sometimes an Abbot of Unreason were chosen by lot and given free rein during the extended Christmas period to run amok and collect 'rents' so that they could lay on entertainments for their 'subjects'. In the Feast of Fools on 1 January, the medieval Church had instituted a custom whose original aim was to instil humility in the highest echelons of the clergy by requiring them to hand over their power briefly to the lowest. It was not long before the lower orders took advantage of the concession by extending their period of licence backwards to Christmas and burlesquing the Church's most solemn rites. So many attempts were made to curb these antics that they clearly caused as much offence as merriment. One complaint from Paris in 1495 describes priests and clerks 'wearing masks and monstrous visages at the hour of office' whilst running and leaping through the church, dancing in the choir dressed as women, eating black puddings at the altar and burning old shoes to make stinking mock incense. Other accounts allude to demon-worship and the throwing of mud during services, so that the congregation 'dissolved into disorderly laughter and illicit mirth'. Nevertheless, although such activities were frowned upon, some cathedral inventories included costumes for the Feast of Fools, suggesting a degree of tolerance. As adults misbehaved, responsibility was delegated to children and a choirboy was chosen to assume the role of bishop. His duties included taking services, even occasionally conducting a mass, and leading a procession round the parish to collect money for laying on a feast in honour of the Holy Innocents on 28 December. Small wild birds like woodcock, plover and snipe were typical fare for this occasion. Miniature vestments were provided by the cathedral, and by all accounts the boy bishops were generally well behaved and greatly loved, fulfilling their duties diligently and occasionally making a well-deserved profit from their efforts.

Throughout this long period, Christmas itself was overshadowed by pagan carnivalesque, partly because Christmas had never been one of the Church's great festivals. If there was to be celebration and feasting, it took place on Christmas Eve, leaving Christmas as a day of quiet churchgoing. Most European countries still have their most important meal on Christmas Eve, though it is a 'fasting feast' since fish, rather than meat or poultry, is the centrepiece. The Tudors, of course, celebrated it in style with much food and good cheer, the Stewarts following suit with masques and feasts, particularly at the more popular occasion of Twelfth Night, where the Bean King's jovial role was similar to that of the Lord of Misrule. Like the Feast of Fools, the custom was absorbed in medieval times from France; and when Christmas feasting was banned by the Puritans, Twelfth Night revelries, being secular, clung on. After the Restoration fashionable people's appetite for Christmas diminished, and the Age of Enlightenment preferred more restrained celebrations. Luckily, however, the less fashionable and country people kept to some of the old traditions; and when they were ripe for resurrection in the nineteenth century, the inclusive Christmas meal and the Twelfth Night cake – last vestiges of bygone merry-making – were revived.[2] Many nineteenth-century engravings illustrate Twelfth Night cakes which, containing a bean and bearing quaint character cards for playing charades, were far more prominent symbols than any Christmas cake.

Queen Victoria and Prince Albert, eager to promote the large family unit, were instrumental in reviving the idea of Christmas. Pictures of

---

2 The *galette du roi*, containing a golden bean, is still eaten throughout France on Twelfth Night. It is a rather dry cake, so needs copious amounts of dessert wine or spirit to wash it down. The person who gets the slice with the bean is the Bean King. This method was one of the ways in which the Lords of Misrule were chosen.

the royal Christmas tree spangled with candles were reproduced in magazines, and accounts of the happy family gathering influenced a public ripe for this type of sentiment. The writings of Charles Dickens emphasised everything that we now regard as being part of an authentic Christmas: the ghost story and the giving of charity, both wrapped up neatly in *A Christmas Carol*; Christmas carols themselves, eagerly researched from archives and country folk; roast goose, to be superseded by stuffed turkey whose size made it more suitable for the large Victorian family; Christmas cards; the wassail bowl; childish party games and dreadful cracker jokes; the flaming Christmas pudding, surely a relic of the fifteenth-century fruit pottage soused in spirit and set forth flickering; and the revival of Snapdragon, a table game where a bowl of raisins was covered in brandy and set alight so that people could risk dipping their fingers into the flames to reach the plumped fruit. Messrs Pickwick, Wardle, Jorrocks and company provided the model atmosphere for the warmest, merriest Christmastide possible. As 'Boz' (Dickens) wrote in 1836, 'A man must be a misanthrope indeed in whose breast something like a jovial feeling is not aroused – in whose mind some pleasant associations are not awakened – by the occurrence of Christmas.'

The swallow: excessive food at Christmas, George Cruikshank, undated, 19th century. The Saturnalian spirit of reversal: food and drink throw themselves down the gullet of a gargantuan figure.

As the Industrial Revolution drew people off the land away from their roots and their families, a nostalgia for the perfect past – a pristine Christmas experience – arose; and despite curmudgeons who, like Ebenezer Scrooge, deplore displays of jollity, there is still a yearning in many people for something they left behind: their childhood, their innocence, perhaps; simple, homely places and people whose remembrance has been dimmed by a different kind of life. Kenneth Grahame, in *The Wind in the Willows*, captures this sentiment perfectly. The Mole, relishing his exciting new life with Ratty, suddenly catches a whiff of his old home and is overcome with longing for its familiar dinginess. After a splendid banquet of sardines, captain's biscuits and German sausage washed down with mulled ale and a 'board set thick with savoury comforts' shared with a group of young field-mice out carol-singing,

> The weary Mole also was glad to turn in without delay, and soon had his head on the pillow, in great joy and contentment. But ere he closed his eyes he let them wander round his old room, mellow in the glow of the firelight that played or rested on familiar and friendly things which had long been unconsciously a part of him, and now smilingly received him back, without rancour … He saw clearly how plain and simple – how narrow, even, – it was; but clearly, too, how much it all meant to him, and the special value of some anchorage in one's existence. He did not at all want to abandon the new life and its splendid places, to turn his back on sun and air and all they offered him and creep home and stay there; the upper world was too strong, it called to him still, even down there, and he knew he must return to the larger stage. But it was good to think he had this to come back to, this place which was all his own, these things which were so glad to see him again and could always be counted on for the same simple welcome.

27

Feasts for the dead: conquering fear

Let us eat and drink; for tomorrow we die.
I CORINTHIANS, 15: 32

Mexico is well known for vibrant colour, but at the end of October, during the lively crescendo that culminates in Días de Muertos, Mexican street markets surpass themselves. The senses are assaulted by masses of brilliant perfumed flowers, scented arrays of ripe fruit, heaped baskets of fiery chillies, vegetables of every possible colour, cacao beans by the sackful, and containers of sweets, their contents spilling out generously under the awnings. There are *alfeñiques* (figurines and medallions moulded out of cacao and maize pounded together with eggs and spices), there is every imaginable shape and size of fancy bread, there are toys, clothes, bundles of candles, pots and pans, bales of cloth and heady incense: in short, everything necessary to provide several days of feasts blazing with colour and pungent with spices. And all this is because everything must be renewed in preparation for honouring the souls of dead relations when they are cheerfully and hospitably welcomed back into the homes of the living.

Los Días de los Muertos, the Days of the Dead, are focussed on 1 and 2 November, the feasts of All Saints and All Souls; but, as might be expected, they are a fiesta that combines indigenous Aztec rituals with Christian ones imported when the Spaniards colonised Mexico in the sixteenth century. All Saints and All Souls were welcomed enthusiastically by the Mexicans, who identified them with two of their own principal feasts which celebrated the Aztec version of life arising out of death. For children there was the Little Feast of the Dead or Offering of Flowers; and for adults there was the Great Feast of the Dead or Fruit Falls. Much to the chagrin of the Church these offerings started to be made at Todos Santos, and there followed a steady integration of the two cultures' celebrations until they merged in a colourful riot of feasting, of which more later.

The Mexican attitude to death could not be more different from our

Mexican Days of the Dead cartoon, anonymous, Mexico, 19th century.

Western secular one. Our own dread of death has not gone away, but we seem to handle it mainly with denial which, it could be argued, only serves to increase people's fear. In the past, though, some people were so anxious to give themselves a really good funeral that their families were left struggling to pay the bills for a funeral feast that was often more lavish than the deceased's wedding had been. The occasion is, after all, a last opportunity to impress your peers who may judge and remember you accordingly. For the same reason, wealthy people left bequests of food to poor people or prisoners, and sometimes they paid for a second celebration thirty days later, known as a 'month's minding'.[1] Those who could not afford such largesse sometimes left provision in their will for the employment of a 'sin-eater'. The antiquary John Aubrey described such an event in 1687:

> In the County of Hereford was an old Custome at funeralls to have
> poor people, who take upon them all the sinnes of the party deceased.
> One of them I remember lived in a cottage on Rosse-high way, he was

---

[1] Similar commemorative events happen elsewhere. In Greece, forty days after a funeral, *kolyva* (a special dish made of soaked grains and seeds, honey, spices and basil) is offered to passers-by and churchgoers by the dead person's family. The association of the pungent smell of basil with death – it was supposed to grow at the entrance to the Underworld – means that basil is rarely used in the Greek kitchen. Jamaicans hold a 'ninth night' nine days after a death when family and friends gather to comfort the bereaved. Songs of hope are sung, usually accompanied by a small percussion band, and traditional foods are served with coffee, rum punch and mugs of hot, spicy chocolate.

a long, leane, ugly, lamentable poor raskal. The Manner was that when
the Corps was brought out of the house and layed on the Biere; a Loafe
of bread was brought out, and delivered to the Sinne eater over the
corps, as also a Mazar-bowle of maple (Gossips bowle) full of beer wch.
he was to drinke up, and sixpence in money, in consideration whereof
he took upon him (ipso facto) all the Sinnes of the Defunct, and freed
him (or her) from walking after they were dead.

Another account, as late as 1825, notes that sin-eaters still existed;
shunned and feared because of their association with evil spirits, they
lived isolated from the community and were only sought out after
a death. When the ceremony had been performed, the sin-eater's
contaminated bowl and platter were burnt. Communal versions of sin-
eating, where no single person had to bear the burden, often involved
a cup of wine being passed over the coffin, either to the mourners, or
to groups of poor people in return for gathering flowers for the burial.

Aubrey's vision of an unhappy spirit wandering the earth with the
potential to wreak havoc is unsettling, and in many countries superstitions and feasts have evolved to keep the dead under control. Chinese
culture is very hospitable towards ghosts and wandering spirits. The
festival of the Hungry Ghosts dates back to the first century AD when
Buddhism was first introduced, and is held to appease the spirits of the
unhappy dead: those who have drowned or died far from home, or
who have no family to perpetuate their memory. A hungry spirit could
seize a living body so must be placated with food. Because this is a
Buddhist tradition, the offerings are always vegetarian. But the Chinese
have a strong sense of enjoyment, so in some regions the festival of the
Hungry Ghosts also involves making huge towers (up to ten metres
high) out of *baozi*, which are ghostly white sticky-rice buns with a red
blob of bean paste in the centre. These towers are assailed by hordes
of young men trying to be the first to reach the top bun. The other
spirit festival, Dong Zhi (the arrival of winter), takes place at the winter
solstice since spirits are busier during long dark evenings. A great
banquet is laid out on the table before the ancestral altar[2] and the spirits

2 As well as an altar to the kitchen god, every Chinese home has a shrine to the ancestors, who are a
major part of their culture. For this reason, old people are very much respected and cared for since they
will soon become ancestors. Food is offered to the ancestors before the main feast at New Year, and in the
spring there is an outing at Qing Ming (it means pure and clean) to the family tomb to tidy it up, followed
by a picnic, also shared with the ancestors. The Japanese, too, have a great respect for their ancestors, as
did the ancient Greeks, who evoked the glory of past heroes through religious rites.

are respectfully invited to join the family at table; empty places are left for them. This ceremony over, the family can enjoy its feast. Amongst the tempting array of dishes, the northern Chinese feast always features *huntun* – a word deriving from chaos, which describes the beginning of the Chinese world. *Huntun* (or *wonton*, to use the better-known Cantonese name) are thin sheets made out of flour, water and egg wrapped round a stuffing, usually of pork and prawn, and then simmered in broth to make a light bite-sized dumpling. *Wonton* means swallowing clouds, and indeed they do look rather like clouds as they float in their clear broth.

To people in the West, ghosts are more likely to conjure up images of Hallowe'en – the night before All Saints' Day – yet another example of a Christian festival being tacked onto an existing pagan one. Samhain, to give it its Druid name, was originally a solemn rite of passage into the spirit world of winter. Modern Hallowe'en games like ducking for apples and the sticky-bun race have their origins in the Celtic ordeals by water and fire which, via the talisman of the apple tree, gave admittance to the land of the Silver Bough: that other world whose chosen people can foretell the future. The ordeal by fire[3] originally employed a rod with an apple at one end and a lighted candle at the other. The rod was hung on a rope and spun round; you had to try to bite the apple without being burnt. This custom has been replaced by the safer if messier sticky-bun race. Hallowe'en made its way over to America with Scots and Irish emigrants; from there it came back to Europe, having lost most of its frightening and sacred overtones and degenerated into a jolly children's festival[4] of skeleton masks, sweets and money. In Italy, crisp little biscuits called *ossi dei morti* (bones of the dead) are made to be eaten at All Souls. Made from ground nuts and sugar bound with flour and egg white, they are formed into bones, arms and noses, and sometimes into beans, in which case they are called *fave dei morti*.

Although All Saints' and All Souls' Days are not holidays in Britain, they are celebrated in many parts of Europe. Cemeteries in Spain are still thronged with people paying respects to their dead, a tradition going back to Roman times when families took food out to their

---

3 Such ordeals play an important role in Mozart's *The Magic Flute*.
4 I notice that in France, however, the witches adorning the streets at *La Toussaint* look considerably more saucy than scary. Clearly they are intended for adult enjoyment.

ancestors' graves to share a picnic with them.[5] Which brings us neatly back to Días de Muertos in Mexico where, in the days around All Saints and All Souls, all the family graves are visited, cleaned and decorated with flowers, sometimes with a little canopy as well, and many an open-air feast is held in the cemetery. Paths of scented petals lead from the grave to the house so that the spirits can find their way to and from the feast which has been prepared for them. In every home the family makes an *ofrenda*, a personalised shrine dedicated to its forefathers. Photographs of deceased relations are surrounded by yellow and orange marigolds (the flower of the dead), copal incense, candles and elaborately frilled decorations. As at Dong Zhi empty places are left at table for the spirits, who are offered clothes and other presents and invited to feast on whatever used to be their favourite food and drink when they were alive. When the spirits have had their fill of the feast by absorbing its essence, the family settles down to eat.

As often as not, you will find a cup of chocolate amongst the offerings. Chocolate is everywhere in Mexico but tends to be relished as a drink rather than as confectionery. Whisked to a hot froth, fragrant and peppered with spices, it is refreshing and invigorating, and tastes quite unlike the insipid, over-sweet chocolate drunk in Europe and North America. Market traders sell more cocoa beans around Días de Muertos than at any other time of the year, for chocolate is also one of the many ingredients of *mole*, the essential Mexican celebration salsa. Family recipes are handed down from generation to generation; some recipes have up to thirty ingredients, no two are the same, and each recipe is the best in the world. It is an immensely complex sauce requiring the individual preparation of chillies, nuts, seeds, fruit, spices, starches and chocolate before they are all pounded to a paste in a heavy stone *metate*. The paste is diluted with broth and cooked and then cooked again until it acquires the right degree of dark, mysterious thickness. The most popular way to serve *mole* at a feast is with *guajolote* (turkey) or red rice or beans, a favourite combination at Días de Muertos. If *mole de guajolote* is not served, then the most likely substitutes are *barbacoa* (slow-roasted lamb cooked overnight in a pit lined

---

5 The families opened up the graves to share their meals and they were occasions of great merriment. In the fourth century, Augustine disapproved of these obviously pagan practices – perpetuated by early Christians because they were such fun – but found that 'a mass of pagans who wished to come to Christianity were held back because their feast days with their idols used to be spent in an abundance of eating and drinking'.

with maguey leaves) or *carnitas* (pork cooked in its own fat with oranges and garlic). The feast continues with a succession of *enchiladas*, *chalupas* and *tamales*: these are concoctions of meat or vegetables or sometimes sweet fillings which are wrapped in maize dough (maize is another time-honoured Mexican staple), some are then wrapped in maize husks or banana leaves before being steamed or baked. There are also fancy breads, biscuits and sugar figures, and there is fruit, both candied and fresh; the latter is also made into thick, sticky pastes – a great favourite. This is all washed down with beer or *atole* (made from maize), and with strong spirits like *pulque* and *tequila*. In some households there will be a tiny table laid for the spirits of children who, in the manner of their Aztec forebears, are supposed to arrive at the feast before the adults; to provide for them, market stalls are full of miniature ceramic pots looking like toys for dolls.

If this festival sounds macabre, it is certainly not morbid, for the Mexican regards death as part of life.[6] In the words of Octavio Paz, the Mexican 'frequents it, mocks it, caresses it, sleeps with it, entertains it, it is one of his favourite playthings and his most enduring love.' And he turns it into a fiesta. The essence of Días de Muertos is its jollity, its carnival atmosphere, dominated by one of its most amusing hallmarks: armies of irreverent little skeletons that scamper crookedly into every part of the celebrations. They may be seen capering in a baker's shop to advertise *los panes de muertos*. Or they may take the form of articulated puppets and grinning paper cut-outs, or pop up as lurid sugary sweets or gesticulating papier-mâché figures, staring vacuously as they mimic everyday human activities. Skeletons can be seen playing football, watching television, smoking, drinking, dancing, making love, anything you like. The device originated in Europe where, in the fifteenth century, skeletons appeared as a *memento mori* during carnival and Lent (see chapter 10). Días de Muertos has removed the menace of the imagery, though, and the irrepressible Mexican skeleton pokes fun at human vanities whilst his living countrymen embrace their loved ones' souls with warmth.

---

6 '*Es una verdad sincera que solo aquél que no nace, no llega a ser calavera,*' runs a Mexican song, 'Truly, only the one who is never born will never become a skull.'

28

Swansong at Hogmanay:
a feast for the millennium

Hogmanay – the Scots word for New Year – seems to be a fusion, or possibly confusion, of *aguillanneuf*, from an old French Druid cry,[1] and the northern word *hoggu-nott*, meaning slaughter-night, since large quantities of cattle were killed in preparation for the great New Year's Day feasts. Hogmanay is the main winter festival in the Protestant North, particularly since John Knox banned the keeping of Christmas in the seventeenth century. Christmas was not made an official holiday in Scotland until 1958, whereas New Year is a two-day affair. As the idea of Christmas was gradually absorbed from England, so Scotland repaid the compliment with Hogmanay which birled down southwards in a cheerful alcoholic roar. Now the whole country celebrates New Year, and never more so than at the turn of the second millennium. The prospect drew forth warnings that the end of the world was nigh, and as though to prove them right, tempests ripped through northern Europe. Commerce went into overdrive as commemorative wine, food, music and trinkets were marketed and many tonnes of fireworks stood ready to be detonated. Some people, weary of the protracted build-up, decided not to celebrate the millennium at all. But, having discovered the efforts people used to make to celebrate momentous events, I thought it churlish not to make a feast – a surprise event where even family members would know only small details. The splendour of historical feasts would clearly be unattainable working single-handed, but I wanted to attempt something memorable for a dozen friends.

Preparations started months ahead, with learning the art of folding napkins from a Portuguese waiter. Silver and glass tableware, cloths and dishes were accumulated. The crucial question, though, was what to serve as a centrepiece. A year beforehand we had by chance been

---

1 According to Jamieson's *Etymological Dictionary of the Scottish Language*, the Druids are supposed to have cried, 'À gui! l'an neuf!', but the transformation does sound a little far-fetched.

given a small flock of female black swans by the artist Ian Hamilton Finlay, who wanted rid of them because they were fouling the lawn in his sculpture garden at Little Sparta. An idea began to form: if wild white swans are protected then perhaps I could breed black swans for the feast. A handsome cob was bought. Unfortunately his ungrateful consorts harried him off the pond into the jaws of a fox, who clearly relished this unusual treat because shortly afterwards he ate all the females as well. So the black-swan feast was not to be, but some months later a different opportunity arose and this is what happened instead.

For the first course I chose vegetable consommé for its simple, clean taste. It is easy to make: a selection of chopped vegetables was roasted and simmered to extract their essence. Clarifying with beaten egg white takes much longer with vegetable broth than with that made from meat or fish, and the liquid needed reducing to intensify its flavour before I added sherry and lemon juice to finish. I cut twos from sliced carrot and zeros from bulb-fennel stalks sliced crossways so that the date 2000 swirled in the clear golden soup.

The fish course consisted of many dozens of whitebait, dusted in spiced flour, deep-fried till crisp and served on a bed of spicy salad leaves and halves of sweet cherry tomatoes drizzled with oil. To go with this, each guest shared with his neighbour[2] a porcelain ramekin containing a yin–yang of bright green tangy watercress salsa and char-coal-coloured caviar. The combination of dusky-flavoured whitebait with its sharp and salty accompaniments turned out to be one of the gastronomic highlights – it achieved *umami*, the state of perfection in food combinations.

Before enjoying these flavours, however, my unsuspecting guests were subjected to the re-enactment of a story in Alexandre Dumas' *Grand Dictionnaire de Cuisine*. A full account is given on page 54, but in brief, the host of a competitive dining club wondered how to make best use of two huge sturgeon his servant had procured. He decided thus: the smaller sturgeon, beautifully decorated and flanked by musicians and kitchen assistants, was carried round the table for the guests to admire. As they retired to serve the fish, disaster struck. A bearer tripped and the whole lot crashed to the floor, to the guests' despair. But the host remained calm, quieting the tumult with 'Serve the other

---

2 The sharing of dishes between pairs of neighbours was usual practice at banquets until the seventeenth century.

one;' whereupon the larger sturgeon (weighing 85 kg/187 lb) was brought in with even greater decorations, pomp and ceremony, to the applause, admiration and gastronomic relief of the company.

My whitebait version relied on quantity (140, twice) rather than size: five fish at a time were skewered onto cocktail sticks to make dozens of small fan shapes. The first batch was cooked and heaped onto a decorated platter which was carried round the table by my elder daughter, the only person to be party to this secret. Everyone had a dish of watercress sauce and caviar and was anticipating the crisp whitebait. Everyone could see how much trouble I had been to. So they were aghast when my daughter engineered the *faux pas* and the pretty fish fans slithered to the floor. An uncomfortable silence reigned as she went off in disgrace to fetch a brush and shovel. And the relief was palpable when she returned, beaming, with the second dish, presented this time on an ornate silver salver holding many more whitebait fans surrounded by far more elaborate and delicious decorations. Perhaps the release of tension provided an extra component that produced *umami*.

Course three also contained surprises. A swan or a peacock in full plumage, borne in between courses as a soteltie, was a favourite medieval feasting treat.[3] Swan used to be esteemed for its excellent flavour, but since the plan to rear black swans failed I had yet to taste it. Some months later, a friend who works with wildlife revealed that he had the sad and regular task of dispatching swans that had crash-landed onto wet roads thinking they were rivers. The carcasses were usually incinerated. So I asked if he would reserve for me the next dead swan that looked fit to eat. In due course a large package arrived and the plan commenced. Although I had plucked, skinned and boned many a waterfowl before, I had never skinned a bird with a view to keeping its plumage. I found it a delicate task but not difficult; a taxidermist would have done it in half the time. Remembering the fifteenth-century instructions, I dusted the inside of the skin liberally with ginger and nutmeg.

Swans and peacocks were presented in a number of ways. Sometimes the skin was simply stuffed and dried, which meant it could be stored and used again. The bird was often carried in on a grand board,

---

3 At Henry V's coronation feast there was a procession of thirty-one swans, roasted and decorated with messages all praising the new monarch.

its beak stuffed with a wad of cloth soaked in spirits and set flaming. Sometimes it was placed on top of a huge pie. The greatest *tour de force* was to cook the skinned carcass first by simmering then by finishing it off on the spit; once it had cooled a little, the feathers and skin were quickly sewn back over the cooked meat, the head and neck were secured by a rod, and the apparition was carried in to everyone's delight. Whilst contamination was not inevitable, the possibility of it must have been quite high – but medieval digestions coped with far more than modern ones can. Judging by my swan's feet and the thickness of its sinews, I decided it was not young and would therefore not be suitable for roasting. A huge pie would be more appropriate, so while the meat marinated I set to work on the plumage. First, a wire-netting cage to stitch the unwieldy skin onto; the interior was lined with foil. A swan's neck is extremely strong, and to obtain the correct curvature I followed the old instructions but used heavy-duty wire instead of a rod. A few stitches secured the neck and wings in the right attitude: swimming. Some touching-up with hydrogen peroxide was necessary to clean the feathers, then I gilded the beak with real gold leaf and tidied round the edge with black paint. Two black beads made very convincing eyes. During the reconstruction I was humbled by the beauty of this creature. I was conscious of the strength of its wings and of its neck, and of what a marvellous piece of design it was. I thought of the contrast between a swan's strength and its ethereal beauty as it swims, neck gently curving, head demurely cast down. Though saddened by this bird's untimely death, I was pleased with my work because I had made it beautiful again and had learnt a lot.[4]

The swan soteltie was carried in on a large foil-covered board, its beak glistering, a golden crown on its head and a silver necklace round its throat. Everyone became excited by this very large spectacle. Bulky though swans are in the context of a private dining room, there is surprisingly little room in the cavity of the carcass so only a very small raised pie could be concealed inside it. Following ancient directions,

---

4 The progress of this feast had been followed by the Guild of Food Writers. I was asked to write an account of how I had managed the various events, but in explaining the technicalities of reconstructing the swan I wrote – perhaps clumsily – that I 'thrust a double piece of high-tensile fence wire down its gullet'. This provoked outrage in a few members, who described the event as repellent, unsavoury, even cruel. Fortunately these views were in the minority; the rest leapt to my defence. The bird was, after all, not alive and I was trying to convey the difficulty of the operation. But it was a lesson learnt that not all those involved in matters as practical as food preparation want to think about reality or the the distinction beteen life and death.

this pie was a fake: it had been baked 'blind' with oatmeal that was emptied out after baking to leave the pie hollow. It had pastry hinges set into its lid with a small pastry swan as a handle, and written in pastry was the message 'LIFT THAT SWAN'. This disappointingly small pie was presented to a guest with the explanation that lifting a swan is the correct medieval term for carving it, and would he please do the honours. As soon as he lifted the lid, two jack-in-the-box springs jumped out; simple surprises like that still make people laugh even after a thousand years.

But it was time to eat once more, and the real raised pie was more satisfying. The swan had yielded about 2 kilos (4½ lb) of dark lean meat, so I added that of a wild goose since the flesh is almost identical. Duck fat and wild-boar belly acted as lubrication, for wild goose and swan meat is almost fatless. The mixture marinated for a couple of days in wine, almond oil and spices. Then I cut the best swan meat into long, thin strips, pounding all the rest into a paste so that the resulting slices formed a pâté studded with pieces of identifiable swan meat. The lid had a crowned pastry swan swimming along, sculpted around a fine metal armature which left the neck rather fragile till it was cooked. The huge pie mould was lent by a music-historian friend who asked for the swan's leg bones in return; apparently Neolithic people used them to make flutes. Now weighing 4 kilos (9 lb), the pie would need about eight hours to cook so I settled down to other seasonal jobs, listening to the sizzle with great pleasure. An hour later the sizzle fizzled out. The stove had run out of oil and the snow was five inches deep outside. The awful implications of this sank in gradually. My pie had started to cook and the juices were running, so the baking could not now be stopped without ruin. No other stoves had ovens big enough to accommodate my pie. A replacement swan was out of the question. It would be days before more oil would be delivered. Disaster had struck the core of my feast. At this point my neighbour turned up. Although her oven was too small for the great pie, she knew that some newly arrived people had a stove like mine. Moments later we were in her car, inching slowly over the snow as the partially cooked pie was carefully and secretly transported a mile downhill to a piping-hot oven. The heroic new neighbour even offered to get up in the middle of the night to remove the pie when it was cooked. I began to appreciate Benjamin Franklin's remark, 'Fools make feasts, wise men eat them.'

To go with the pie we needed some medieval colour so, in recognition of the recently reinstated Scottish Parliament, mashed potatoes were made into a shallow flag-shaped dish to resemble the saltire. Its background was made from Blue Congo potatoes, which have deep blue flesh, and the white cross was made from mashed celeriac. A carrot-and-orange purée and bright green spinach completed the palette. The excitement over the swan and pies, however, resulted in the other items cooling, so this course was not as gastronomically satisfying as it should have been even though the temperature must have been authentically medieval. We enjoyed it much better heated up on subsequent days.

Before two dessert courses there was a cheese board containing farmhouse English Cheddar, the famous Lanark Blue, soft Cooleeny from Ireland, a hard Spanish *manchego*, and a runny Coulommiers from a street market in France. Home-made oatcakes had been cut into little stars and crescents. The dessert, made by my younger daughter, was refreshingly tangy. She brushed filo pastry with butter and baked it into undulating layers. Many passion fruits were sieved and the pulp made into a sweetened reduced purée. The pastry layers were filled with cream mixed with crunchy passion-fruit pips, and drizzled with the purée. The '*Deux Millefeuilles*' were dredged with snowy icing sugar and strewn with twinkling silver-coated almonds. A simple, tangy, crunchy, dessert.

In the Renaissance and Elizabethan periods, the word banquet referred to the final dessert course consisting of sweetmeats and a sweet spiced wine called hippocras. Entertainments were laid on as well and some sotelties of this period were edible. For our banquet, therefore, we had dried fruit and nuts with vintage port and a dessert wine from Hungary in a delicate glass flask with a leaping glass stag inside it. These wines glowed like rich jewels in the candlelight. Gleaming silver platters held sweetmeats whose shapes represented the number 2000. Twos were cut out of orange peel and crystallised, and the zeros were made of sugared almonds, round chocolates and *calissons d'Aix*, which are iced sweetmeats made in Provence out of ground almonds and fruit pulp; they would have been recognised by any Elizabethan.

Besides the sweetmeats and wine there was a final subtlety for the company's amusement. Sitting in the middle of the table throughout the meal was a white hart (symbol of renewal) made of pastry with a sword sticking out of his breast and a resigned expression on his face.

This reconstruction was the one that had puzzled me most. It was just one small part of an elaborate soteltie described by Robert May in *The Accomplisht Cook* of 1660. May was a chef and his descriptions are far more lucid than many of his contemporaries'; evidently he had made or supervised this impressive construction himself. This passage includes the instructions for making pies with live birds in them. At the end is a wistful comment, making it clear that although the book was published after the monarchy was restored, Cromwell's Puritan reign had put an end to many such spectacles as this. May wrote, apparently without stopping for breath:

Triumphs and Trophies in Cookery, to be used at Festival Times, as in Twelfth-Day, &c.

Make the likeness of a Ship in paste-board, with Flags and Streamers, the Guns belonging to it of Kickses[5] binde them about with packthred, and cover them with course paste proportionable to the fashion of a Cannon with Carriages, lay them in places convenient, as you see them in Ships of War; with such holes and trains of Powder that they may all take fire; Place your Ship firm in a great Charger; then make a salt round about it, and stick therein egg-shells full of sweet water; you may by a great Pin take out all the meat of the Egg by blowing, and then fill it with rose-water. Then in another Charger have the proportion of a Stag made of course paste, with a broad arrow in the side of him, and his body filled up with claret wine. In another Charger at the end of the Stag have the proportions of a Castle with Battlements, Percullices, Gates, and Draw-bridges made of Paste-board, the Guns of Kickses, and covered with course paste as the former; place it at a distance from the Ship to fire at each other. The Stag being plac't betwixt them with the egg-shells full of sweet water (as before) placed in salt. At each side of the Charger wherein is the Stag, place a Pie made of course Paste, in one of which let there be some live Frogs, in the other live Birds; make these Pies of course Paste filled with bran, and yellowed over with Saffron or Yolks of Eggs, gild them over in spots, as also the Stag, the Ship and Castle; bake them, and place them with gilt bay-leaves on the turrets and tunnels of the Castle and Pies; being baked, make a hole in the bottom of your pies, take out the bran, put in your Frogs and Birds,

---

5 A corruption of *quelquechoses*, i.e. something or other. Paste-board was a kind of stiff flour-and-water pastry used to make table-decoration sotelties like this. It was not designed to be eaten.

and close up the holes with the same course paste; then cut the Lids neatly up, to be taken off by the Tunnels:[6] being all placed in order upon the Table, before you fire the trains of powder, order it that some of the Ladies may be perswaded to pluck the Arrow out of the Stag, then will the Claret wine follow as blood running out of a wound. This being done with admiration to the beholders, after some short pawse, fire the train of the Castle, that the pieces all of one side may go off; then fire the trains of the Ship as in a battle; next turn the Chargers, and by degrees fire the trains of each other side as before. This done, to sweeten the stink of the powder, let the Ladies take the egg shells full of sweet waters, and throw them at each other. All dangers being seemingly over, by this time you will suppose they will desire to see what is in the Pies; where lifting first the lid off one pie, out skips some Frogs, which makes the Ladies to skip and shreek; next after another Pie, whence comes out the Birds; who by a natural instinct flying at the light, will put out the Candles; so that what with the flying Birds, and skipping Frogs, the one above, the other beneath, will cause much delight and pleasure to the whole company: at length the Candles are lighted, and a banquet brought in, the musick sounds, and every one with much delight and content rehearses their actions in the former passages. These were formerly the delights of the Nobility, before good House-keeping had left England, and the Sword really acted that which was only counterfeited in such honest and laudable Exercises such as these.

Not knowing in what attitude Robert May made his stag, I made mine in a classic heraldic position, couchant with one leg bent forward – for stability, and so it would fit in my oven. I made a metal armature and some salt-crust paste, and settled down to three hours' sculpting; five years at art college helped this process. I made a metal plug to fit on the end of a tiny sword so that it would make a big enough hole to allow the wine to escape, and then fitted it into place in the stag's chest. Then I glazed him with egg white and milk and baked him for two days in a slow oven. The leverage of the sword (propped up with wine corks) made the construction extemely fragile, for the slightest crack would allow wine to escape. The greatest puzzle was how Robert May's stag had been made watertight with a sword sticking out of the

---

6 Tunnels are pastry funnels to let the steam out and for use as handles. They are also known as Bristols which, according to some sources, is rhyming slang (Bristol City = titty). Others maintain it is a corruption of bristles – the hog's hairs that surgeons left in a stitched wound to allow it to drain.

pastry; tantalisingly, he did not divulge his method. I concluded that the only way to do it was to glaze the cavity with egg yolk, twice over, in the hope that, once baked, it would form a kind of waterproof enamel and prevent the wine from staining the pastry. I made a little hole in his back into which the wine was poured through a funnel on the day, and afterwards disguised the hole with spare paste. And it worked. My younger daughter was asked to pull out the arrow and the wine really did flow 'as blood running out of a wound', pulsing like a heartbeat. A year later I saw an early eighteenth-century German engraving of instructions for decorating a pie with a pastry stag. The animal was in exactly the same position as mine. When I wrote to the librarian with this story, she told me she slipped my description into the book of engravings for someone else to discover one day. The stag now sits on the dresser in our kitchen, reminding us all of that strange meal, after which we lit a beacon on top of the hill and watched below us a mesmerising display of fireworks exploding all around, lighting up the darkness in thanksgiving for an old era and in hope for the future.

'Die Hirsch Pastet', Conrad Hagger, *Neues Saltzbergisches Koch-Boch*, 1719. The paste stag on Hagger's pie was in exactly the same pose as the author's; a satisfying end to the story.

29

Charlemagne's tablecloth:
a postscript

Every feast has its last course.
CHINESE PROVERB

The story of Charlemagne's asbestos tablecloth[1] was too intriguing to leave unresearched. The first clue came from Norman Travis, a retired minerals expert, who wrote that the Romans used asbestos sheets as winding cloths for their cremations so that the ashes could be recovered afterwards. He also provided a reference to the Greek geographer Strabo, who lived from about 64 BC to AD 45. Strabo wrote: 'In Carystus is produced also asbestos, which stone is combed and woven, so that the woven material is made into napkins, and, when these are soiled, they are thrown into fire and cleansed, just as linens are cleansed by washing.' Not long after, Pliny made the same observation, as Samuel Johnson's entry for asbestos in his *Dictionary of the English Language* reveals: 'Paper as well as cloth has been made of this stone; and Pliny says he has seen napkins made of it, which, being taken foul from the table, were thrown into the fire and better scoured than if they had been washed in water.'

So far, so good. Surely, as king of the Franks and Holy Roman Emperor, Charlemagne would have been educated in the classics and more than likely would have read Pliny's works? The *Encyclopaedia Britannica*, 11th edition, implied that Charlemagne could read Latin and Greek and, encouragingly, stated: 'Asbestos was formerly spun and woven into fabrics as a rare curiosity. Charlemagne is said to have possessed a tablecloth of this material, which when soiled was purified by being thrown into the fire.'

---

[1] The Emperor Charlemagne apparently had an asbestos tablecloth. He would impress his dinner guests by throwing it in the fire after the feast so all the crumbs would burn away and he could put it back on the table clean and white.

A Roman Noble 'Magician' casts his asbestos table cover into the fire. Leonard Summers, *Asbestos and the Asbestos Industry,* 1919.

A hunt for more sources led to a small book by Leonard Summers, published in 1919, called *Asbestos and the Asbestos Industry.* Mr Summers was an unashamed evangelist for the mineral, describing innumerable tragic deaths in theatre fires all over Europe which would have been avoided had asbestos been used. He wrote approvingly of Holkham Hall, 'the famous old Norfolk mansion, which enjoys a reputation for its fireproof construction, and has never been insured for the very good reason that *it will not burn!*' Then, complete with illustration, he describes the ex-Kaiser's 'portable asbestos cottage, in which he resided when taking part in military manoeuvres. It contained a reception room, the ex-Kaiser's bedroom, and bedrooms for the staff as well as a bathroom. The cottage required only three hours to erect. A pumping and filtering engine on wheels enabled water to be laid on with constant hot and cold supplies.' Mr Summers' enthusiasm for asbestos even extended to its virtue as a constituent of baking powder.

As far as ancient history goes, he writes in similar vein to the other authors:

> The form in which asbestos was used by the ancients was usually as a cloth, of rather coarse texture (probably hand-woven), for wrapping material of durable quality – such as that in which they buried distinguished personages. A specimen of this old-world fabric may possibly

still be seen in the Vatican, Rome. In his thirteenth-century travels, Marco Polo refers to a fire-resisting material, which he believed to be made from the skin of the Salamander – the little animal popularly supposed to be immune from fire – but which proved to be asbestos cloth.

A footnote underneath a drawing entitled 'A Roman Noble "Magician"' runs 'Prominent hosts – including Charlemagne – sometimes entertained and mystified their guests by committing their table covers (asbestos) to the flames.' Tantalisingly, none of these references give an authoritative source.

Whenever I am stuck for references on medieval or classical subjects I turn to my cousin Oliver Nicholson. He advised me to read two books, both entitled *Life of Charlemagne*, one written by Einhard the Frank and the other by a monk called Notker the Stammerer. Einhard's version is fairly modest and his style is supposed to have been heavily influenced by Suetonius' *Lives of the Twelve Caesars*. He clearly wished to present Charlemagne in a noble light and is at pains to point out how modest this illustrious person was in his personal habits, so there was no mention of tablecloths, asbestos or otherwise. Notker the Stammerer's account is full of lively stories illustrating the emperor's great wisdom and ability to astonish anyone he wanted to impress, sometimes by outwitting them, sometimes by his perceptiveness, sometimes by bravery and sometimes by displaying his enormous wealth. He describes Charlemagne, 'of all kings the most glorious ... standing by a window through which the sun shone with dazzling brightness. He was clad in gold and precious stones and he glittered himself like the sun at its first rising.'

The emperor even managed to impress a group of Persian envoys by making them wait till Easter for their audience, so that they could see him dressed in all his glory for the most important festival of the year. Usually, as chapter 2 points out, it was the rest of the world that was impressed by Persia. The ruse worked: 'Until now we had only seen men of clay, now we have seen golden men,' they said, and were apparently quite content to stay gazing at Charlemagne and his nobles for several days. The emperor's great banquet left them so impressed by its strangeness that they left almost hungry.[2] Surely this would have

---

2 This is a nice parallel to Chardin's account of the French ambassador's party being entertained in Persia in the seventeenth century. The display of wealth excited them so much that they 'fed apon the Admiration of the Magnificence of [the] Service' while everyone else busied themselves with the food.

been a perfect occasion for the tablecloth trick? But nowhere is it mentioned.

Further reading about the emperor revealed other stories and some facts, one of which was that, although he could speak Latin, Charlemagne had difficulty in reading it. Another is that, after he died, innumerable legends gathered around the memory of the great man. Increasingly frustrated, I consulted Oliver again; he told me that right on my doorstep I had an authority on Charlemagne: Donald Bullough, Emeritus Professor of St Andrews University. Clearly Oliver had decided to hold on to this gem until I had exhausted my own researches. In answer to my enquiry, Professor Bullough wrote: 'Alas! Charlemagne's "asbestos tablecloth" is the purest of pure myths, one of the many that were added to the ones inherited from the Middle Ages in the late eighteenth century and early nineteenth centuries, particularly in France – by-products of the Enlightenment and its Napoleonic reflections, as the "scientific" element in this one suggests. It isn't, in fact, in my file of "modern Charlemagne myths" which is both eclectic and voluminous!'

So ended my quest and the research for the first two sentences of this book. I couldn't help feeling a little bit flat. But at least I had made a small contribution to Professor Bullough's collection of myths. And time spent delving into books, like time spent with friends at the feasting table, is never wasted. 'When you sit at the table with your brothers, sit long,' wrote a Shi'ite imam, 'for it is a time that is not counted against you as part of your ordained lifespan' – a comforting thought. And as long as we remember that, I am confident that our feasts – modest or magnificent – will be remembered long after the more mundane parts of our lives have been forgotten.

BIBLIOGRAPHY AND SOURCES

1. What is a feast?

Beeton, Isabella, *Book of Household Management*, Ward, Lock & Tyler, London, 1868.

Dalby, Andrew, *Empires of Pleasure: Luxury and indulgence in the Roman world*, Routledge, London, 2000.

Dietler, M., & Hayden, B., *Feasts*, Smithsonian Institution Press, Washington, 2001.

Edgerton, March, *Since Eve Ate Apples*, Tsunami Press, Portland, 1994.

'Expositions Universelles', in *Public Eating*, Prospect Books, Totnes, 1998.

Graves, Robert, *The Twelve Caesars*, Penguin Books, London, 1957.

Hay, J. Stuart, *The Amazing Emperor Heliogabalus*, 1911.

Larousse Gastronomique, Paul Hamlyn, London, 1991.

Latham, R., & Matthews, W. (eds.), *The Diary of Samuel Pepys, a new and complete transcription*, Bell, London, 1976.

Soyer, Alexis, *The Pantropheon*, Simpkin, Marshall & Co., London, 1853.

Timbs, John, *Club Life of London . . .*, 2 vols., Richard Bentley, London, 1866.

Tschumi, Gabriel, *Royal Chef*, William Kimber, 1954.

2. Paradise: the origin of feasts

Particular thanks for advice on this chapter go to Margaret Shaida, who introduced me to Chardin's book as well as to the joy of Persian cuisine.

Chardin, Sir John, *Travels in Persia, 1673–1677*, London, Argonaut Press, 1927.

Levi, Primo, *If This Is a Man*, Penguin, 1979.

Mintz, Sidney W., *Sweetness and Power*, Penguin, 1986.

Perry, Charles, 'Elements of Arab Feasting', in *Feasting and Fasting*, Prospect Books, London, 1990.

Rawlinson, G., *History of Herodotus*, 1862.

Shaida, Margaret, *The Legendary Cuisine of Persia*, Grub Street, 2000.

Soyer, Alexis, *Soyer's Culinary Campaign*, G. Routledge, London, 1857.

Van Gelder, Geert Jan, *God's Banquet: Food in classical Arabic literature*, Columbia University Press, New York, 2000.

Wills, C. J., MD, *In the Land of the Lion and Sun*, Ward, Lock & Co., 1891.

3. The golden age: medieval feasting

Innumerable people have contributed to this chapter but I would particularly like to mention Gillian Riley, Oliver Nicholson and Bishopthorpe Palace in York, as well as many speakers at the Leeds Symposia on Food and History and the Oxford Symposia on Food and Cookery.

Anon., *Sir Gawain and the Green Knight*, tr. Keith Harrison, Oxford University Press, 1998.

Anon., *Two Books of Cookerie and Carving*, 1650.

Black, Maggie, *A Taste of History*, British Museum Press, London, 1993.

Blüchel, Kurt, *Die Jagd*, Könemann, Cologne, 1996.

Boscolo, R., & Savio, C., *The Great Book of Decorations for Buffets*, ISAC Étoile, Venice, 1995.

Bradley Martin, E. & C., *Run Rhino Run*, Chatto & Windus, London, 1982.

Bynum, Caroline W., *Holy Feast and Holy Fast*, University of California Press, 1987.

Chambers, E. K., *The English Folk-Play*, Oxford: The Clarendon Press, 1933.

Chaucer, Geoffrey, *The Canterbury Tales*, ed. A. K. Hiatt & C. Hiatt, Bantam, London, 1982.

Flandrin, J.-L., & Lambert, C., *Fêtes gourmandes au Moyen-Age*, Imprimerie Nationale, Paris, 1998.

Froissart, Sir John, *The Chronicles*, ed. G. C. Macaulay, Macmillan & Co., London, 1895.

Furnivall, F. J. (ed.), *The Babees Boke*, Roxburghe Club, London, 1868.

— *Feste for a Bryde*, Roxburghe Club, London, 1868.

— *The Forme of Cury*, c.1390, Roxburghe Club, London, 1867.

— *The Boke of Kervynge of Wynken de Worde*, 1513, Roxburghe Club, London, 1867.

— *The Boke of Nurture of John Russell*, c.1460, Roxburghe Club, London, 1867.

Gray, Patience, *Honey from a Weed*, Prospect Books, London, 1986.

Hammond, Paul, *Food and Feast in Medieval England*, Wrens Park Publishing, London, 1993.

Hartley, Dorothy, *Food in England*, Macdonald & Co., London, 1963.

Henisch, Bridget Ann, *Fast and Feast*, The Pennsylvania State University Press, 1976.

Holinshed, Raphael, *Chronicles: Richard II, Henry IV and Henry V*, Oxford, 1923.

La Marche, Olivier de, *Mémoires*, ed. H. Beaune and J. d'Arbaumont, 4 vols., Paris, 1883–88.

Jeanneret, Michel, *A Feast of Words*, Polity Press, Cambridge, 1991.

Kendall, Paul Murray, *The Yorkist Age*, George Allen & Unwin, London, 1962.

Kurath, Robert Lewis, *Oxford Middle English Dictionary*, University of Michigan Press, Ann Arbor, 1988.

Laroque, François, *Shakespeare's Festive World*, tr. Janet Lloyd, Cambridge University Press, 1991.

Laurioux, Bruno, *Le Moyen-Age à table*, Éditions Adam Biro, Paris, 1989.

Luard, Elisabeth, *European Festival Food*, Bantam Press, 1990.

Luke, Harry, *The Tenth Muse*, The Rubicon Press, 1992 (originally published 1954).

Mars, Gerald & Valerie (eds.), *The London Food Seminar*, Food, Culture, and History, 1993.

Markham, Gervase, *The English House-wife*, Wilson, London, 1649.

Mason, Laura (ed.), *Food and the Rites of Passage*, Prospect Books, Totnes, 2002.

May, Robert, *The Accomplisht Cook*, Nathaniel Brooke, London, 1671.

Mintz, Sidney W., *Sweetness and Power*, Penguin, 1986.

Montaigne, Michel de, *The Complete Works: Essays*, tr. Charles Cotton, J. Templeman, London, 1842.

Montanari, Massimo, *The Culture of Food*, Blackwell, Oxford, 1994.

Monteil, Amans-Alexis, *Histoire des Français des divers états aux cinq derniers siècles*, Paris, 1842.

Pullar, Philippa, *Consuming Passions*, Hamish Hamilton Ltd, London, 1970.

Rabelais, François, *Five books of the lives, heroic deeds and sayings of Gargantua and his son Pantagruel*, tr. Sir Thomas Urquhart of Cromarty, London, 1904.

Scappi, Bartholomeo, *Opera di M. B. Scappi: Cuoco secreto di Pappa Pio Quinto*, 1570.

Sitwell, Sacheverell, *Primitive Scenes and Festivals*, Faber & Faber, London, 1942.

Soyer, Alexis, *The Pantropheon*, London, 1853.

Stowe, John, *A Summarye of the chronicles of England*, Thomas Marshe, London, 1573.

Stowe, John, & Gairdner, James, *Three Fifteenth century Chronicles with historical memoranda by John Stowe . . .*, 1880.

Tannahill, Reay, *Food in History*, Penguin, 1988.

Vischer, Isabelle, *Now to the Banquet*, Victor Gollancz, London, 1953.

Warner, Richard, *Antiquitates Culinariae*, R. Blamire, London, 1791.

Wartburg, Walter von, & Bloch, Oscar, *Dictionnaire étymologique de la langue française* (10th edition), Presses Universitaires de France, Paris, 1994.

Wheaton, Barbara, *Savouring the Past*, Chatto & Windus, London, 1983.

Wilson, C. Anne, *Food and Drink in Britain*, Constable, 1973.

Winder, Simon, *Feasts*, Penguin Books, 1998.

4. Competitive feasts: disconcerting elements

My thanks to Richard Carmichael of Carmichael for recounting the story of James IV's feast. It was given at Carmichael in Lanarkshire, since James was having an affair with Carmichael's sister.

Boas, Franz, 'Ethnology of the Kwakiutl', *Bureau of American Ethnology: 35th Annual Report*, part 1, Washington, 1913–14

— *Contributions to the Ethnology of the Kwakiutl*, Columbia University Press, New York, 1925.

Dietler, M., & Hayden, B., *Feasts*, Smithsonian Institution Press, Washington, 2001.

Jonaitis, Aldona, *Chiefly Feasts: The enduring Kwakiutl potlatch*, University of Washington Press, Seattle, 1991.

Kazuko, Emi, *Japanese Food and Cooking*, Lorenz Books, London, 2001.

Lang, George, *The Cuisine of Hungary*, Atheneum Press, 1971; Penguin Books, 1985.

Morrison, Alick, *The Chiefs of Clan MacLeod*, Associated Clan MacLeod Societies, Edinburgh, c.1986.

Rain, Eden, 'A sumptuous meal: navigating the laws restricting wedding banquets of 14th-century Florence', Oxford Symposium paper, 2001 (in publication).

Runyon, Damon, 'A Piece of Pie', in *Guys and Dolls*, Penguin, Harmondsworth, 1956.

Warner, Richard, *Antiquitates Culinariae*, R. Blamire, London, 1791.

5. King Midas' last feast

Information for this chapter was generously provided by Patrick McGovern, archaeologist at the University of Pennsylvania Museum, and by Daphne Derwen, archaeologist and food historian.

Derwen, Daphne, 'A feast of gold', in *Gastronomica*, vol. 1, no.3, 2001.

More information can be found at

http//:www.upenn.edu/museum/Wine/wineintro.html.

6. Ingredients of the feast: fish

Barnes, D., & Rose, P., *Matters of Taste: Food and drink in 17th-century Dutch art*, Syracuse University Press, 2002.

Bynum, Caroline W., *Holy Feast and Holy Fast*, University of California Press, 1987.

Dalby, Andrew, *Empires of Pleasure: Luxury and indulgence in the Roman world*, Routledge, London, 2000.

— *Siren feasts: A history of food and gastronomy in Greece*, Routledge, London, 1996.

Davidson, Alan and Jane, *Dumas on Food*, Oxford University Press, 1978.

Davidson, James N., *Courtesans and Fishcakes*, HarperCollins, 1997.

Dumas, Alexandre, *Grand Dictionnaire de cuisine*, Alphonse Lemerre, Paris, 1873.

Hay, J. Stuart, *The Amazing Emperor Heliogabalus*, 1911.

Kurlansky, Mark, *Cod*, Jonathan Cape, London, 1998.

Lawson, John, *Modern Greek Folklore and Ancient Greek Religion*, Cambridge University Press, 1910.

Lissarrague, François, *The Aesthetics of the Greek Banquet*, tr. Andrew Szegedy-Maszak, Princeton University Press, 1990.

Luard, Elisabeth, *European Festival Food*, Bantam Press, 1990.

Mars, Valerie, 'Little fish and large appetites', in *Fish, Food from the Waters*, Prospect Books, Totnes, 1998.

Montaigne, Michel de, *The Complete Works: Essays*, tr. Charles Cotton, J. Templeman, London, 1842.

Murray, Venetia, *High Society: A Social History of the Regency 1788–1830*, Viking, 1988.

Paterson, Wilma, *The Regency Cookery Book*, Dog & Bone, Glasgow, 1990.

Pullar, Philippa, *Consuming Passions*, Hamish Hamilton Ltd, London, 1970.

Raphael, Chaim, *The Festivals: A History of Jewish Celebration*, Weidenfeld & Nicolson, London, 1991.

Riley, Gillian, 'Fish in art', in *Food in the Arts*, Prospect Books, Totnes, 1999.

Roden, Claudia, *The Book of Jewish Food*, Viking, London, 1997.

Shaida, Margaret, *The Legendary Cuisine of Persia*, Grub Street, London, 2000.

Soyer, Alexis, *The Gastronomic Regenerator*, Simpkin Marshall & Co., London, 1846.

Timbs, John, *Club Life of London . . .*, 2 vols., Richard Bentley, London, 1866.

Walker, Harlan (ed.), *Oxford Symposium on Food and Cookery, 1990: Feasting and Fasting*, Prospect Books, London, 1990.

Walker, Harlan (ed.), *Oxford Symposium on Food and Cookery, 1997: Fish, food from the waters*, Prospect Books, Totnes, 1998.

Wheaton, Barbara, *Savouring the Past*, Chatto & Windus, 1983.

Wilkins, John, *Social Status and Fish in Greece and Rome*, London Food Seminar, 1993.

7. Chinese banquets: an ancient food culture

My thanks to Beth McKillop and Frances Wood of the Oriental Department of the British Library for their corrections and helpful suggestions, and especial thanks to Deh-ta Hsiung, food writer, generous tutor, and enthusiastic ambassador for Chinese cooking and culture.

Chang, K. C., *Food in Chinese Culture*, Yale University Press, New York, 1997.

Cotterell, Yong Yap, *The Chinese Kitchen*, Weidenfeld & Nicolson, 1986.

Gavin, John, Private and business letter books from John Gavin, an engineer from Edinburgh in Hankow and Shanghai, 1863–4, British Library, Asia, Pacific and Africa Collections, private papers, MSS. Eur. C 871.

Hahn, Emily, *The Cooking of China*, Time Life International, 1969.

Hom, Ken, *The Taste of China*, Pavilion Books Ltd, 1990.

Hsiung, Deh-ta, *The Festive Food of China*, Kyle Cathie, London, 1991.

— *The Chinese Kitchen*, Kyle Cathie, London, 1999.

Ju Lin, Hsiang & Tsuifeng, *Chinese Gastronomy*, 1969, Nelson, London.

Luke, Harry, *The Tenth Muse*, Rubicon Press, 1992 (originally published 1954).

So, Yan-kit, *Yan-kit's Classic Chinese Cookbook*, Dorling Kindersley, 1984.

— *The Chinese Kitchen*, Kyle Cathie, London, 1999.

— *Yan-kit So's Chinese Cookery*, Walker Books, 1988.

Wood, Frances, *No Dogs and Not Many Chinese*, John Murray, London, 1988.

8. Ingredients of the feast: meat

Anon., *Sir Gawain and the Green Knight*, tr. Keith Harrison, Oxford University Press, 1998.

Arnold, Walter, *The Life and Death of the Sublime Society of Beef Steaks*, Bradbury Evans & Co., London, 1871.

Beeton, Isabella, *Book of Household Management*, Ward, Lock & Tyler, London, 1868.

Black, Maggie (ed.), *A Taste of History*, British Museum Press, London, 1993.

Castelvestro, Giacomo, *The Fruit, Herbs and Vegetables of Italy*, tr. Gillian Riley, Viking, London, 1989.

Chardin, Sir John, *Travels in Persia, 1673–1677*, London, Argonaut Press, 1927.

Cordain, L., et al., 'Fatty acid analysis of wild ruminant tissues: evolutionary implications for reducing diet-related chronic disease', *European Journal of Clinical Nutrition*, 2002.

Crawford, Michael, & Vergroesen, A. J., *The Role of Fats in Human Nutrition*, Academic Press, London, 1989.

Epstein, Jason, 'Burger heaven', *New York Times*, 9 June 2002.

Furnivall, F. J. (ed.), *The Boke of Nurture of John Russell*, c.1460, Roxburghe Club, London, 1867.

Lang, George, *The Cuisine of Hungary*, Penguin Books, Harmondsworth, 1985.

Le Jeune, P., *Relation de ce qui s'est passé en la Nouvelle France ...*, S. Cramoisy, Paris, 1634.

Llewelyn Davies, Margaret, *Life as We Have Known It*, Hogarth Press, 1931.

Masson, L. R., *Les Bourgeois de la Compagnie du Nord-Ouest*, Quebec, 1889, cited in *The North American Buffalo*, by F. G. Roe.

Montanari, Massimo, *The Culture of Food*, Blackwell, Oxford, 1994.

Roe, Frank Gilbert, *The North American Buffalo*, University of Toronto Press, 1951.

Soyer, Alexis, *The Pantropheon*, Simpkin Marshall, London, 1853.

Topsell, Edward, *The History of Four-footed Beasts and Serpents ...*, London, 1658.

Varro, Marcus, *De Re Rustica (On Agriculture)*, William Heinemann, London, 1960.

Walker, Harlan (ed.), *Oxford Symposium of Food and Cookery, 1990: Feasting and Fasting*, Prospect Books, London, 1990.

Warner, Richard, *Antiquitates Culinariae*, R. Blamire, London, 1791.

9. Feasting in adversity: enhancing the ordinary

Brunet, G. (ed.), *Mémoires-journaux de Pierre de l'Estoile*, Paris, 1875–96.

Cherry-Garrard, Apsley, *The Worst Journey in the World*, Constable & Co., London, 1922.

Dickens, Charles, *A Christmas Carol*, Ward Lock & Co., London, 1885.

Lang, George, *The Cuisine of Hungary*, Atheneum Press, 1971; Penguin Books, 1985.

Levi, Primo, *If This Is a Man*, Penguin, Harmondsworth, 1979.

Llewelyn Davies, Margaret, *Life as We Have Known It*, Hogarth Press, 1931.

Roden, Claudia, *The Book of Jewish Food*, Viking, London, 1997.

Roelker, Nancy L. (ed.), *The Paris of Henry of Navarre as Seen by Pierre de l'Estoile*, Harvard University Press, Cambridge Mass., 1958.

Sterne, Laurence, *A Sentimental Journey ... by Mr Yorick*, P. Miller & J. White, London, 1774.

Stroud, M., *Survival of the Fittest*, Jonathan Cape, London, 1998.

Szathmary, Louis I., 'A symbolic dinner', in *Feasting and Fasting*, Prospect Books, London, 1990.

Tschumi, Gabriel, *Royal Chef*, William Kimber, London, 1954.

Wheaton, Barbara, *Savouring the Past*, Chatto & Windus, London, 1983.

10. The banquet from hell

Bober, Phyllis, 'The black or Hell banquet', in *Feasting and Fasting*, Prospect Books, London, 1990.

Sanuto, Marino, *I Diari*, Venice, 1896.

Vasari, Giorgio, *Lives of the Painters, Sculptors and Architects*, tr. A. B. Hind, Dent, London, 1927.

Wheaton, Barbara, *Savouring the Past*, Chatto & Windus, London, 1983.

11. Feasting and fasting: Mardi Gras

Bynum, Caroline W., *Holy Feast and Holy Fast*, University of California Press, 1987.

Byrne, Muriel St Clare, *The Lisle Letters*, Secker & Warburg, London, 1983.

Chambers, E. K., *The English Folk-Play*, Oxford: The Clarendon Press, 1933.

Dekker, Thomas, *The Shoemaker's Holiday*, 1600.

Froissart, Sir John, *The Chronicles*, ed. G. C. Macaulay, Macmillan & Co, London, 1895.

Furnivall, F. J. (ed.), *The Forme of Cury*, c.1390, Roxburghe Club, London, 1867.

Fussell, Betty, *The Story of Corn*, Knopf, New York, 1992.

Gundersheimer, W. L., *Ferrara, the Style of a Despotism*, Princeton University Press, 1973.

Henish, Bridget Ann, *Fast and Feast*, The Pennsylvania State University Press, 1976.

Hutton, Ronald, *The Stations of the Sun: A history of the ritual year in Britain*, Oxford University Press, 1996.

Hyman, T., & Malbert, R., *Carnivalesque*, Hayward Gallery Publishing, London, 2000.

Jeanneret, Michel, *A Feast of Words*, Polity Press, Cambridge, 1991.

Laroque, François, *Shakespeare's Festive World*, tr. Janet Lloyd, Cambridge University Press, 1991.

Laurioux, Bruno, *Le Moyen-Age à table*, Éditions Adam Biro, Paris, 1989.

Montaigne, Michel de, *The Complete Works: Essays*, tr. Charles Cotton, J. Templeman, London, 1842.

Paterson, Wilma, *The Regency Cookery Book*, Dog & Bone, Glasgow, 1990.

Pullar, Philippa, *Consuming Passions*, Hamish Hamilton Ltd, London, 1970.

Rabelais, François, *Five books of the lives, heroic deeds and sayings of Gargantua and his son Pantagruel*, tr. Sir Thomas Urquhart of Cromarty and Peter Antony Motteux, London, 1904.

Spencer, Colin, *The Heretic's Feast*, Fourth Estate, London, 1993.

Topsell, Edward, *The History of Four-footed Beasts and Serpents ...*, London, 1658.

Walker, Harlan (ed.), *Oxford Symposium of Food and Cookery, 1990: Feasting and Fasting*, Prospect Books, London, 1990.

Walker, Harlan (ed.), *Oxford Symposium on Food and Cookery, 1997: Fish, food from the waters*, Prospect Books, Totnes, 1998.

Warner, Richard, *Antiquitates Culinariae*, R. Blamire, London, 1791.

12. The Feast of St Hubert: hunting, and a nine-course venison feast

Grateful thanks to John, my resource for anything to do with deer.

Anon., *Sir Gawain and the Green Knight*, c.1385.

Bath, Michael, *The Image of the Stag*, Verlag Valentin Koerner, Baden-Baden, 1992.

Baxter Brown, Michael, *Richmond Park*, Robert Hale, London, 1985.

Beeton, Isabella, *Book of Household Management*, Ward, Lock & Tyler, London, 1868.

Blüchel, Kurt, *Die Jagd*, Könemann, Cologne, 1996.

Boorde, Andrew, *A Compendyous Regyment or a Dyetary of Helth* (1542), edited for the Early English Text Society, N. T. Trubner & Co., London, 1870.

Cantor, Leonard, *The Medieval Parks of England: a Gazetteer*, Loughborough University, Loughborough, 1983.

Champlain Society, *The Works of Samuel de Champlain*, University of Toronto Press, Toronto, 1971.

Columella, L., *Of Husbandry, in Twelve Books*, London, 1745.

Cummins, John, *The Hound and the Hawk: The art of mediaeval hunting*, Weidenfeld & Nicolson, London, 1988.

Dierkens, A., & Duvosquel, J.-M., *Le Culte de saint Hubert en Namurois*, Crédit Communal, 1992.

Fletcher, John, *A Life for Deer*, Victor Gollancz/Peter Crawley, London, 2000.

Fletcher, Nichola, *Venison, the Monarch of the Table*, Auchtermuchty, 1983.

Fortemps, Jean-Luc Duvivier de, *Le Brame, images et rituel*, Éditions Perron & Hatier, n.d.

Deer, Journal of the British Deer Society.

Furnivall, F. J. (ed.), *The Boke of Nurture of John Russell*, c.1460, Roxburghe Club, London, 1867.

Gilbert, John, *Hunting and Hunting Reserves in Medieval Scotland*, John Donald, Edinburgh, 1979.

Hackett, Francis, *Henry the Eighth*, Jonathan Cape, 1929.

Hartley, Dorothy, *Food in England*, Macdonald, London, 1963.

Manwood, John, *Treatyse of the Laws of the Forest*, Company of Stationers, London, 1665.

McNeill, F. Marian, *The Silver Bough*, MacLellan, Glasgow, 1957.

Murray, Venetia, *High Society: A Social History of the Regency 1788–1830*, Viking, 1988.

Ortega y Gasset, José, *Meditations on Hunting* (1942), tr. H. B. Wescott, New York, Charles Scribner's Sons, 1972.

Powers, Jo Marie, 'L'Ordre de Bontemps', in *Feasting and Fasting*, Prospect Books, London, 1990.

Scruton, Roger, *On Hunting*, Yellow Jersey, London, 1998.

Shakespeare, William, *Twelfth Night*, HarperCollins, Glasgow, 1994.

Soyer, Alexis, *The Gastronomic Regenerator*, Simpkin Marshall, London, 1846.

Thiebaux, Marcelle, *The Stag of Love: The chase in mediaeval literature*, Cornell University Press, Ithaca and London, 1974.

Thorpe, Lewis, *Two Lives of Charlemagne*, Penguin, Harmondsworth, 1969.

Timbs, John, *Club Life of London* . . ., 2 vols., Richard Bentley, London, 1866.

Topsell, Edward, *The History of Four-footed Beasts and Serpents* . . ., London, 1658.

Turbevile, George, *The Noble Arte of Venerie or Hunting* (1576), Tudor and Stuart Library reprint, Oxford, 1908.

World Cancer Research Fund and American Institute for Cancer Research, *Food, Nutrition and the Prevention of Cancer – a Global Perspective*, Washington, 1997.

13. Ephemera at the feast: perfume and flowers

Aikin, Lucy, *Memoirs of the Court of Queen Elizabeth*, London, 1819.

Andersen, Hans Christian, *Imprivatoren, or Travels in Italy*, tr. Mary Howitt, London, 1845.

Anon., *The Epicure's Yearbook*, Bradbury Evans, London, 1868 and 1869.

Anon., *Mesnagier de Paris (The Goodman of Paris)*, tr. Eileen Powers, London, 1928.

Anon., *Two Books of Cookerie and Carving*, 1650.

Armstrong, Lucie Heaton, *Etiquette and Entertaining*, John Lang, London, 1913.

Chardin, Sir John, *Travels in Persia, 1673–1677*, Argonaut Press, London, 1927.

Chauncey, Mary (ed.), *The Floral Gift. From Nature and the Heart*, Leavitt & Allen, New York, 1853.

Cooper, Joseph, *The Receipt Book of Joseph Cooper, Cook to Charles I*, 1654.

Culpeper, Nicholas, *The English Physician*, 1653.

Digby, Kenelm, *The closet of the eminently learned Sir Kenelme Digbie Kt. opened* (1669), ed. Jane Stevenson and Peter Davidson, Prospect Books, Totnes, 1997.

Esquivel, Laura, *Like Water for Chocolate*, Black Swan, London, 1993.

Gerard, John, *The Herball or Generall Historie of Plants*, 1597.

Greenaway, Kate, *Language of Flowers*, George Routledge and Sons, London, 1884.

Huish, Robert, *An Authentic History of the Coronation of King George the Fourth*, J. Robins & Co., London, 1821.

May, Robert, *The Accomplisht Cook*, Nathaniel Brooke, London, 1671.

Mercure galant, Le, janvier 1680, 2ème partie, Paris, Au Palais, 1680.

Stead, Jennifer, 'Bowers of Bliss', in *Banquetting Stuffe*, Edinburgh University Press, 1991.

Wheaton, Barbara, *Savouring the Past*, Chatto & Windus, 1983.

White, Florence, *Flowers as Food*, Jonathan Cape, London, 1934.

14. The Feast of St Antony: pigs – the peasants' feast

Special thanks to Sue Style for her descriptions of the Metzgete *and the* Treberwurstfrass, *and to Margaret Shaida for her description of* Escudella.

Beeton, Isabella, *Book of Household Management*, Ward, Lock & Tyler, London, 1868.

Cobbett, William, *Cottage Economy*, C. Clement, London, 1822.

Hippisley Coxe, A. & A., *Book of Sausages*, Victor Gollancz/Peter Crawley, London, 1997.

Hunt, P., & Morrison, J., *Christmas Customs and Cooking*, Wiltshire Folk Life Society, 1984.

Malcolmson, R., & Mastoris, S., *The English Pig*, Hambledon Press, London, 1998.

Mason, Laura (ed.), *Food and the Rites of Passage*, Prospect Books, Totnes, 2002.

Mayle, Peter, *Toujours Provence*, Hamish Hamilton, London, 1991.

Strang, Jeanne, *Goose Fat and Garlic*, Kyle Cathie, 1991.

Topsell, Edward, *The History of Four-footed Beasts and Serpents ...*, London, 1658.

Varro, Marcus, *De Re Rustica (On Agriculture)*, William Heinemann, London, 1960.

Verroust, J., Pastoureau, M., & Buren, R., *Le Cochon*, Éditions Sang de la Terre, Paris, 1987.

15. A beastly feast

Encyclopaedia Britannica (11th edition), Cambridge University Press, 1910.

Horne, Alistair, *The Fall of Paris*, London, Macmillan & Co., 1965.

Wheaton, Barbara, *Savouring the Past*, Chatto & Windus, London, 1983.

16. The Renaissance: evolution of European banquets

Baroni, Daniele, *Design and the Rite of Dining*, Gruppo Editoriale Electra SpA, Milan, 1981.

Black, Maggie (ed.), *A Taste of History*, British Museum Press, London, 1993.

Boscolo, R., & Savio, C., *The Great Book of Decorations for Buffets*, ISAC Étoile, Venice, 1995.

Dawson, Thomas, *The Good Huswife's Jewell*, 1597.

Evelyn, John, *Diaries*, ed. E. S. De Beer, Oxford University Press, 2000.

Fawcett, Richard, *Stirling Castle, the Restoration of the Great Hall*, Council for British Archaeology, York, 2001.

Fowler, William, *A True Reportarie of the most Triumphant . . . Baptism of . . . Prince Henry Frederick*, John Reid Younger, Edinburgh, 1703.

Geigher, Mattia, *Trattato*, 1639.

Hibbert, Christopher, *George IV*, Penguin, London, 1976.

Huish, Robert, *An Authentic History of the Coronation of King George the Fourth*, J. Robins & Co., London, 1821.

Ingram, R. W. (ed.), *Records of Early English Drama: Coventry*, Manchester University Press, 1981.

Latham, R., & Matthews, W. (eds.), *The Diary of Samuel Pepys, a new and complete transcription*, Bell, London, 1976.

Latini, Antonio, *Lo Scalco Moderna*, 1692.

Lynch, Michael, 'Queen Mary's Triumph: the baptismal celebrations at Stirling in December 1566', *Scottish Historical Review*, no. 69.

Messibugo, Cristoforo, *Banchetti*, Venice, 1557.

Montanari, Massimo, *The Culture of Food*, Blackwell, Oxford, 1994.

Platina, Bartholomeo Sacchi de', & Maestro Martino, *De Honesta Voluptate et Valetudine*, Venice, 1475.

Platt, Sir Hugh, *Delightes for Ladies*, Humphrey Lownes, London, 1609.

Pullar, Philippa, *Consuming Passions*, Hamish Hamilton Ltd, London, 1970.

Scappi, Bartholomeo, *Opera di M. B. Scappi: Cuoco secreto di Pappa Pio Quinto*, 1570.

Strong, Roy, *Art and Power*, Boydell, Woodbridge, 1984.

Warner, Richard, *Antiquitates Culinariae*, R. Blamire, London, 1791.

Wheaton, Barbara, *Savouring the Past*, Chatto & Windus, London, 1983.

Wilson, C. Anne, *Food and Drink in Britain*, Constable, 1973.

— *The Appetite and the Eye*, Edinburgh University Press, 1991.

— *Banquetting Stuffe*, Edinburgh University Press, 1991.

17. Thanksgivings: celebrating relief

Fussell, Betty, *The Story of Corn*, Knopf, New York, 1992.

Mourt's Relation, or *Iournall of the beginning and proceedings of the English Plantation settled at Plimouth in New England*, by certain English adventurers both merchants and others, 1622.

Raphael, Chaim, *The Festivals: A history of Jewish celebration*, Weidenfeld & Nicolson, London, 1991.

Roden, Claudia, *The Book of Jewish Food*, Viking, London, 1997.

Saberi, Helen, *Noshe Djan: Afghan food and cookery*, Prospect Books, Totnes, 2000.

— 'Public Eating in Afghanistan', in *Public Eating*, Prospect Books, Totnes, 1991.

18. A Victorian banquet: dinner for the Acclimatisation Society of Great Britain

My thanks to Valerie Mars for her helpful discussions on dining à la russe.

Anon., *The Epicure's Yearbook*, Bradbury Evans, London, 1868 and 1869.

Armstrong, Lucie Heaton, *Etiquette and Entertaining*, John Lang, London, 1913.

Day, Ivan, *Eat, Drink and Be Merry*, Philip Wilson Ltd., London, 2000.

Lever, Christopher, *They Dined on Eland*, Quiller Press, London, 1992.

Markham, Gervase, *The English House-wife*, Wilson, London, 1649.

Montaigne, Michel de, *The Complete Works: Essays*, tr. Charles Cotton, J. Templeman, London, 1842.

Soyer, Alexis, *The Pantropheon*, Simpkin, Marshall & Co., London, 1853.

Tannahill, Reay, *Food in History*, Penguin, 1988.

The Field magazine, 1860–65.

Timbs, John, *Club Life of London* . . ., 2 vols., Richard Bentley, London, 1866.

Tschumi, Gabriel, *Royal Chef*, William Kimber, London, 1954.

Wilson, C. Anne (ed.), *Luncheon, Nuncheon and other meals*, Alan Sutton Publishing, Stroud, 1994.

19. *Cha-kaiseki*: a vegan feast at the Japanese tea ceremony

Grateful thanks to Emi Kasuko for her beautiful calligraphy and for her exhaustive help in preparing this chapter, and to Alex Fraser for introducing me to the Way of Tea.

Fraser, Alex, *A Tea House for Glasgow*, exhibition notes, 2000.

Kazuko, Emi, *Japanese Food and Cooking*, Lorenz Books, London, 2001.

Tsuji, Shizuo, *Japanese Cooking, a Simple Art*, Kodansha International, Tokyo, 1980.

Turay, Mohamed, *Chanoyu: Symbols and Rituals*, Savannah State University thesis, n.d.

20. A feast in the bath: how not to behave

My thanks to Agnes Kruger for completing my search for the picture, and in particular to the Staatsbibliothek in Berlin for their generous permission to use it, and to Oliver Nicholson for translating the text.

Valerius Maximus, *Facta et Dicta Memorabilia*, Philippe de Mazerolles, c.1407.

Wright, Lawrence, *Clean and Decent*, Routledge & Kegan Paul, London, 1960.

21. Rites of passage: universal symbols

Capalbo, Carla, *The Food and Wine Lover's Companion to Tuscany*, Chronicle Books, 2002.

Fawcett, Richard, *Stirling Castle, the Restoration of the Great Hall*, Council for British Archaeology, York, 2001.

Huish, Robert, *An Authentic History of the Coronation of King George the Fourth*, J. Robins & Co., London, 1821.

Lang, George, *The Cuisine of Hungary*, Atheneum Press, 1971; Penguin Books, 1985.

Mason, Laura (ed.), *Food and the Rites of Passage*, Prospect Books, Totnes, 2002.

May, Robert, *The Accomplisht Cook*, Nathaniel Brooke, London, 1671.

Montijn, Ileen, 'Dutch Treats', in *Feasting and Fasting*, Prospect Books, London, 1990.

Musacchio, Jacqueline, *The Art and Ritual of Childbirth in Renaissance Italy*, Yale University Press, 1999.

Paterson, Wilma, *The Regency Cookery Book*, Dog & Bone, Glasgow, 1990.

Pavord, Anna, *Tulip*, Bloomsbury, London, 1999.

Riley, Gillian, personal communication.

Short, R., & Potts, M., *Ever Since Adam and Eve*, Cambridge University Press, 1999.

Warner, Richard, *Antiquitates Culinariae*, R. Blamire, London, 1791.

Woolley, Hannah, *The Gentlewoman's Companion*, Edward Thomas, London, 1674.

22. A pollen feast for Ruskin: banqueting in the high forests

Kesseler, Rob, *Pollinate*, The Wordsworth Trust and Grizedale Arts, Cumbria, 2001.

Ruskin, John, *The Works of John Ruskin*, Catalogue of the Educational Series, 1871.

— *Proserpina, Studies of Wayside Flowers*, Sunnyside, 1879.

Wordsworth, Dorothy, *The Grasmere Journals*, ed. Pamela Woof, Oxford, The Clarendon Press, 1991.

Wordsworth, William, *The Prelude, or Growth of a Poet's Mind*, Book 1, London, 1850.

Shakespeare, William, *The Tempest*, HarperCollins, Glasgow, 1994.

23. Burns Supper: feasts of fraternity, and men behaving badly

Burns, Robert, *Complete Poetical Works*, ed. James MacKay, Darvel, Alloway, 1993.

Crawford, Robert (ed.), *Robert Burns and Cultural Authority*, Edinburgh University Press, 1997.

Jamieson, John, *An Etymological Dictionary of the Scottish Language*, Alexander Gardner, Paisley, 1825.

McCormick, Donald, *The Hell-Fire Club*, Jarrolds, London, 1958.

Murray, Venetia, *High Society: A Social History of the Regency 1788–1830*, Viking, 1988.

Pullar, Philippa, *Consuming Passions*, Hamish Hamilton Ltd, 1970.

Stevenson, David, *The First Freemasons*, Aberdeen University Press, 1988.

— *The Origins of Freemasonry: Scotland's Century, 1590–1710*, Cambridge University Press, 1988.

Suster, Gerald, *The Hell-Fire Friars*, Robson Books, London, 2000.

Timbs, John, *Club Life of London . . .*, 2 vols., Richard Bentley, London, 1866.

24. Eating people: cannibal feasts

Clancy, Jeremy, *Consuming Culture*, Chapmans, London, 1992.

Coe, Michael, *The Maya*, Thames & Hudson, 1993.

Korn, D., Radice, M., & Hawkes, C., *Cannibal*, Channel 4 Books, London, 2001.

Sheridan, Alison (ed.), *Heaven and Hell*, NMS Publishing, Edinburgh, 2000.

Tannahill, Reay, *Flesh and Blood*, Abacus, London, 1976.

25. A feast on horseback

My grateful thanks to Mike Wallace for his researching, and to Leila Hadley Luce for sending me the photograph of her grandfather at this feast.

Ingram, R. W. (ed.), *Records of Early English Drama: Coventry*, Manchester University Press, 1981.

26. Midwinter feasts: light in the darkness

Alcock, Joan P., 'The Festival of Christmas', in *Feasts and Fasts*, Prospect Books, 1990.

Dickens, Charles, *A Christmas Carol*, Ward Lock & Co., London, 1885.

— 'A Christmas Dinner', in *Sketches by Boz*, 1836.

Grahame, Kenneth, *The Wind in the Willows*, Methuen, London, 1908.

Henisch, Bridget Ann, *Cakes and Characters*, Prospect Books, London, 1984.

Hunt, P., & Morrison, J., *Christmas Customs and Cooking*, Wiltshire Folk Life Society, 1984.

Hutton, Ronald, *The Stations of the Sun: A history of the ritual year in Britain*, Oxford University Press, 1996.

Hyman T., & Malbert, R., *Carnivalesque*, Hayward Gallery Publishing, London, 2000.

Levy, Paul, *The Feast of Christmas*, Kyle Cathie, 1992.

Luard, Elisabeth, *European Festival Food*, Bantam Press, 1990.

27. Feasts for the dead: conquering fear

Adapon, Joy, 'The presence or absence of *mole* in Mexican feasts', in *Petits Propos Culinaires 67*, Prospect Books, Totnes, 2001.

Aubrey, John, *Remaines of Gentilisme and Judaisme*, 1687.

Bober, Phyllis, 'The black or Hell banquet', in *Feasting and Fasting*, Prospect Books, London, 1990.

Carmichael, E., & Sayer, C., *The Skeleton at the Feast*, British Museum Press, 1991.

Hsiung, Deh-ta, *The Festive Food of China*, Kyle Cathie, London, 1991.

Kendall, Paul Murray, *The Yorkist Age*, George Allen & Unwin, London, 1962.

Livingstone, Sheila, *Scottish Festivals*, Birlinn Press, Edinburgh, 1997.

Mason, Laura (ed.), *Food and the Rites of Passage*, Prospect Books, Totnes, 2002.

McNeill, F. Marian, *The Silver Bough*, MacLellan, Glasgow, 1957.

Paz, Octavio, *El Laberinto de la Soledad* (*The Labyrinth of Solitude: Life and thought in Mexico*), Buenos Aires, 1959.

Rossiter, Evelyn, *The Book of the Dead*, Minerva SA, Geneva, 1984.

Sheridan, Alison (ed.), *Heaven and Hell*, NMS Publishing, Edinburgh, 2000.

28. Swansong at Hogmanay: a feast for the millennium

Davidson, Alan and Jane, *Dumas on Food*, Oxford University Press, 1978.

Dumas, Alexandre, *Grand Dictionnaire de cuisine*, Alphonse Lemerre, Paris, 1873.

Furnivall, F. J. (ed.), *The Boke of Kervynge of Wynken de Worde*, *1513*, Roxburghe Club, London, 1867.

— *The Boke of Nurture of John Russell*, c.1460, Roxburghe Club, London, 1867.

Hagger, Conrad, *Neues Saltzburgisches Koch-Buch*, Johann Jacob Lotter, Augsburg, 1719.

Jamieson, John, *An Etymological Dictionary of the Scottish Language*, Alexander Gardner, Paisley, 1825.

May, Robert, *The Accomplisht Cook*, Nathaniel Brooke, London, 1671.

— *The Accomplisht Cook: Facsimile of 1685 edition*, Prospect Books, Totnes, 2000.

Wilson, C. Anne, *The Appetite and the Eye*, Edinburgh University Press, 1991.

— *Banquetting Stuffe*, Edinburgh University Press, 1991.

29. Charlemagne's tablecloth: a postscript

Bullough, Donald, FSA, FRPSL, Professor Emeritus, personal communication.

Einhard the Frank, *Life of Charlemagne*, tr. Lewis Thorpe, Penguin, Harmondsworth, 1969.

Encyclopaedia Britannica (11th edition), Cambridge University Press, 1910.

Johnson, Samuel, *Dictionary of the English Language*, London, 1775.

Jones, H. L., *The Geography of Strabo*, Heinemann, Loeb Classical Library, 1917–33.

Notker the Stammerer, *Life of Charlemagne*, tr. Lewis Thorpe, Penguin, Harmondsworth, 1969.

Summers, A. Leonard, *Asbestos and the Asbestos Industry*, Isaac Pitman, London, 1919.

INDEX

education 7
Edward I 176
Edward IV 29
Edward VII 81, 153
eel 49
eggs 31, 172, 179
Elagabalus 48–9, 118–19
eland 74
Eleanor of Provence 176
elephants 131
Elizabeth I 111, 116, 180
Elizabeth II, coronation 143
emigration 148
entremets 33
entremets mouvant 33
Epstein, Jason 65
eroticism 7
Escudella 125
etiquette 27
Etiquette and Entertaining (Armstrong) 117, 156
eulachon oil 41
euphoria 91
Evelyn, John 138
exotic animals 131–2
eye feasts 61

fasting 51–2, 90–8
fats 64–5, 67–8, 74
Feast of Fools 206–7
Feast of the Pheasant 6, 32
feasts
    defined 1–8
    largest 6
    solitary 3–4
fennel 135
Ferrara, Duke 93
fertility 6, 10, 50, 172, 178–9, 181
Field of the Cloth of Gold 36
Fiennes, Sir Ranulph 76
Fijian Islands 199–200
fingers, eating with 27
fire 30, 34–6, 41–2
fireworks 15
fish 47–55, 96, 178–9
flambéing 35
Florida Creek people 91–2
flowers 26, 115–17
food poisoning 28
fools 33

forks 133, 134, 200
Forme of Cury, The 17, 18
Fowler, William 139
Freemasonry 189–91
French style 155–6
Froissart, Sir John 19–20, 24, 28, 29, 32, 35, 98
fruit 59
    fertility symbol 10, 178, 179
    suspicion of 31
fruit cake 181
frumenty 31
funeral settings 86–7, 89
funerals 211
fungi 147–8

galette du roi 208
Gaozong, Emperor 58–9
garam masala 11
Gasset, José Ortega y 104
Gavin, John 59
generosity 6–7
gentleman's clubs 189–92
George IV 143–5
Ghirardacci, Cherubino 134
Giegher, Mattia 134
gilding 134
glassware 134
gluts 6
gluttony 93, 134
gold leaf 26, 29, 112, 114, 219
goldfish 50
gondolas 39–40
Good Huswifes Jewell, The (Dawson) 136
gossips 174
Grahame, Kenneth 209
grains 179
Grand Dictionnaire de Cuisine (Dumas) 54–5, 217–18
graves 213–14
gravy browning 26
Great Exhibition 152
Green, Tony 178
Green Corn ceremony 92
green fat 53, 153
Grimond de La Reynière, A.-B.-L. 83–7, 88–9
Grizedale Forest feast 184–8
Guisay, Hugonin de 35